TER: **BRIAN MICHAEL BENDIS**   PENCILER: **MARK BAGLEY**

ER: **ANDY LANNING** WITH **ANDREW HENNESSY** (#160)

ORIST: **JUSTIN PONSOR**   LETTERERS: **VC'S CORY PETIT** & **JOE SABINO**

ER ART: **MARK BAGLEY, ANDY LANNING** & **JUSTIN PONSOR**

ISTANT EDITOR: **SANA AMANAT**   SENIOR EDITOR: **MARK PANICCIA**

LECTION EDITOR: **JENNIFER GRÜNWALD**

ISTANT EDITORS: **ALEX STARBUCK** & **NELSON RIBEIRO**

TOR, SPECIAL PROJECTS: **MARK D. BEAZLEY**

IOR EDITOR, SPECIAL PROJECTS: **JEFF YOUNGQUIST**

IOR VICE PRESIDENT OF SALES: **DAVID GABRIEL**

OF BRAND PLANNING & COMMUNICATIONS: **MICHAEL PASCIULLO**

OK DESIGNER: **RODOLFO MURAGUCHI**

TOR IN CHIEF: **AXEL ALONSO**   CHIEF CREATIVE OFFICER: **JOE QUESADA**

BLISHER: **DAN BUCKLEY**   EXECUTIVE PRODUCER: **ALAN FINE**

ATE COMICS SPIDER-MAN VOL. 4: DEATH OF SPIDER-MAN. Contains material originally published in magazine form as ULTIMATE COMICS SPIDER-MAN #156-160. First printing 2012. ISBN# 978-0-7851-5275-
shed by MARVEL WORLDWIDE, INC., a subsidiary of MARVEL ENTERTAINMENT, LLC. OFFICE OF PUBLICATION: 135 West 50th Street, New York, NY 10020. Copyright © 2011 and 2012 Marvel Characters, Inc. All
eserved. $19.99 per copy in the U.S. and $21.99 in Canada (GST #R127032852); Canadian Agreement #40668537. All characters featured in this issue and the distinctive names and likenesses thereof, and all
indicia are trademarks of Marvel Characters, Inc. No similarity between any of the names, characters, persons, and/or institutions in this magazine with those of any living or dead person or institution is intended,
y such similarity which may exist is purely coincidental. **Printed in the U.S.A.** ALAN FINE, EVP - Office of the President, Marvel Worldwide, Inc. and EVP & CMO Marvel Characters B.V.; DAN BUCKLEY, Publisher &
nt - Print, Animation & Digital Divisions; JOE QUESADA, Chief Creative Officer; DAVID BOGART, SVP of Business Affairs & Talent Management; TOM BREVOORT, SVP of Publishing; C.B. CEBULSKI, SVP of Creator &
t Development; DAVID GABRIEL, SVP of Publishing Sales & Circulation; MICHAEL PASCIULLO, SVP of Brand Planning & Communications; JIM O'KEEFE, VP of Operations & Logistics; DAN CARR, Executive Director
ishing Technology; SUSAN CRESPI, Editorial Operations Manager; ALEX MORALES, Publishing Operations Manager; STAN LEE, Chairman Emeritus. For information regarding advertising in Marvel Comics or on
.com, please contact John Dokes, SVP Integrated Sales and Marketing, at jdokes@marvel.com. For Marvel subscription inquiries, please call 800-217-9158. **Manufactured between 3/14/2012 and 4/2/2012**
. DONNELLEY, INC., SALEM, VA, USA.

7654321

156

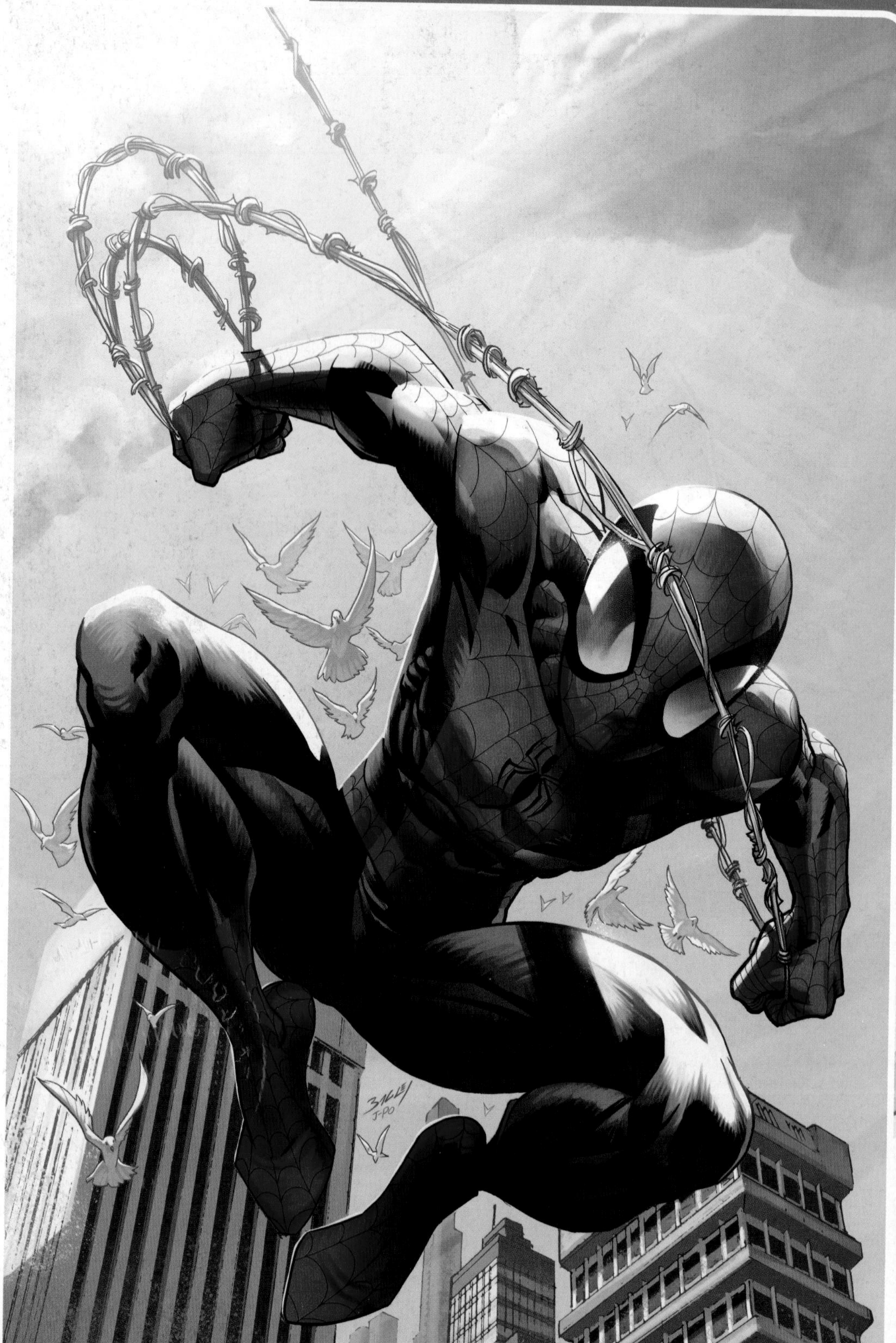

MARVEL COMICS PROUDLY PRESENTS

Does he still have his powers?

It doesn't *seem* so.

Does that answer sound good enough?

There is absolutely no evidence that he is anything but a normal physical specimen of his age.

Wake him up.

THE DEATH OF SPIDER-MAN

He is up.

Okay, then...

For acts of treason against your government...

For acts of terrorism against your fellow man...

As director of S.H.I.E.L.D. I am hereby tasked to inform you, legally, that you are under arrest.

There will be no trial, and there will be no hearing...

You are in S.H.I.E.L.D. custody for the duration of your days...

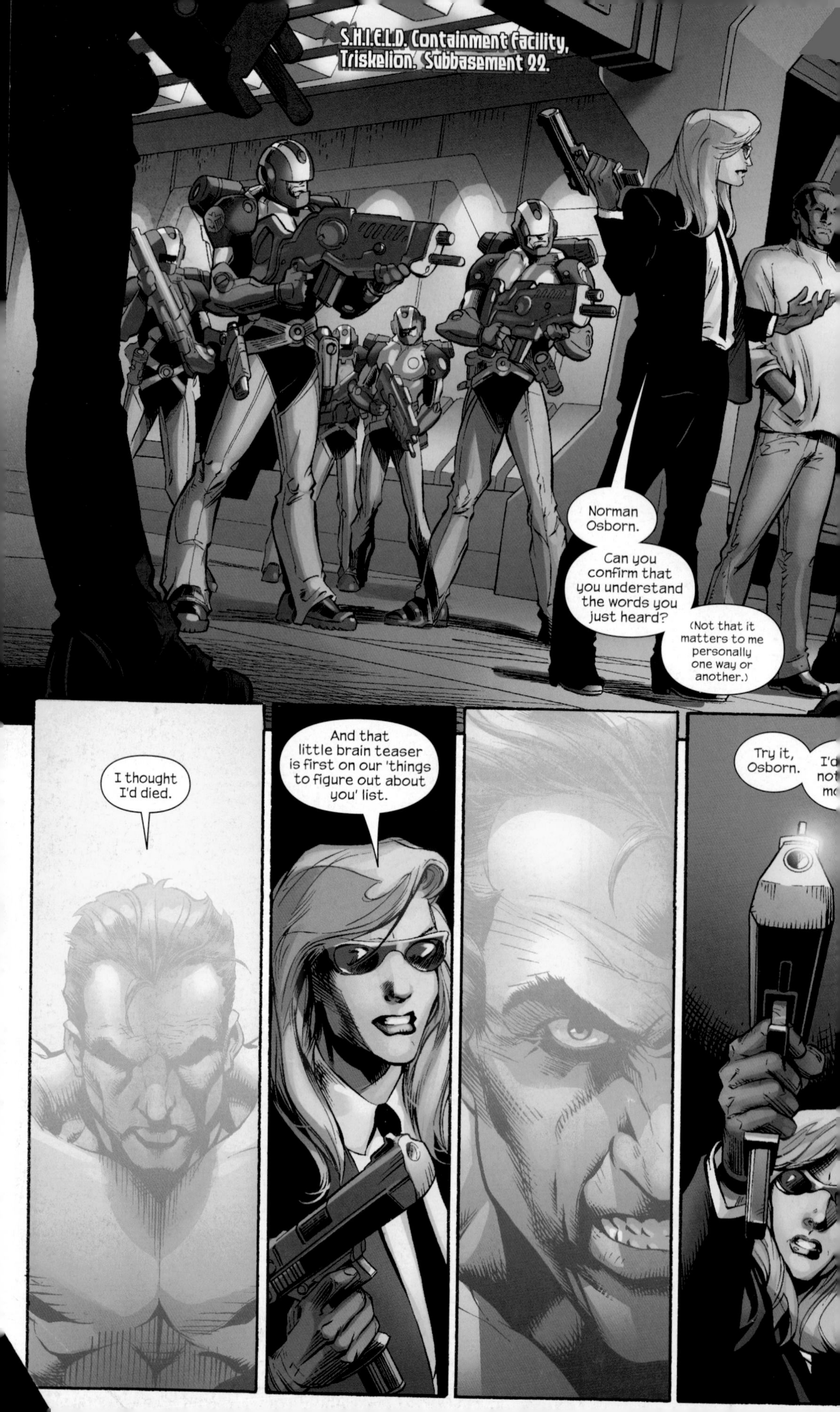
S.H.I.E.L.D. Containment Facility, Triskelion. Subbasement 22.
Norman Osborn.
Can you confirm that you understand the words you just heard?
(Not that it matters to me personally one way or another.)
I thought I'd died.
And that little brain teaser is first on our 'things to figure out about you' list.
Try it, Osborn.

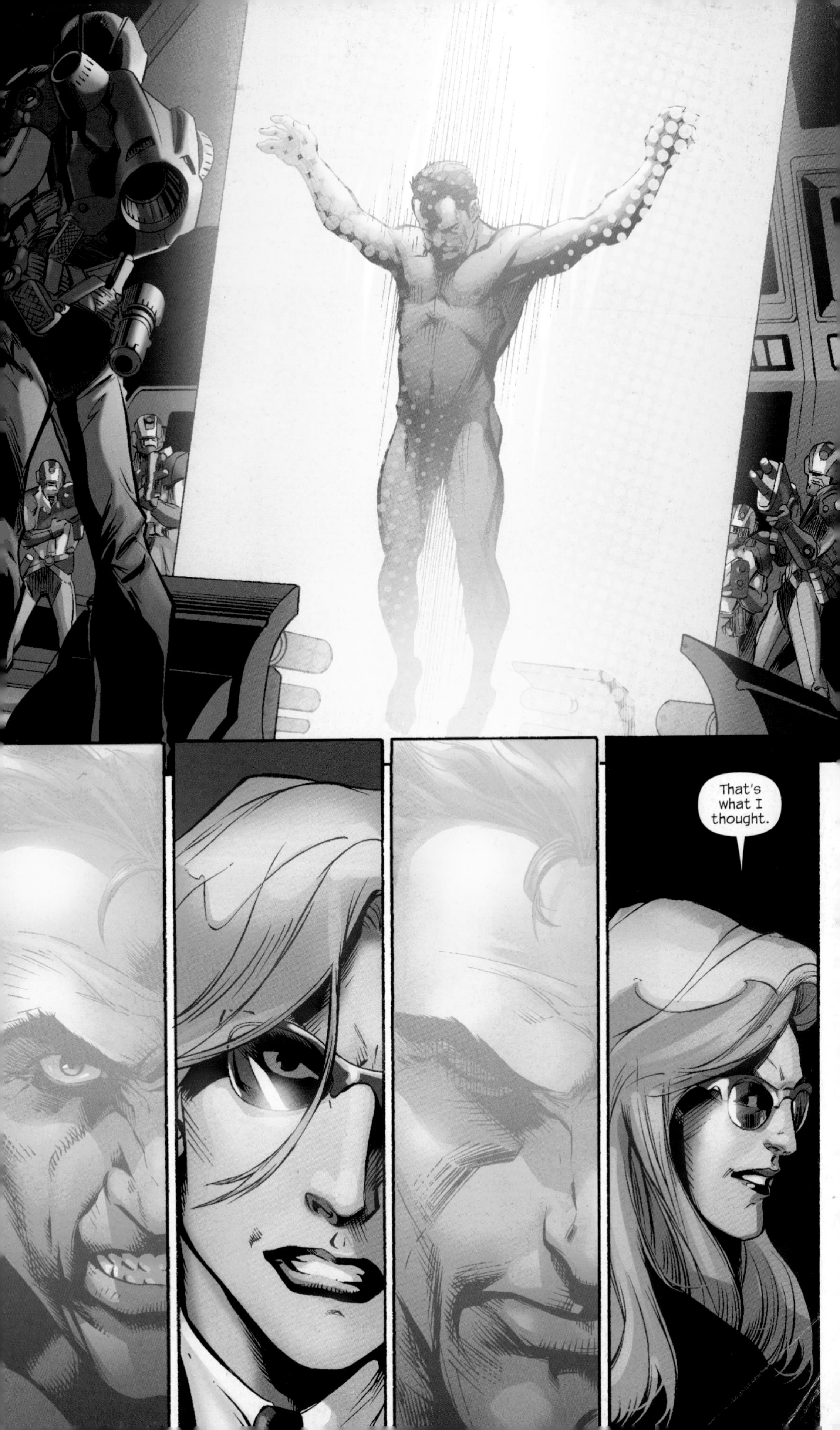
That's what I thought.

The bite of a genetically altered spider granted high school student Peter Par
incredible arachnid-like powers. When a burglar killed his beloved Uncle Be
grief-stricken Peter vowed to use his amazing abilities to protect his fellow m
He learned the invaluable lesson that with great power there must also com
great responsibility.

Now the fledgling super hero tries to balance a full high school curriculum,
night job, a relationship with Mary Jane, and swing time as the misundersto
web-slinging Spider-Man!

PREVIOUSLY IN ULTIMATE SPIDER-MAN:

The world peacekeeping task force S.H.I.E.L.D. has decided to put th
foot down as far as all things Spider-Man are concerned. Spider-M
is told that he must undergo afterschool super hero training if he is
continue fighting crime.

After a tumultuous year, Mary Jane and Peter Parker find themselv
back together again.

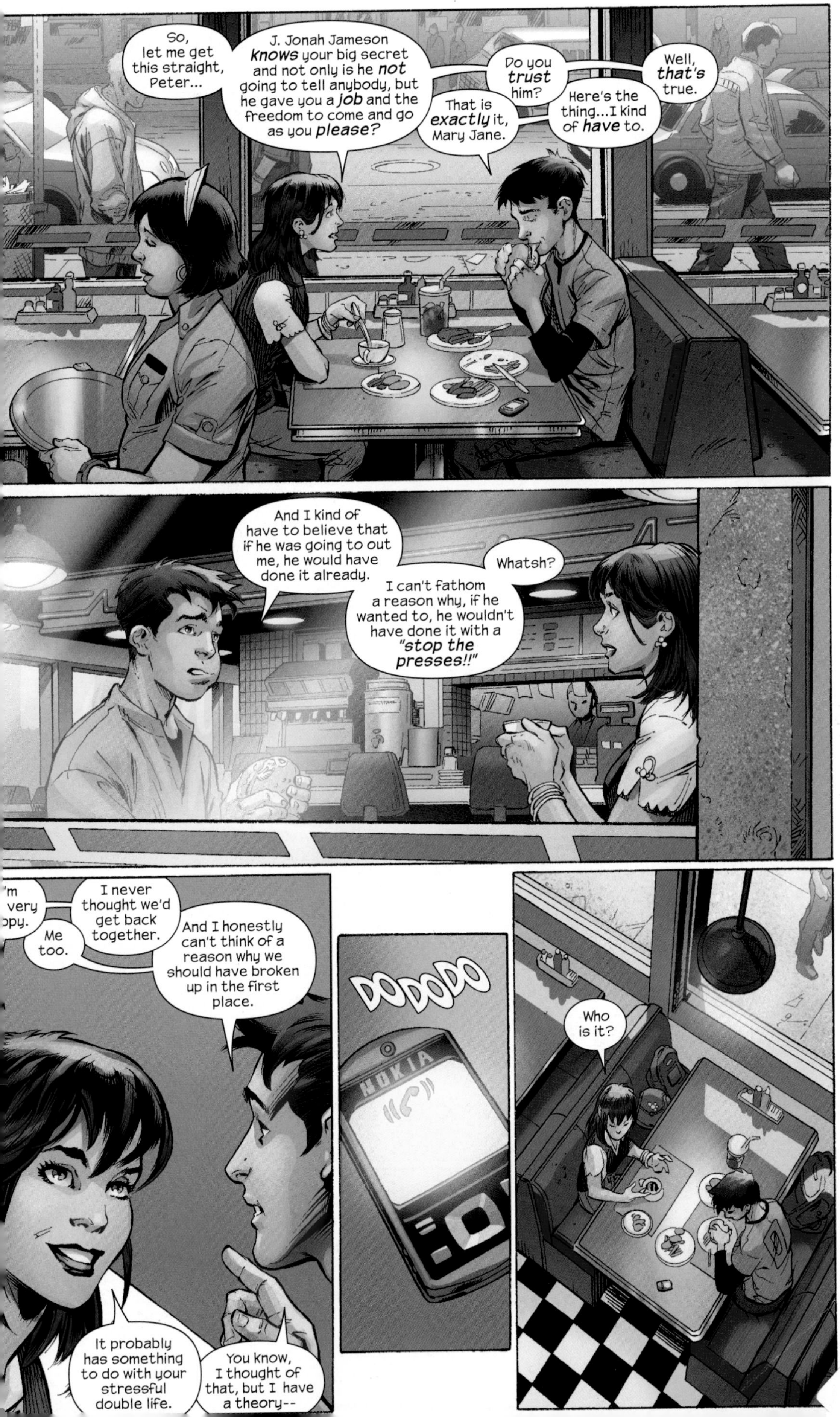

So, let me get this straight, Peter...
J. Jonah Jameson knows your big secret and not only is he not going to tell anybody, but he gave you a job and the freedom to come and go as you please?
That is exactly it, Mary Jane.
Do you trust him?
Here's the thing...I kind of have to.
Well, that's true.
And I kind of have to believe that if he was going to out me, he would have done it already.
Whatsh?
I can't fathom a reason why, if he wanted to, he wouldn't have done it with a "stop the presses!!"
'm very ppy.
I never thought we'd get back together.
Me too.
And I honestly can't think of a reason why we should have broken up in the first place.
It probably has something to do with your stressful double life.
You know, I thought of that, but I have a theory--
DODODO
NOKIA
Who is it?

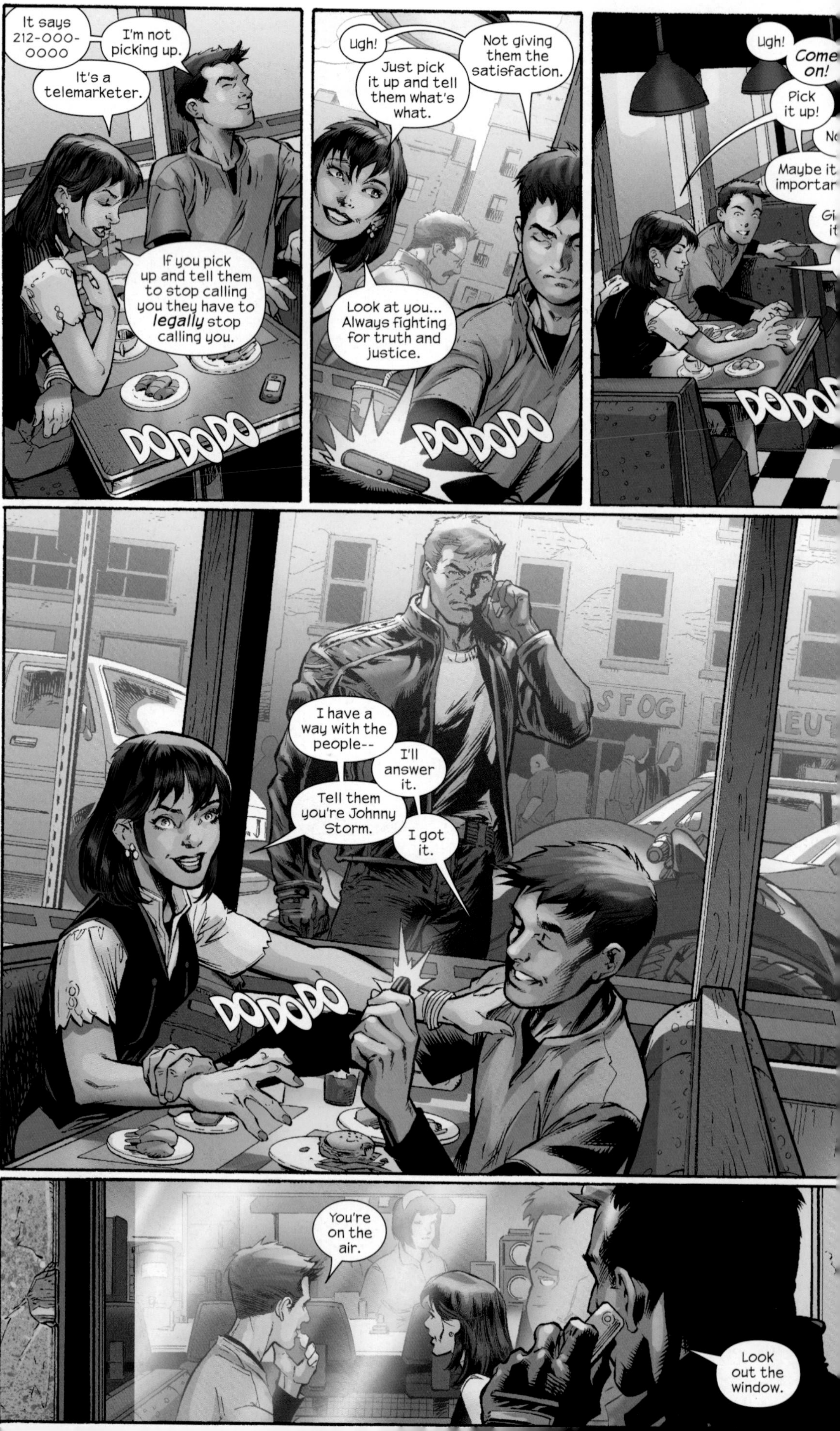
It says 212-000-0000
I'm not picking up.
It's a telemarketer.
If you pick up and tell them to stop calling you they have to *legally* stop calling you.
DODODO
Ugh!
Not giving them the satisfaction.
Just pick it up and tell them what's what.
Look at you... Always fighting for truth and justice.
DODODO
Ugh!
Come on!
Pick it up!
Maybe it
DODO
I have a way with the people--
I'll answer it.
Tell them you're Johnny Storm.
I got it.
SFOG
DODODO
You're on the air.
Look out the window.

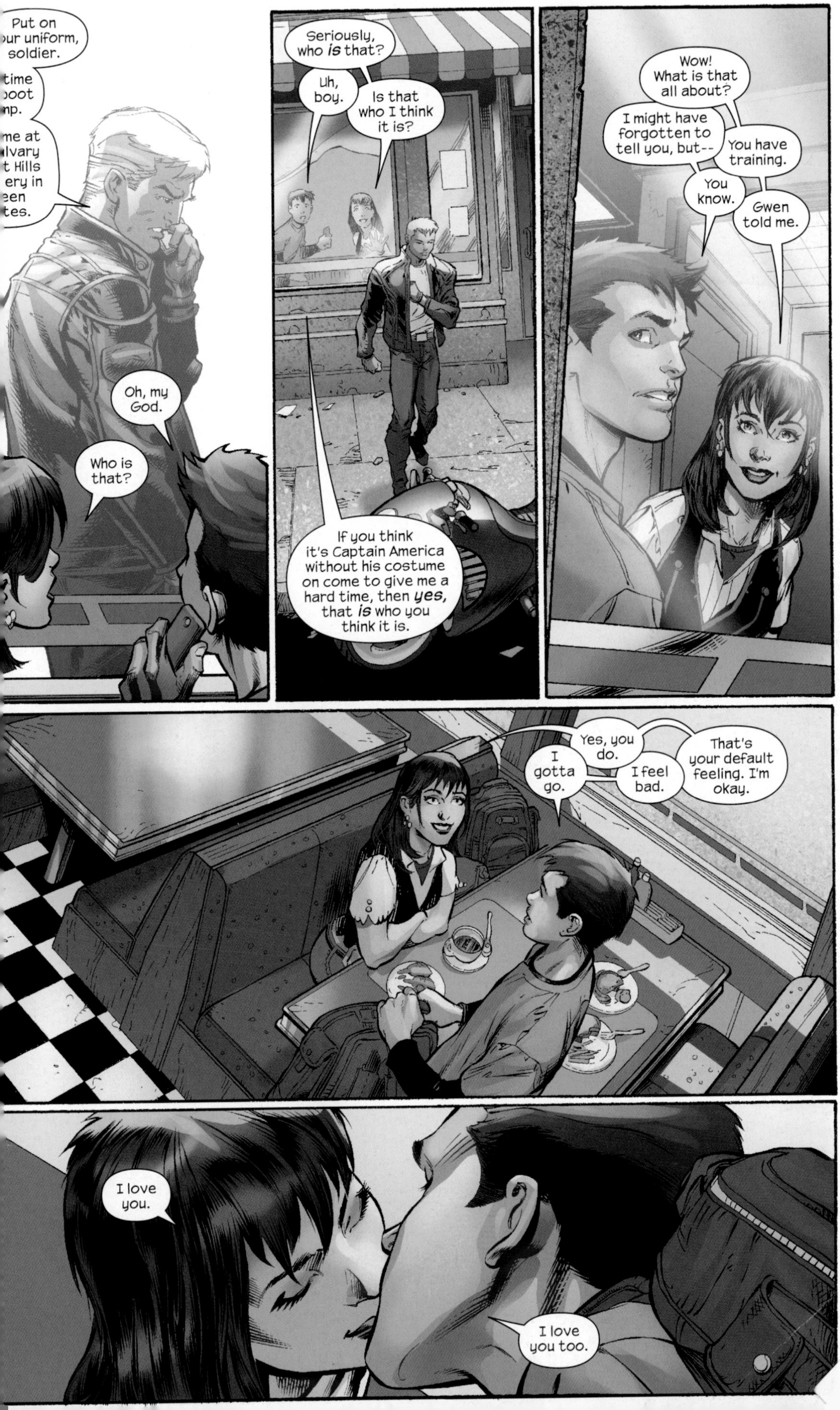
Put on
ur uniform, soldier.
time
oot
np.
me at
lvary
t Hills
ery in
een
tes.
Oh, my God.
Who is that?
Seriously, who *is* that?
Uh, boy.
Is that who I think it is?
If you think it's Captain America without his costume on come to give me a hard time, then *yes,* that *is* who you think it is.
Wow! What is that all about?
I might have forgotten to tell you, but--
You have training.
You know.
Gwen told me.
I gotta go.
Yes, you do.
I feel bad.
That's your default feeling. I'm okay.
I love you.
I love you too.

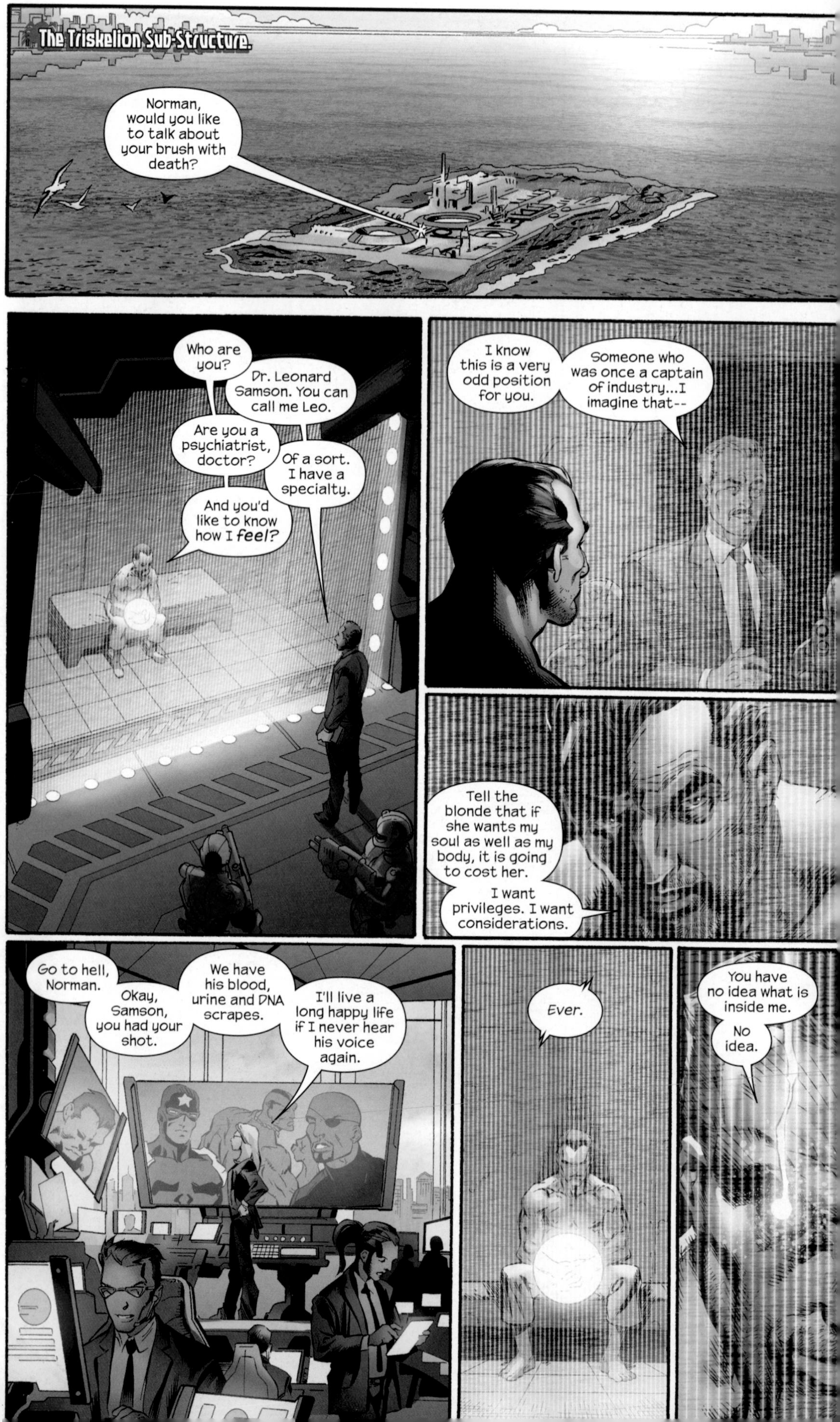
The Triskelion Sub-Structure.
Norman, would you like to talk about your brush with death?
Who are you?
Dr. Leonard Samson. You can call me Leo.
Are you a psychiatrist, doctor?
Of a sort. I have a specialty.
And you'd like to know how I *feel*?
I know this is a very odd position for you.
Someone who was once a captain of industry...I imagine that--
Tell the blonde that if she wants my soul as well as my body, it is going to cost her.
I want privileges. I want considerations.
Go to hell, Norman.
Okay, Samson, you had your shot.
We have his blood, urine and DNA scrapes.
I'll live a long happy life if I never hear his voice again.
Ever.
You have no idea what is inside me.
No idea.

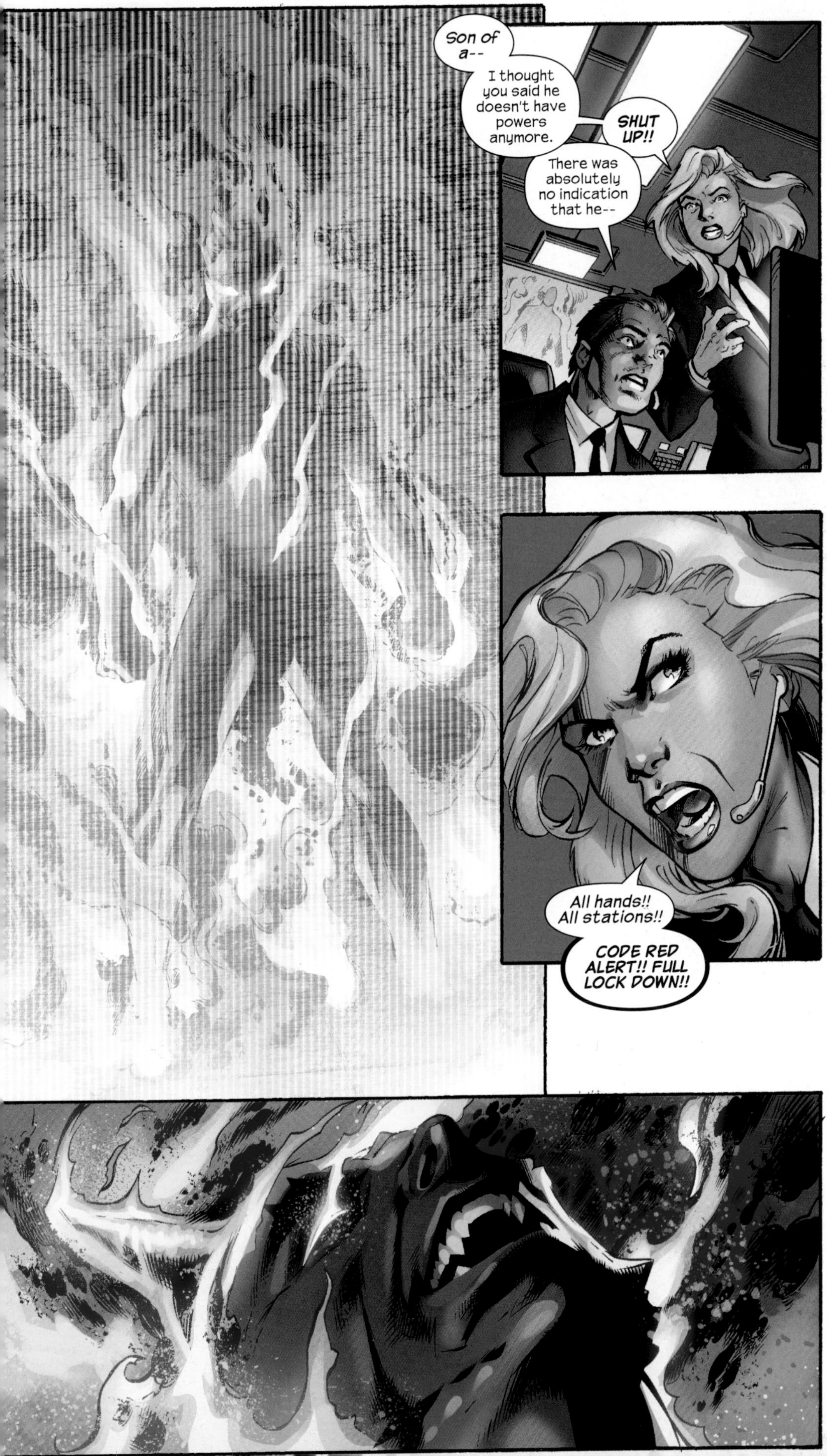
Son of a--
I thought you said he doesn't have powers anymore.
SHUT UP!!
There was absolutely no indication that he--
All hands!! All stations!!
CODE RED ALERT!! FULL LOCK DOWN!!

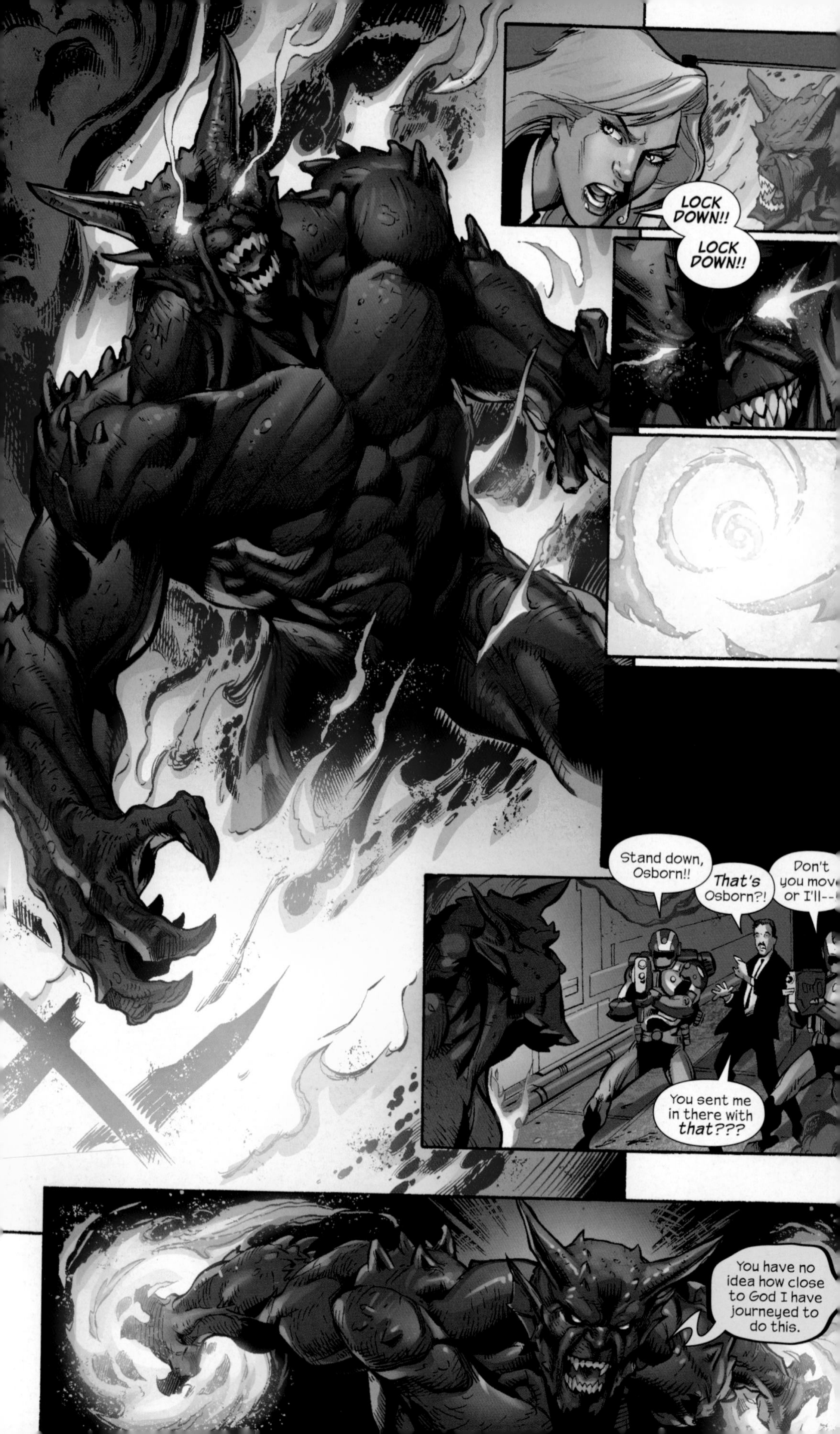
LOCK DOWN!!
LOCK DOWN!!
Stand down, Osborn!!
That's Osborn?!
Don't you move or I'll--
You sent me in there with that???
You have no idea how close to God I have journeyed to do this.

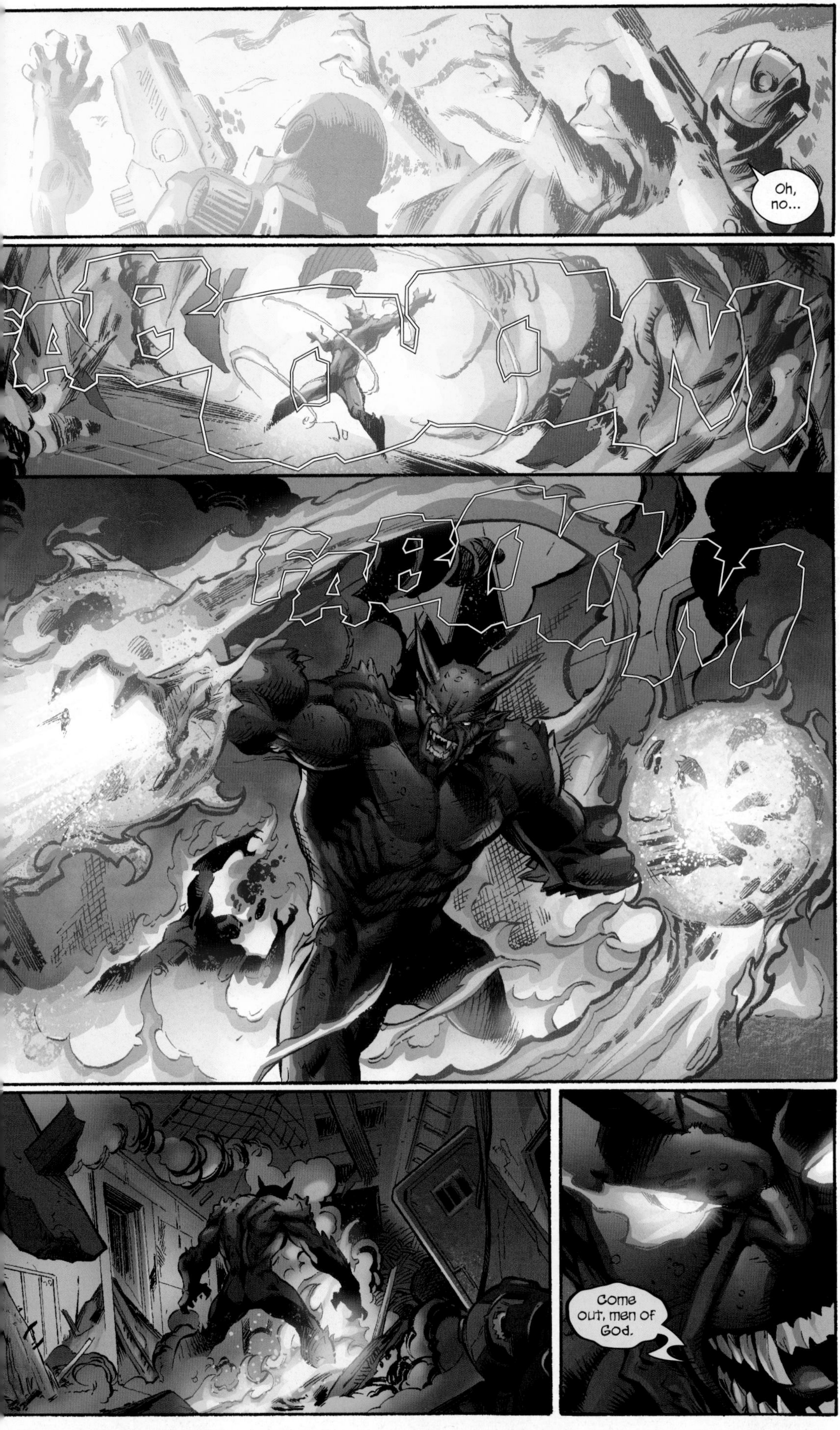
Oh, no...
Come out, men of God.

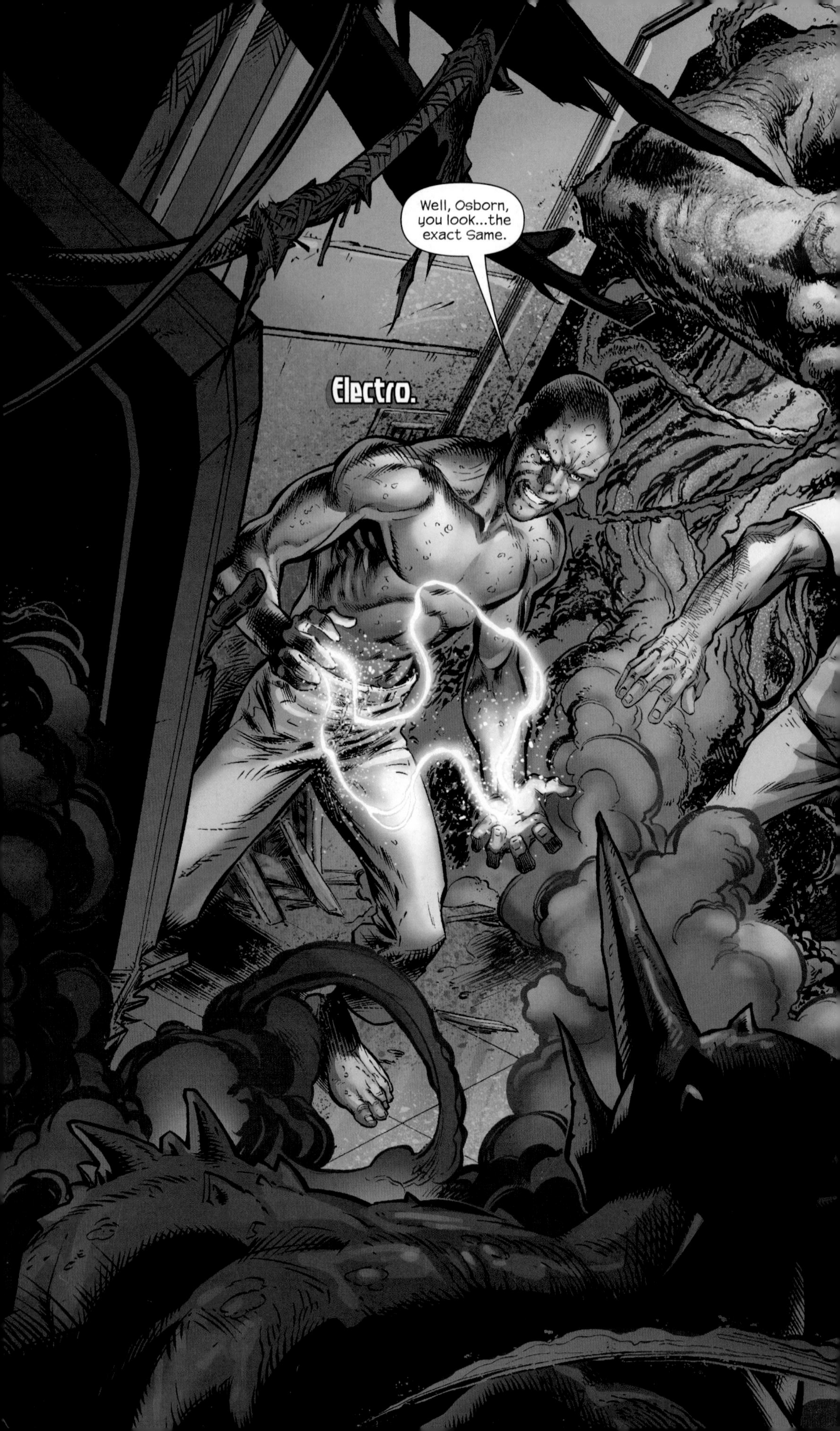
Well, Osborn, you look...the exact Same.
Electro.

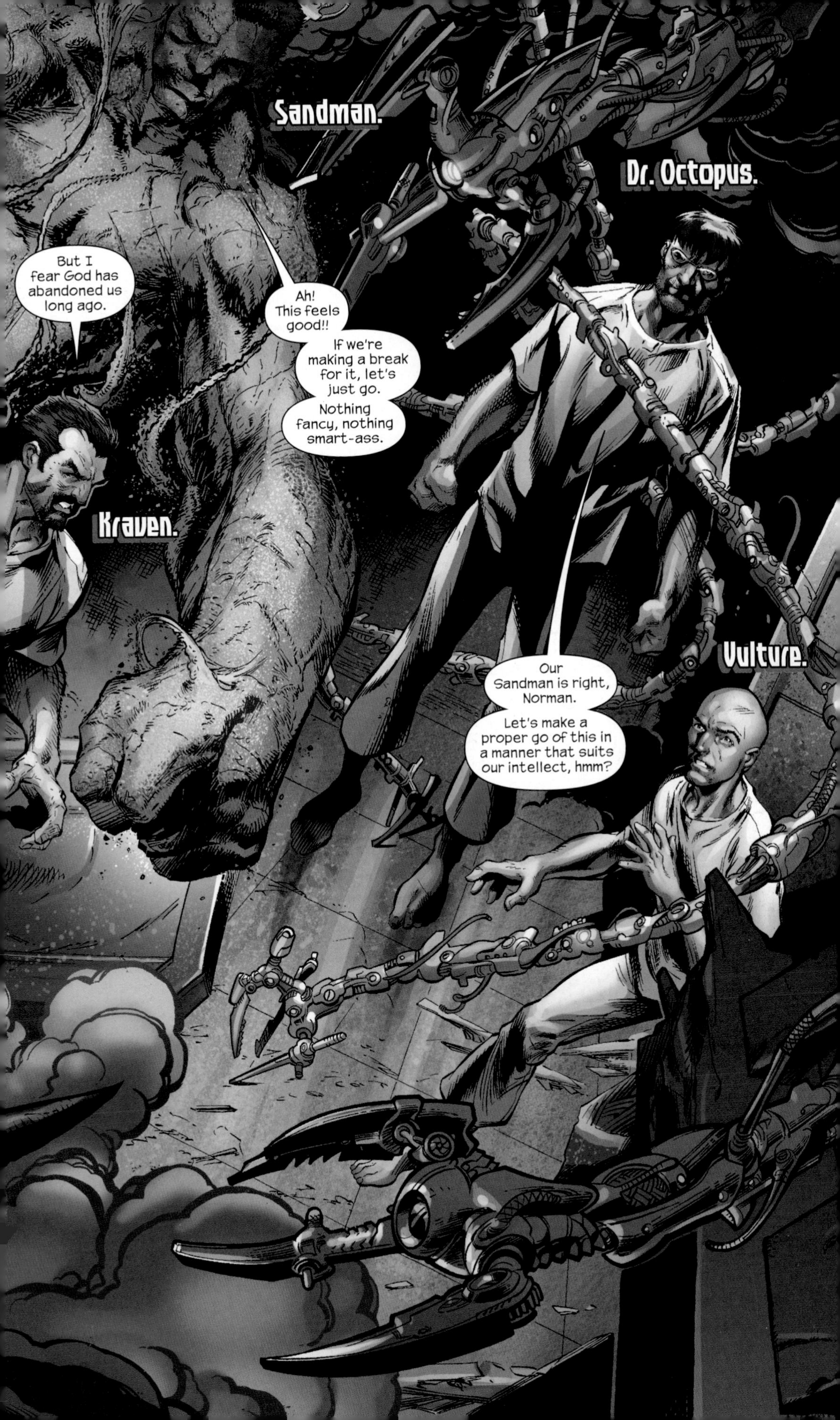
Sandman.
Dr. Octopus.
But I fear God has abandoned us long ago.
Ah! This feels good!!
If we're making a break for it, let's just go.
Nothing fancy, nothing smart-ass.
Kraven.
Vulture.
Our Sandman is right, Norman.
Let's make a proper go of this in a manner that suits our intellect, hmm?

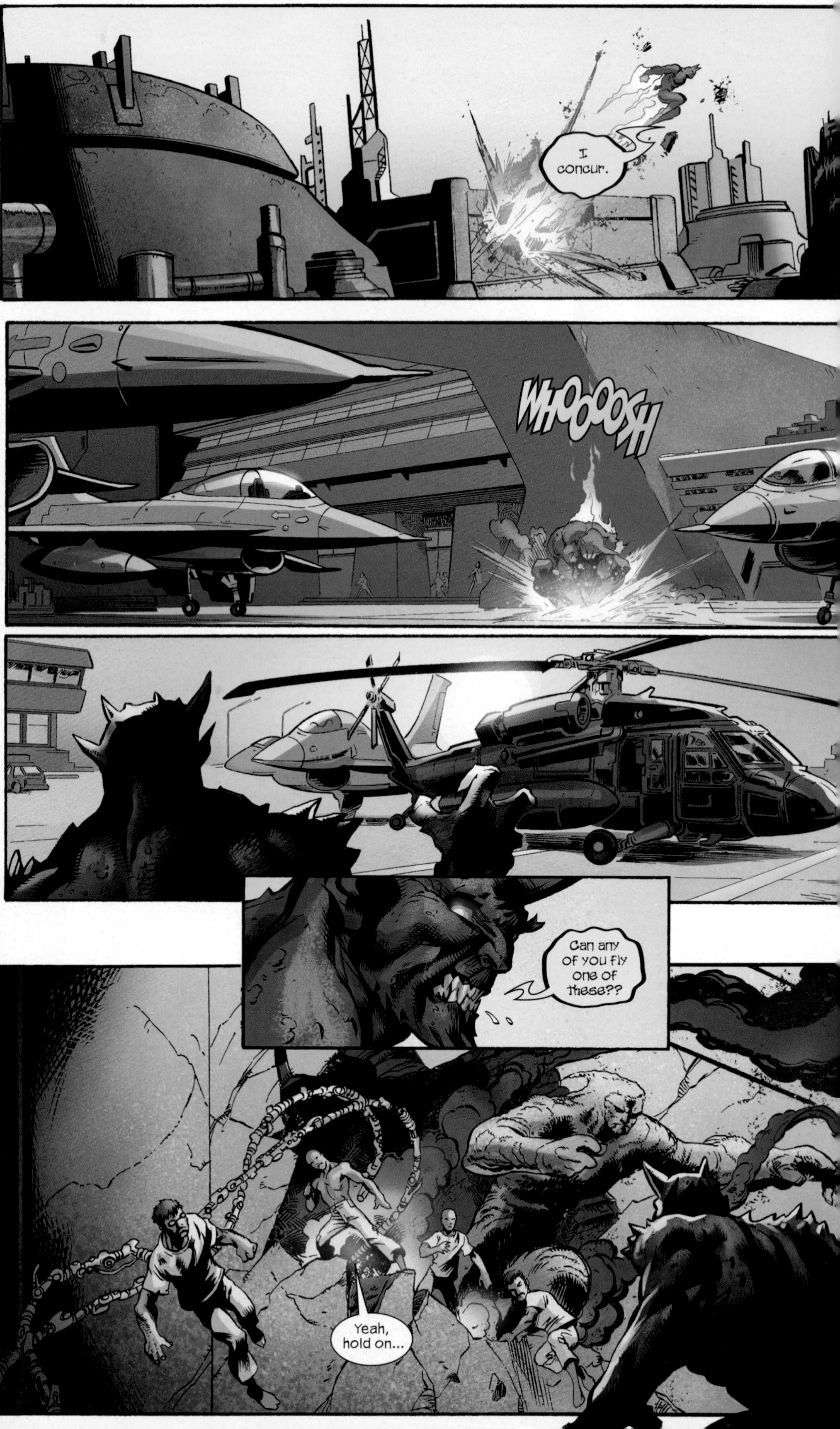
I concur.
WHOOOOSH
Can any of you fly one of these??
Yeah, hold on...

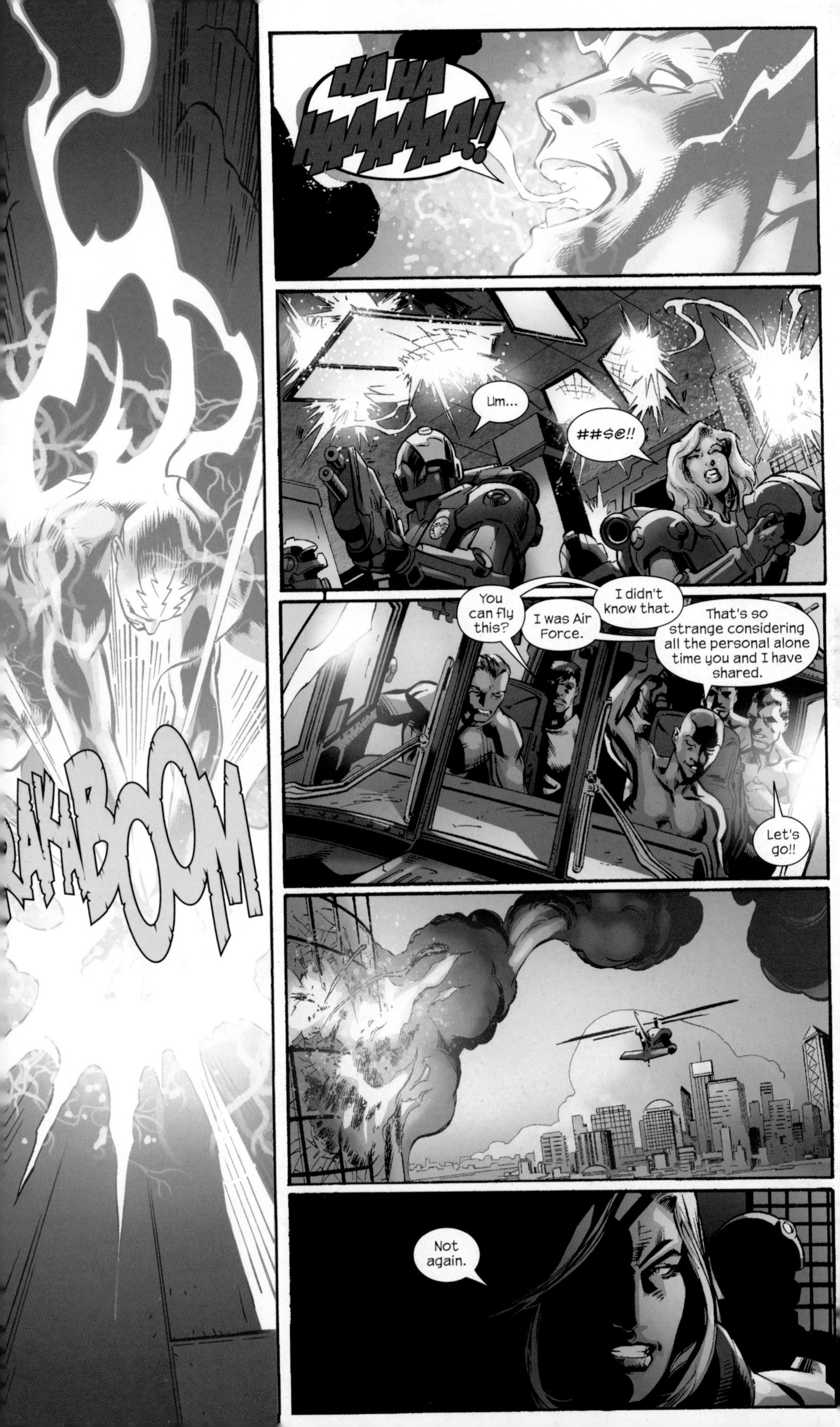

KAHBOOM
HA HA HAHAHAHA!!
Um...
##$@!!
You can fly this?
I was Air Force.
I didn't know that.
That's so strange considering all the personal alone time you and I have shared.
Let's go!!
Not again.

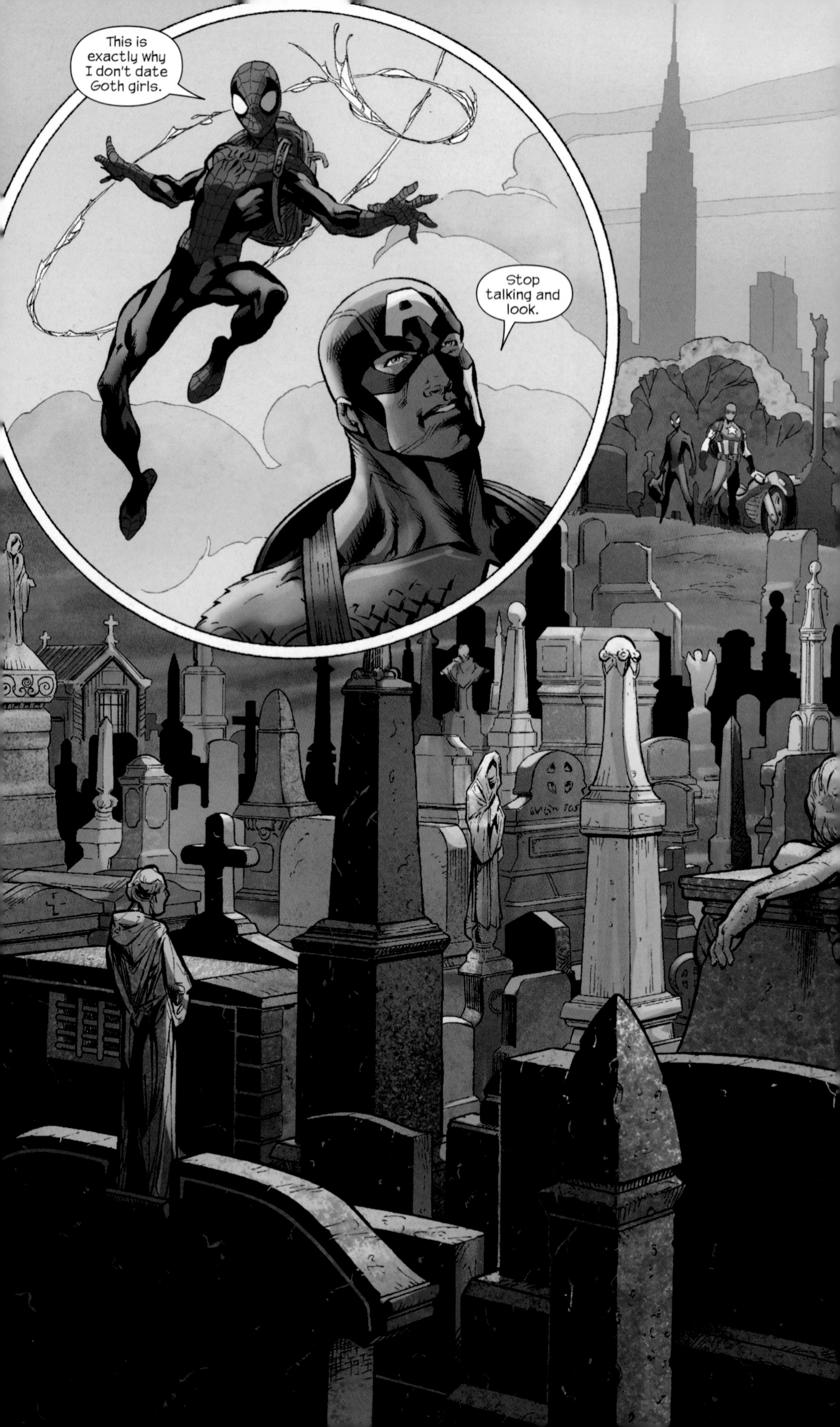
This is exactly why I don't date Goth girls.
Stop talking and look.

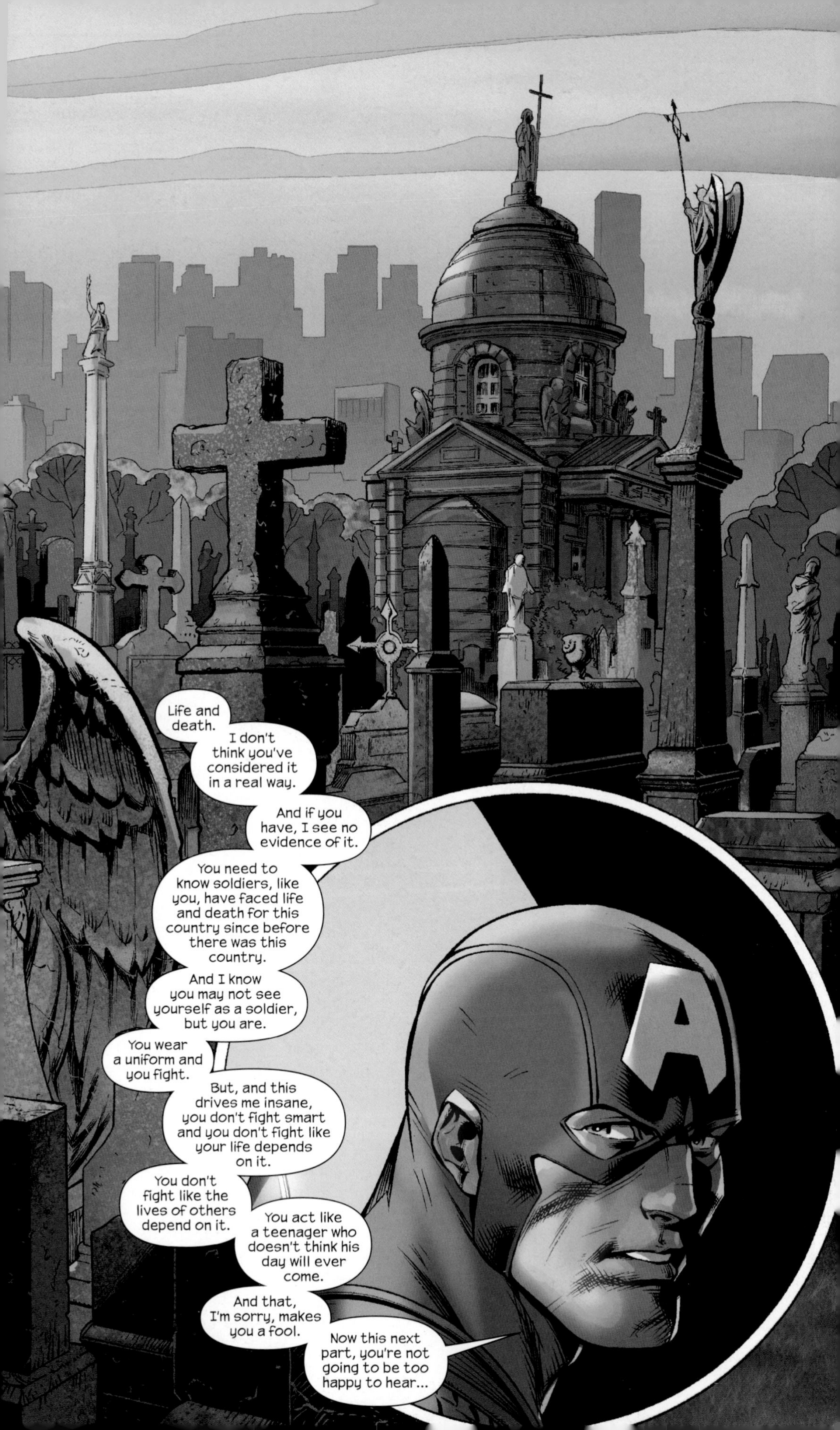
Life and death.
I don't think you've considered it in a real way.
And if you have, I see no evidence of it.
You need to know soldiers, like you, have faced life and death for this country since before there was this country.
And I know you may not see yourself as a soldier, but you are.
You wear a uniform and you fight.
But, and this drives me insane, you don't fight smart and you don't fight like your life depends on it.
You don't fight like the lives of others depend on it.
You act like a teenager who doesn't think his day will ever come.
And that, I'm sorry, makes you a fool.
Now this next part, you're not going to be too happy to hear...

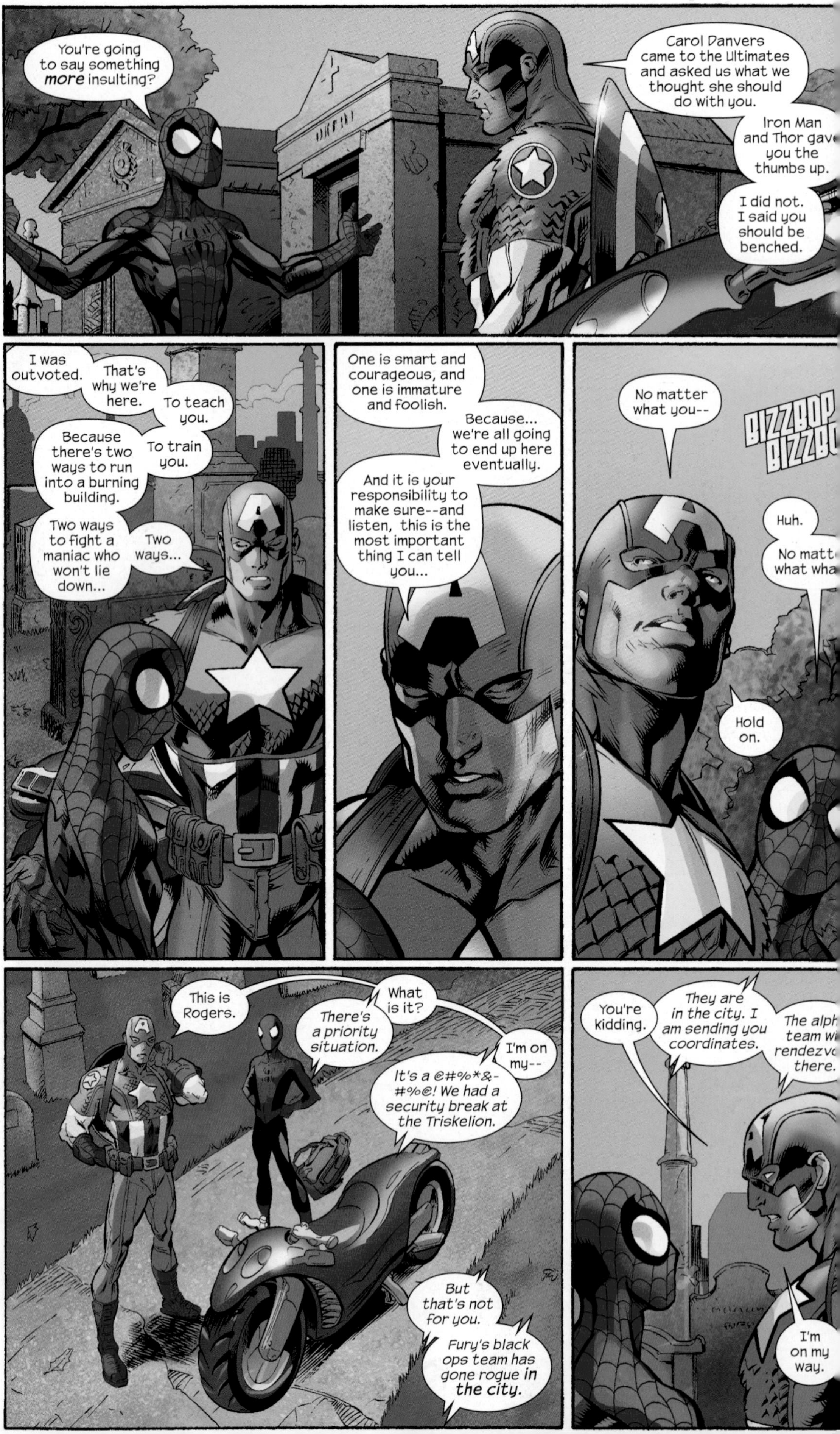

You're going to say something *more* insulting?
Carol Danvers came to the Ultimates and asked us what we thought she should do with you.
Iron Man and Thor gav you the thumbs up.
I did not. I said you should be benched.
I was outvoted.
That's why we're here.
To teach you.
To train you.
Because there's two ways to run into a burning building.
Two ways to fight a maniac who won't lie down...
Two ways...
One is smart and courageous, and one is immature and foolish.
Because... we're all going to end up here eventually.
And it is your responsibility to make sure--and listen, this is the most important thing I can tell you...
No matter what you--
BIZZBOP
BIZZBO
Huh.
No matt what wha
Hold on.
This is Rogers.
What is it?
There's a priority situation.
I'm on my--
It's a @#%*&-#%@! We had a security break at the Triskelion.
But that's not for you.
Fury's black ops team has gone rogue **in the city.**
You're kidding.
They are in the city. I am sending you coordinates.
The alph team w rendezv there.
I'm on my way.

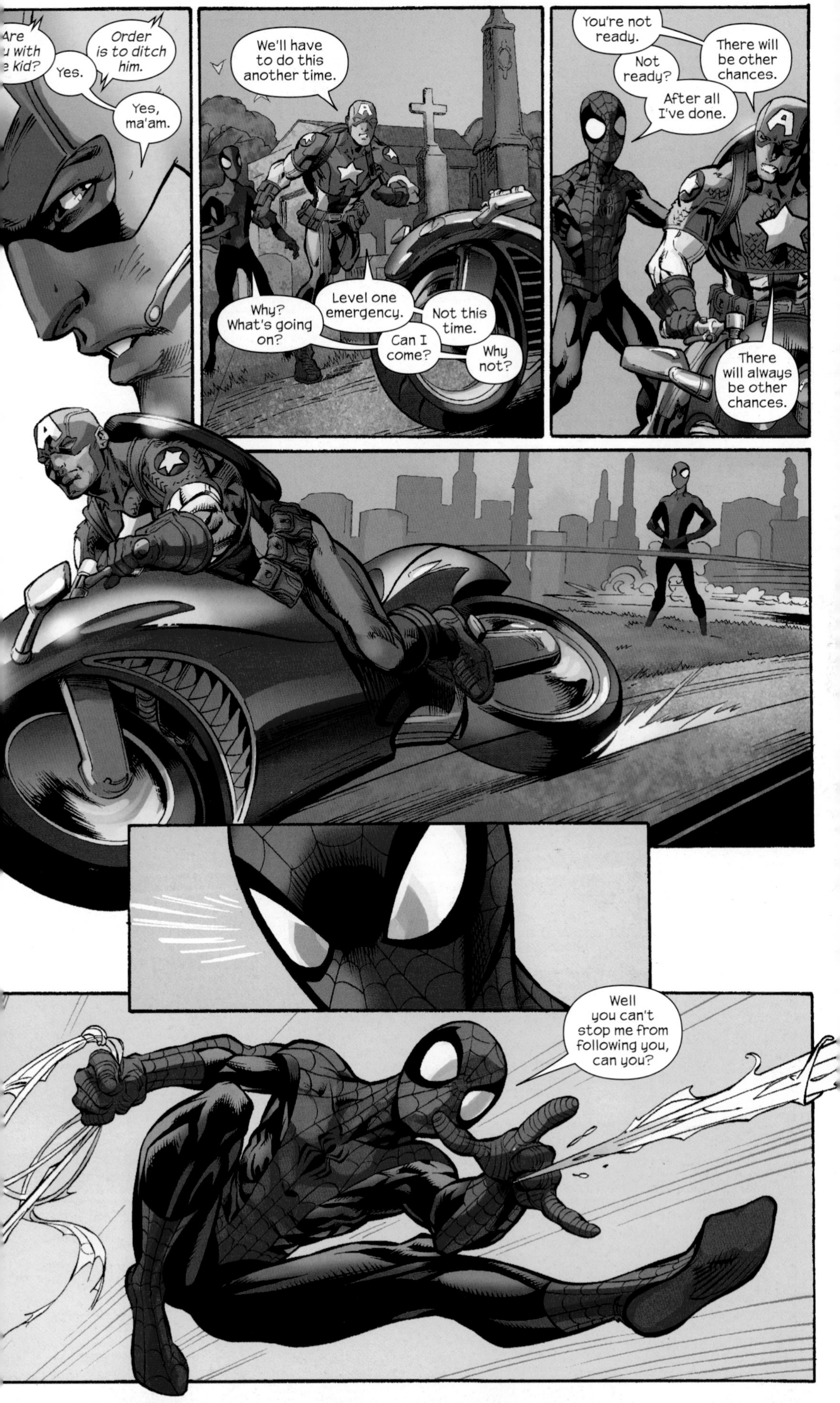
Are u with e kid?
Yes.
Order is to ditch him.
Yes, ma'am.
We'll have to do this another time.
Why? What's going on?
Level one emergency.
Can I come?
Not this time.
Why not?
You're not ready.
Not ready?
After all I've done.
There will be other chances.
There will always be other chances.
Well you can't stop me from following you, can you?

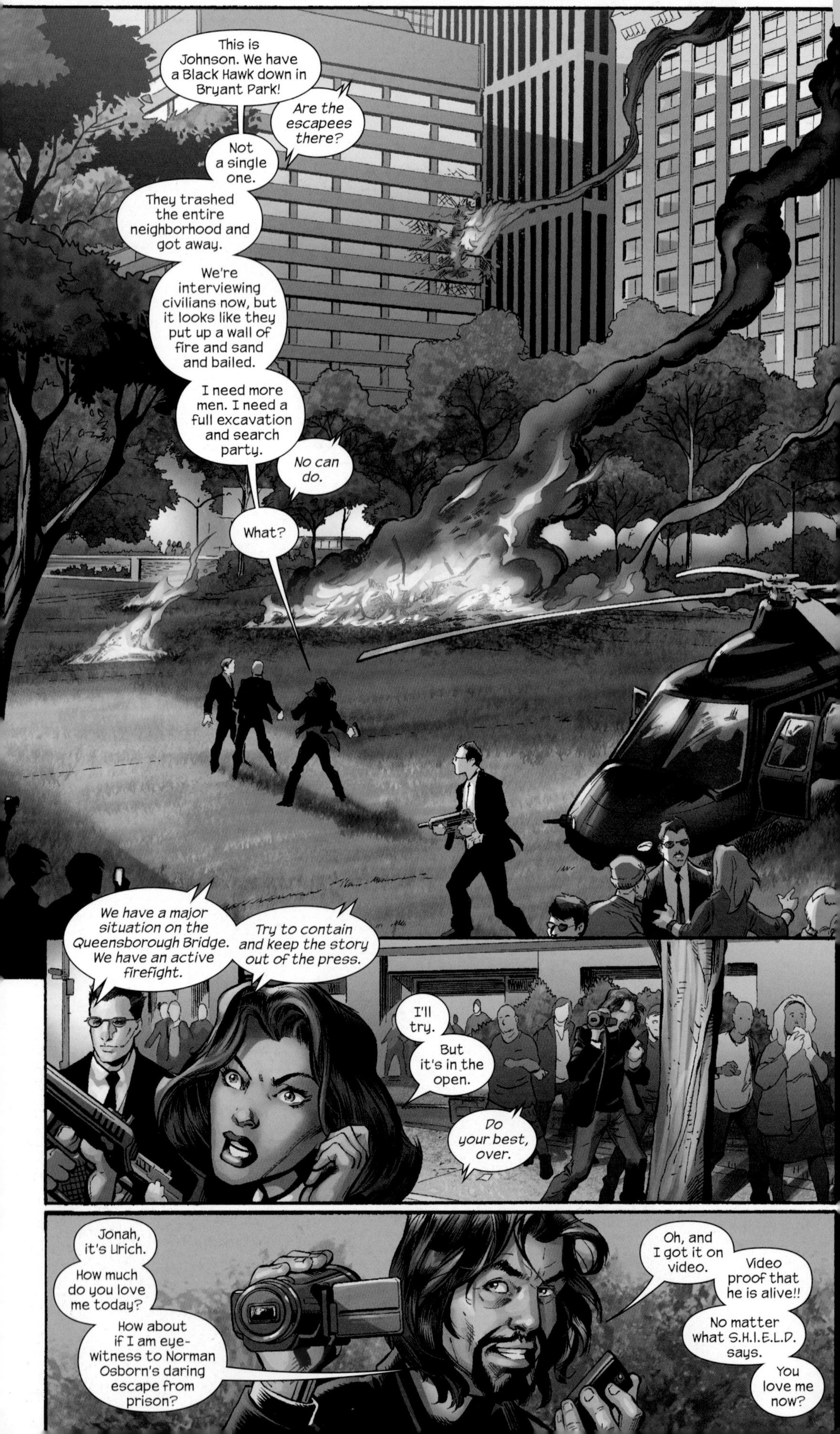
This is Johnson. We have a Black Hawk down in Bryant Park!
Are the escapees there?
Not a single one.
They trashed the entire neighborhood and got away.
We're interviewing civilians now, but it looks like they put up a wall of fire and sand and bailed.
I need more men. I need a full excavation and search party.
No can do.
What?
We have a major situation on the Queensborough Bridge. We have an active firefight.
Try to contain and keep the story out of the press.
I'll try.
But it's in the open.
Do your best, over.
Jonah, it's Urich.
How much do you love me today?
How about if I am eye-witness to Norman Osborn's daring escape from prison?
Oh, and I got it on video.
Video proof that he is alive!!
No matter what S.H.I.E.L.D. says.
You love me now?

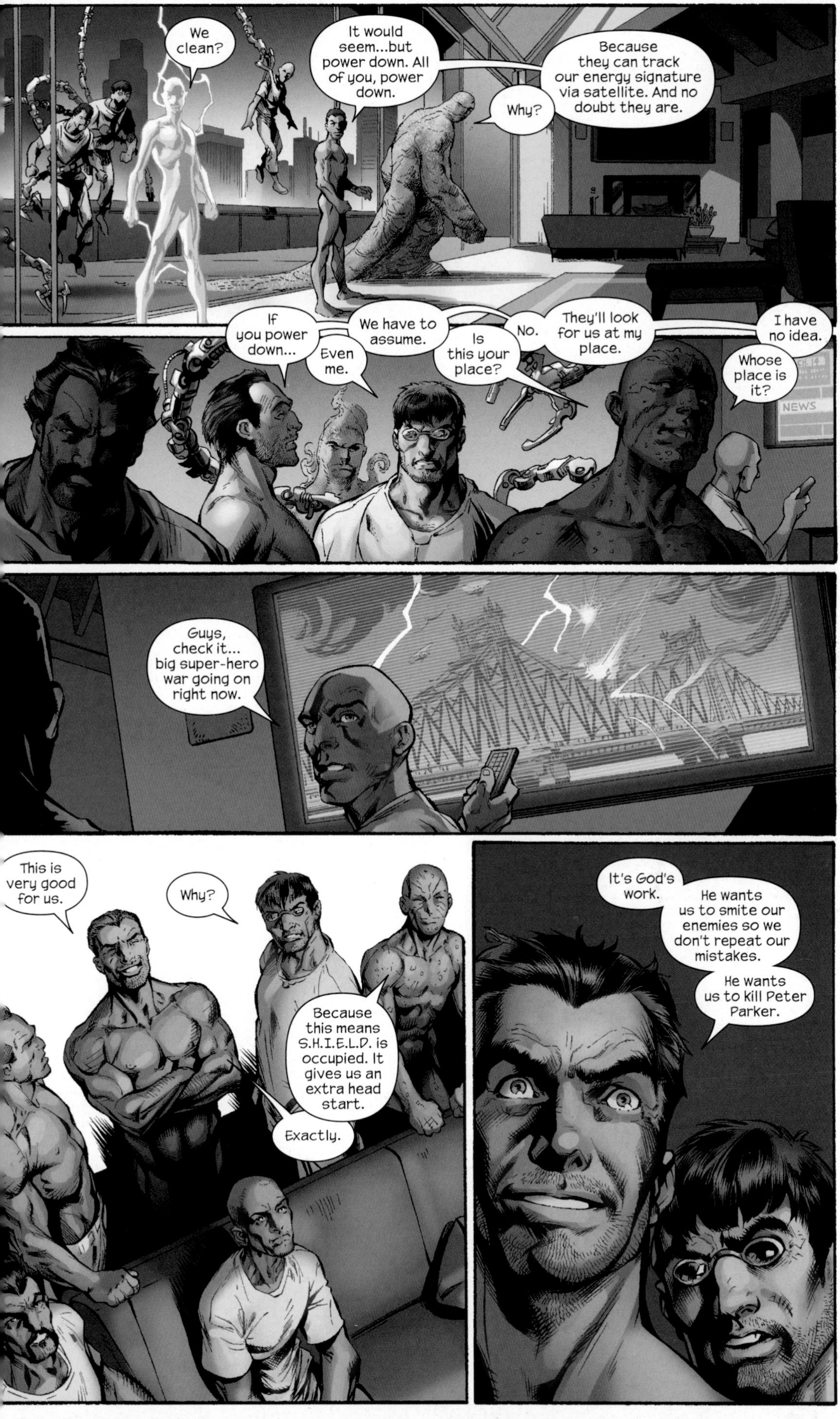
We clean?
It would seem...but power down. All of you, power down.
Why?
Because they can track our energy signature via satellite. And no doubt they are.
If you power down...
Even me.
We have to assume.
Is this your place?
No.
They'll look for us at my place.
Whose place is it?
I have no idea.
NEWS
Guys, check it... big super-hero war going on right now.
This is very good for us.
Why?
Because this means S.H.I.E.L.D. is occupied. It gives us an extra head start.
Exactly.
It's God's work.
He wants us to smite our enemies so we don't repeat our mistakes.
He wants us to kill Peter Parker.

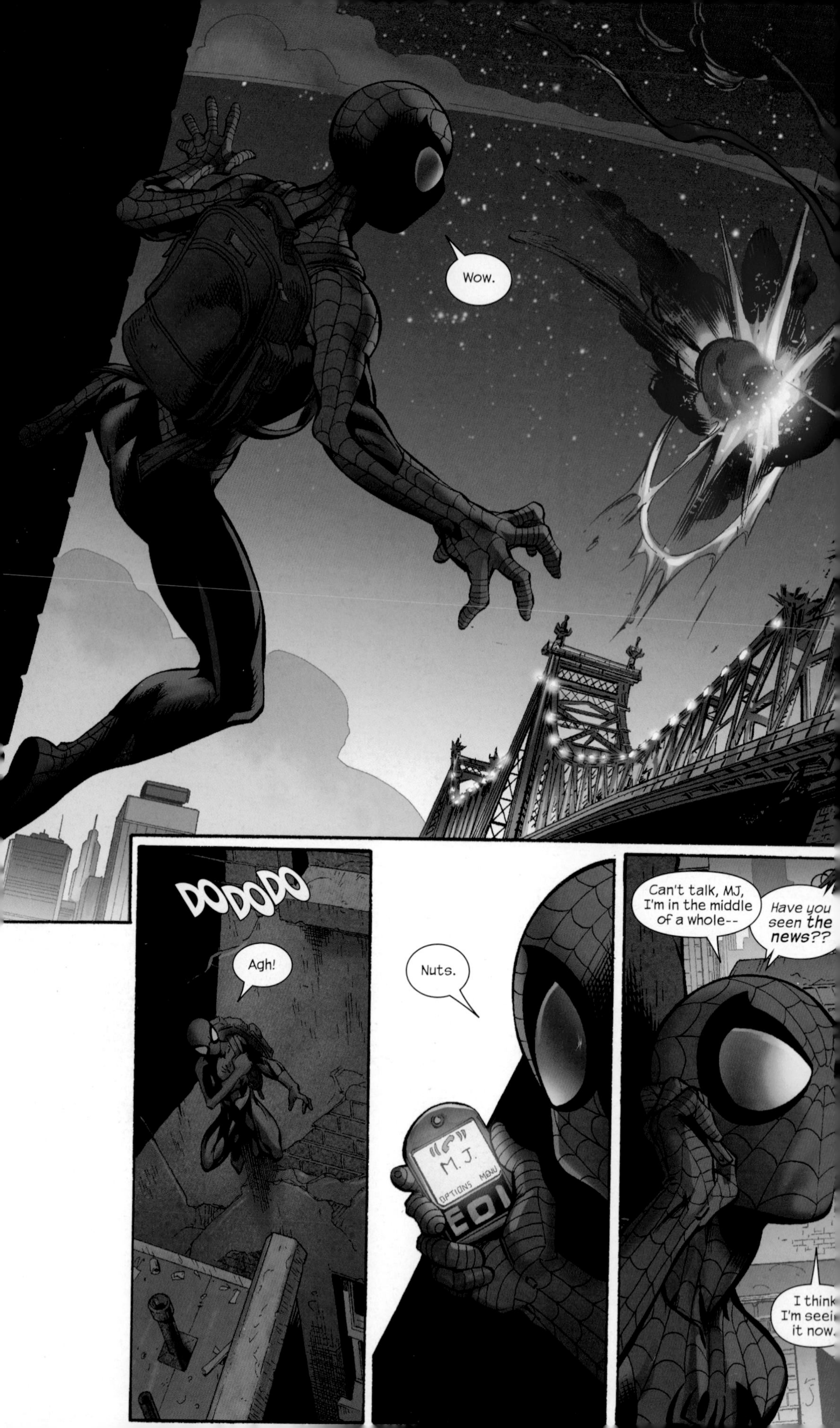
Wow.
DODODO
Agh!
Nuts.
M.J.
OPTIONS MENU
Can't talk, MJ, I'm in the middle of a whole--
Have you seen the news??
I think I'm seei it now.

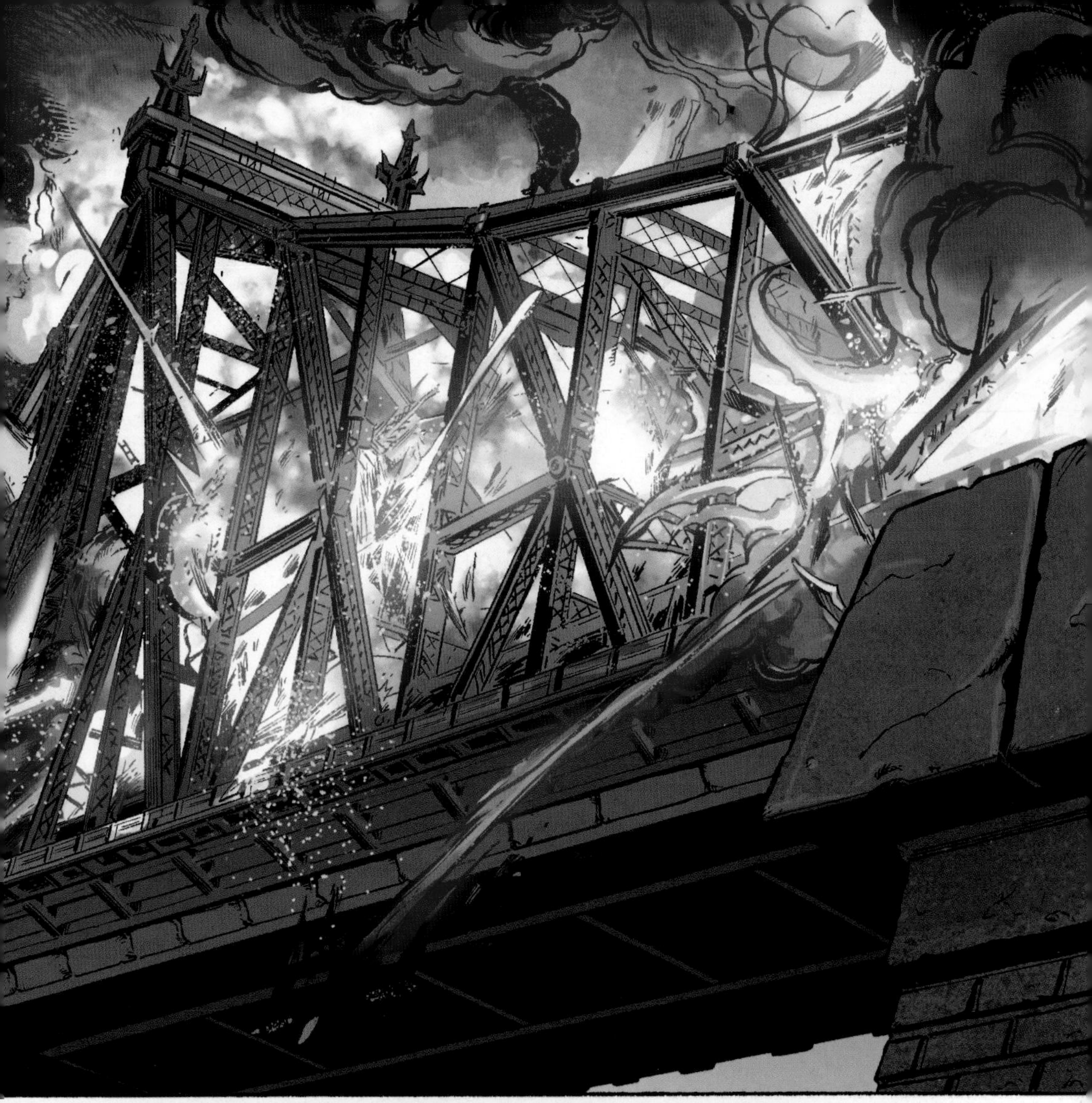

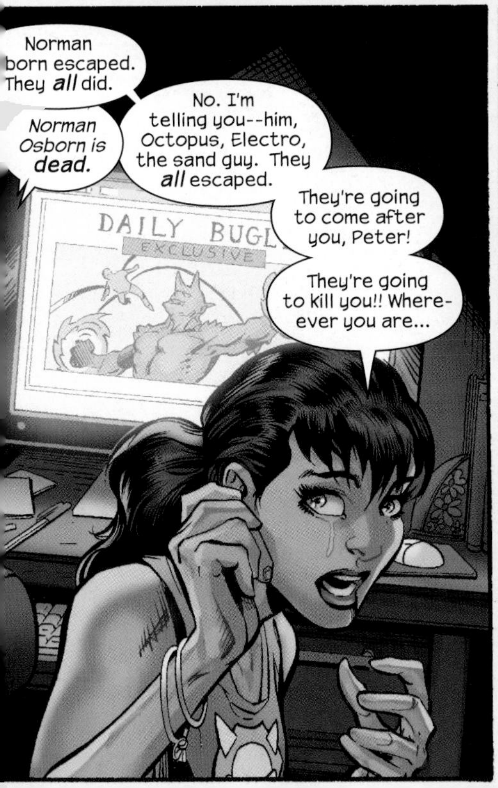

Norman born escaped. They all did.
Norman Osborn is dead.
No. I'm telling you--him, Octopus, Electro, the sand guy. They all escaped.
They're going to come after you, Peter!
They're going to kill you!! Where-ever you are...
DAILY BUGL
EXCLUSIVE

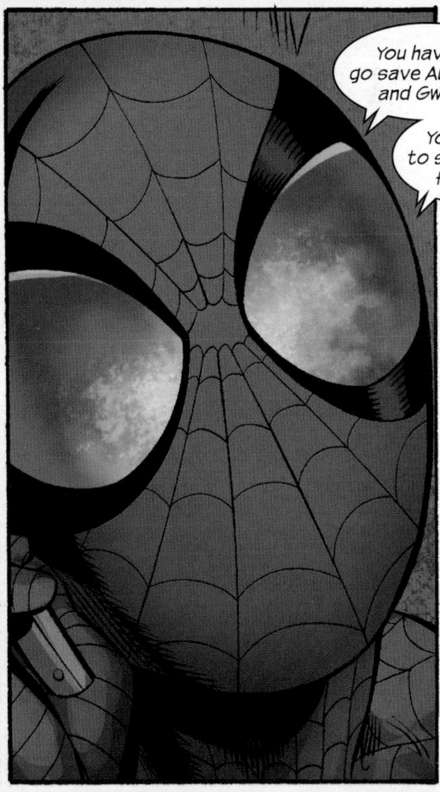

You have to go save Aunt May and Gwen.
You have to save your family.

#156 VARIANT
BY KAARE ANDREWS

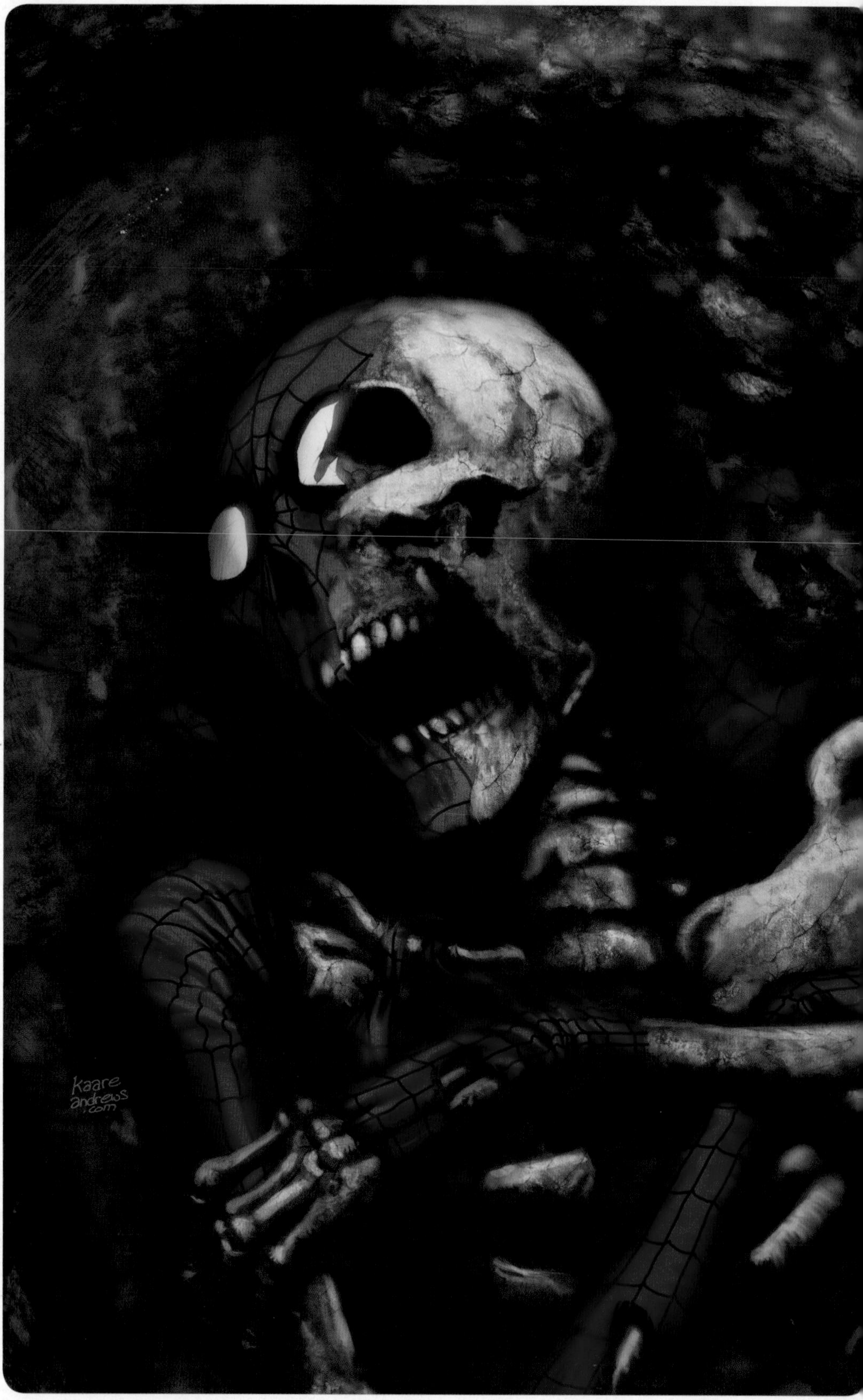
kaare
andrews
.com

157

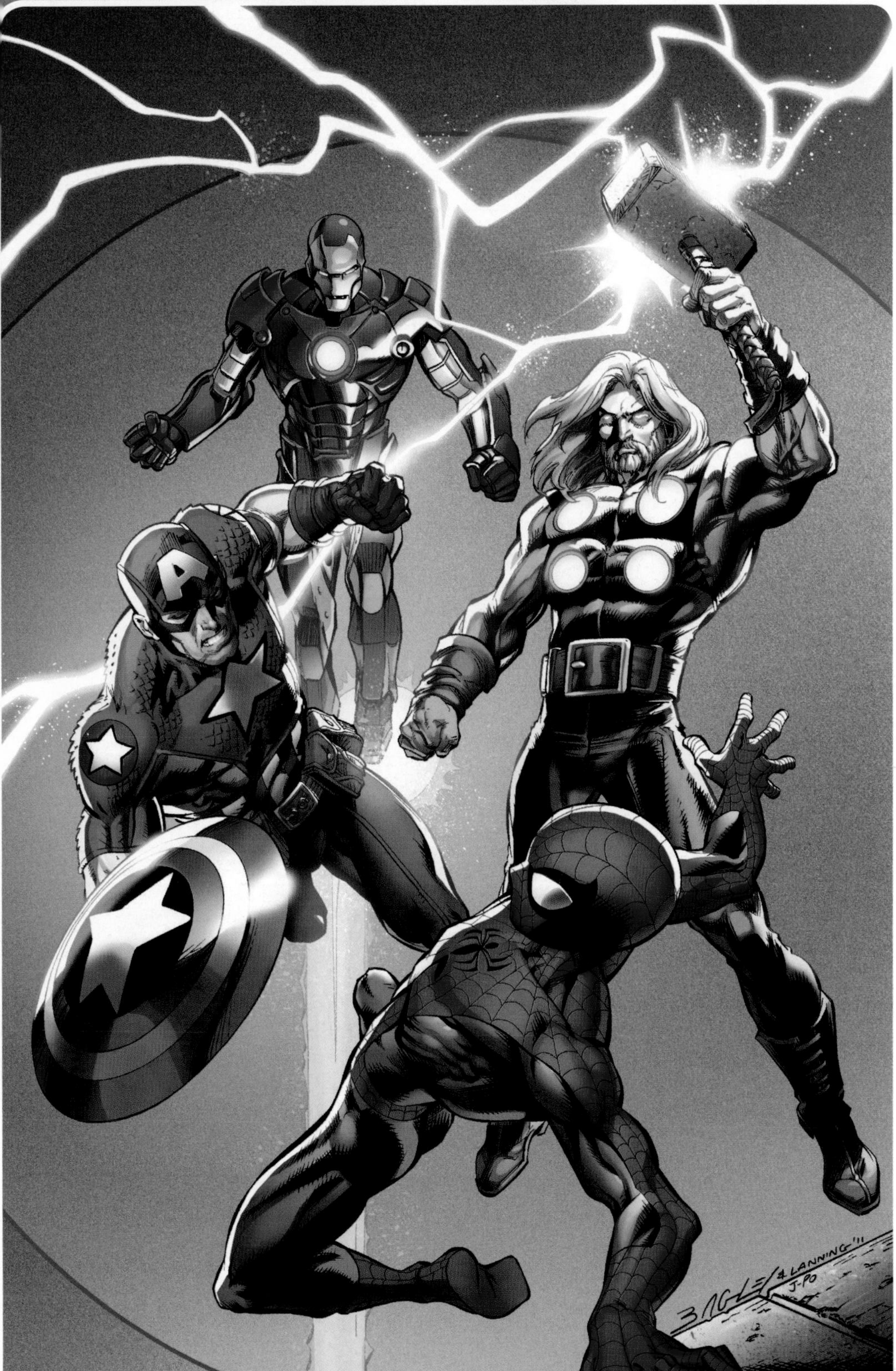
BAGLEY & LANNING '11
J-PO

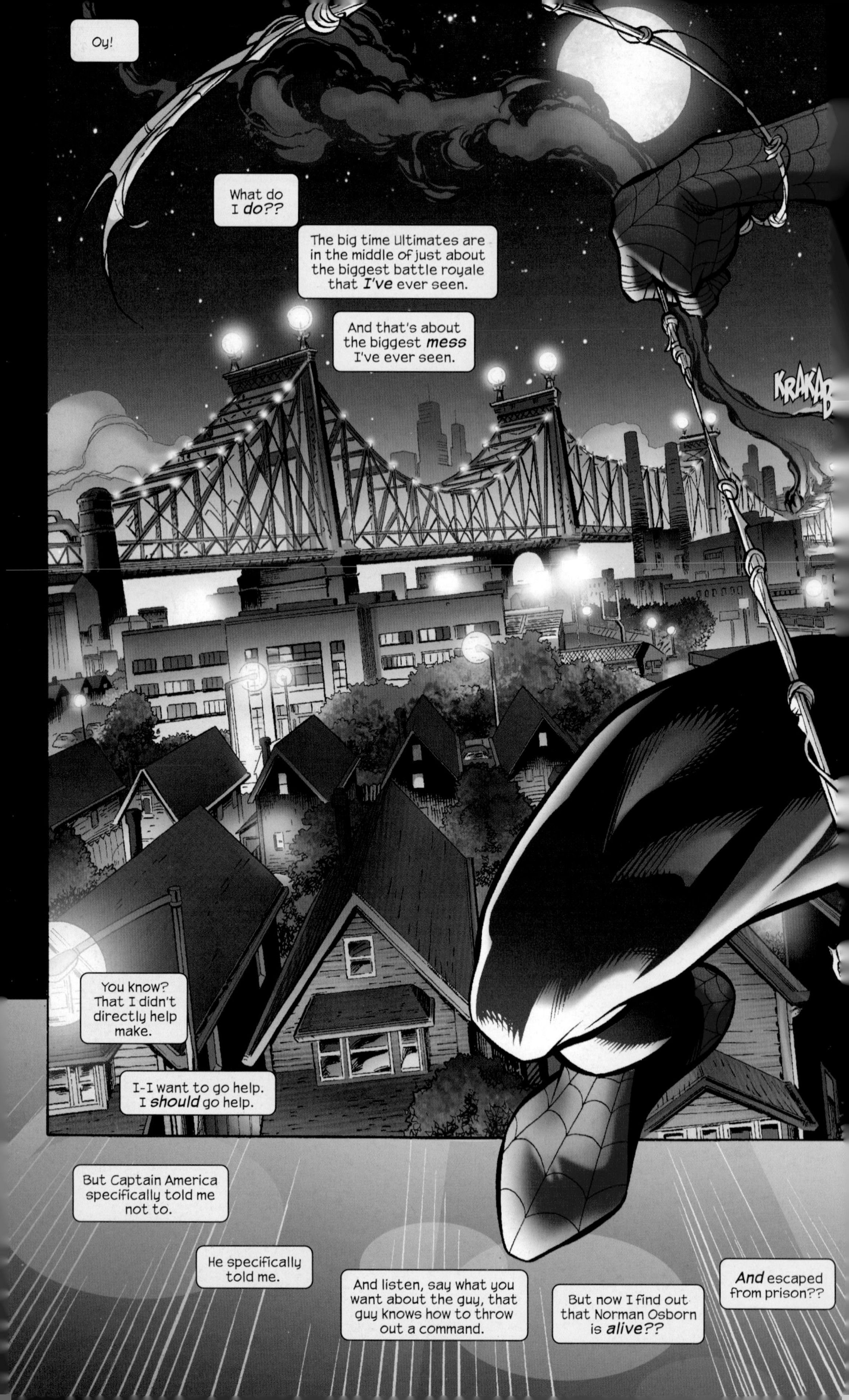
Oy!
What do I *do??*
The big time Ultimates are in the middle of just about the biggest battle royale that *I've* ever seen.
And that's about the biggest *mess* I've ever seen.
KRAKABB
You know? That I didn't directly help make.
I-I want to go help. I *should* go help.
But Captain America specifically told me not to.
He specifically told me.
And listen, say what you want about the guy, that guy knows how to throw out a command.
But now I find out that Norman Osborn is *alive??*
And escaped from prison??

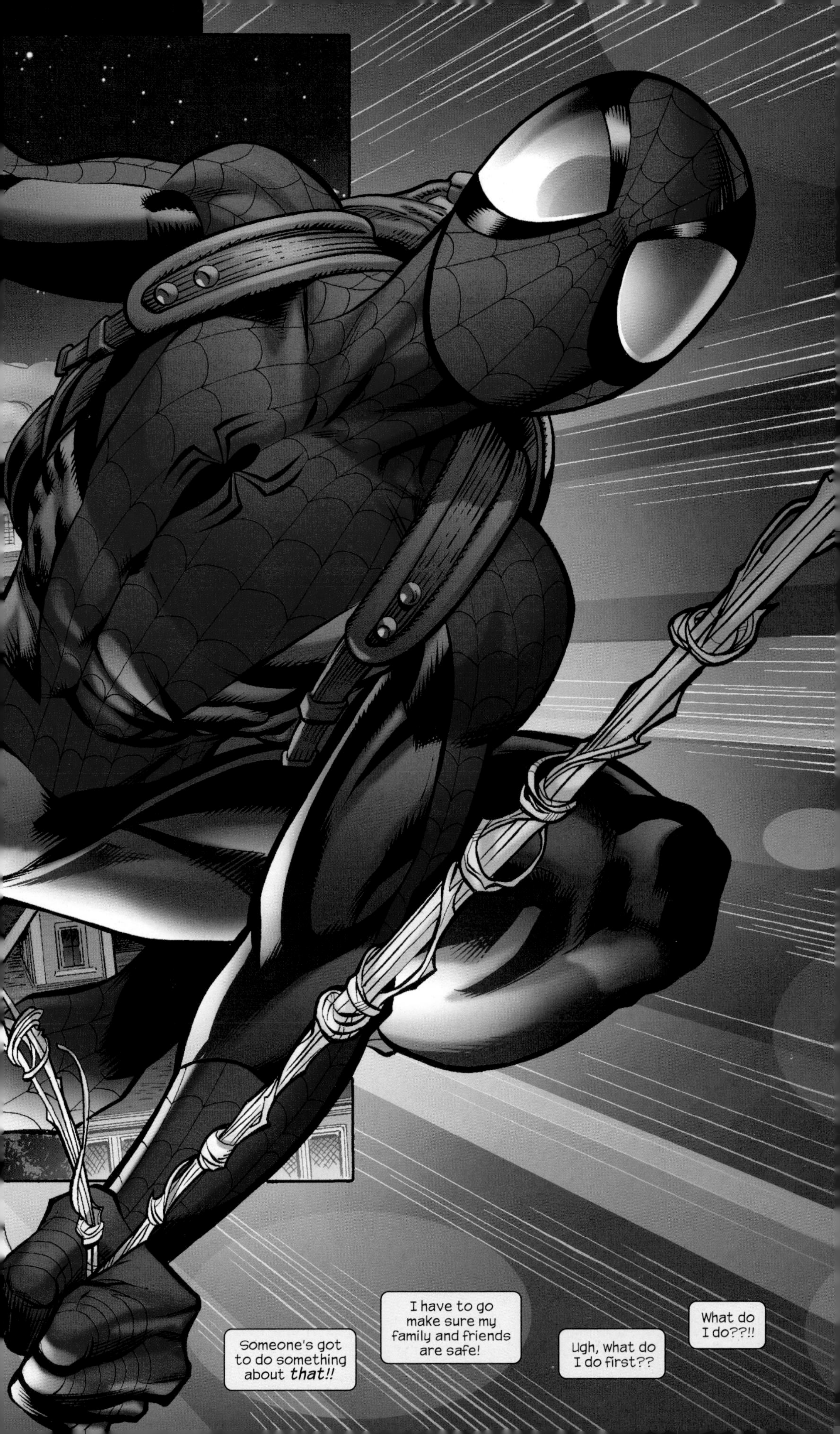
Someone's got to do something about *that!!*
I have to go make sure my family and friends are safe!
Ugh, what do I do first??
What do I do??!!

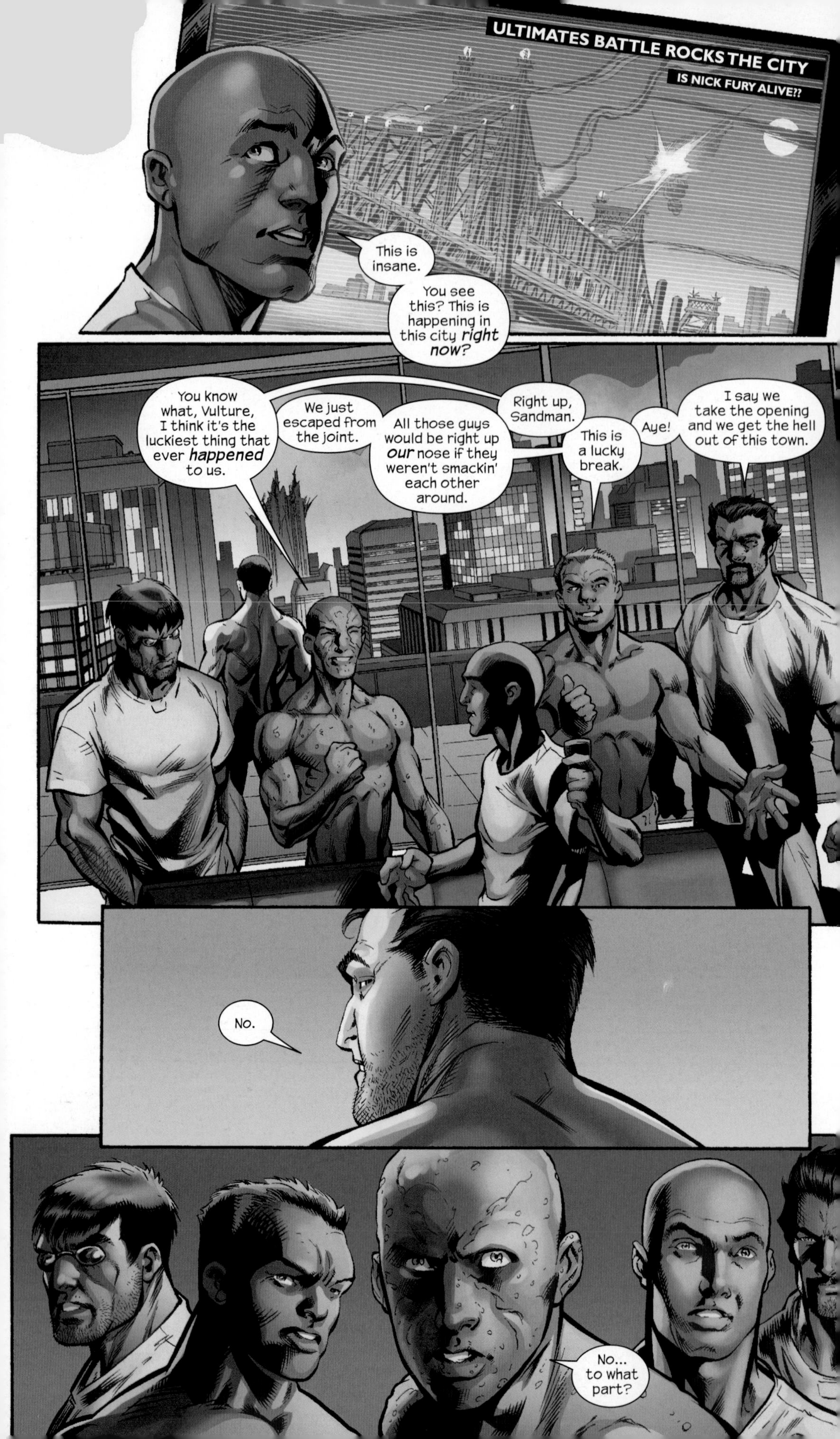
ULTIMATES BATTLE ROCKS THE CITY
IS NICK FURY ALIVE??
This is insane.
You see this? This is happening in this city right now?
You know what, Vulture, I think it's the luckiest thing that ever happened to us.
We just escaped from the joint.
All those guys would be right up our nose if they weren't smackin' each other around.
Right up, Sandman.
This is a lucky break.
Aye!
I say we take the opening and we get the hell out of this town.
No.
No... to what part?

stay ere.

What we need to do is here in New York.

Listen, Osborn, I appreciate everything you've done for me in the past...

And I appreciate you getting me out of prison even though we've had our differences but...

I'm out.

Out, Otto?

I know that look.

You have revenge in your eyes.

You're ready to get everyone.

I'm--I'm just not there. That's not where my head is at.

I want to get back to my work.

Your work?

I'm a scientist, Osborn.

I want-- I just want to be a scientist.

I'm not a career criminal or some bio-terrorist or whatever it is you're trying to accomplish here.

t rk.

ve seen since the e you and eamed ether.

see ngs rently w.

ow s I now e.

jes, I've hings, ble js.

I know.

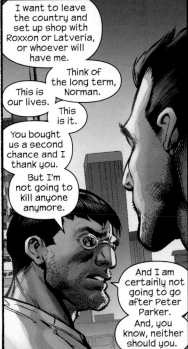

I want to leave the country and set up shop with Roxxon or Latveria, or whoever will have me.

Think of the long term, Norman.

This is our lives.

This is it.

You bought us a second chance and I thank you.

But I'm not going to kill anyone anymore.

And I am certainly not going to go after Peter Parker.

And, you know, neither should you.

End of the day, if you really think about it, Peter Parker is our greatest achievement.

We birthed Spider-Man into the world.

We did.

We should take insane pride in that and leave it alone.

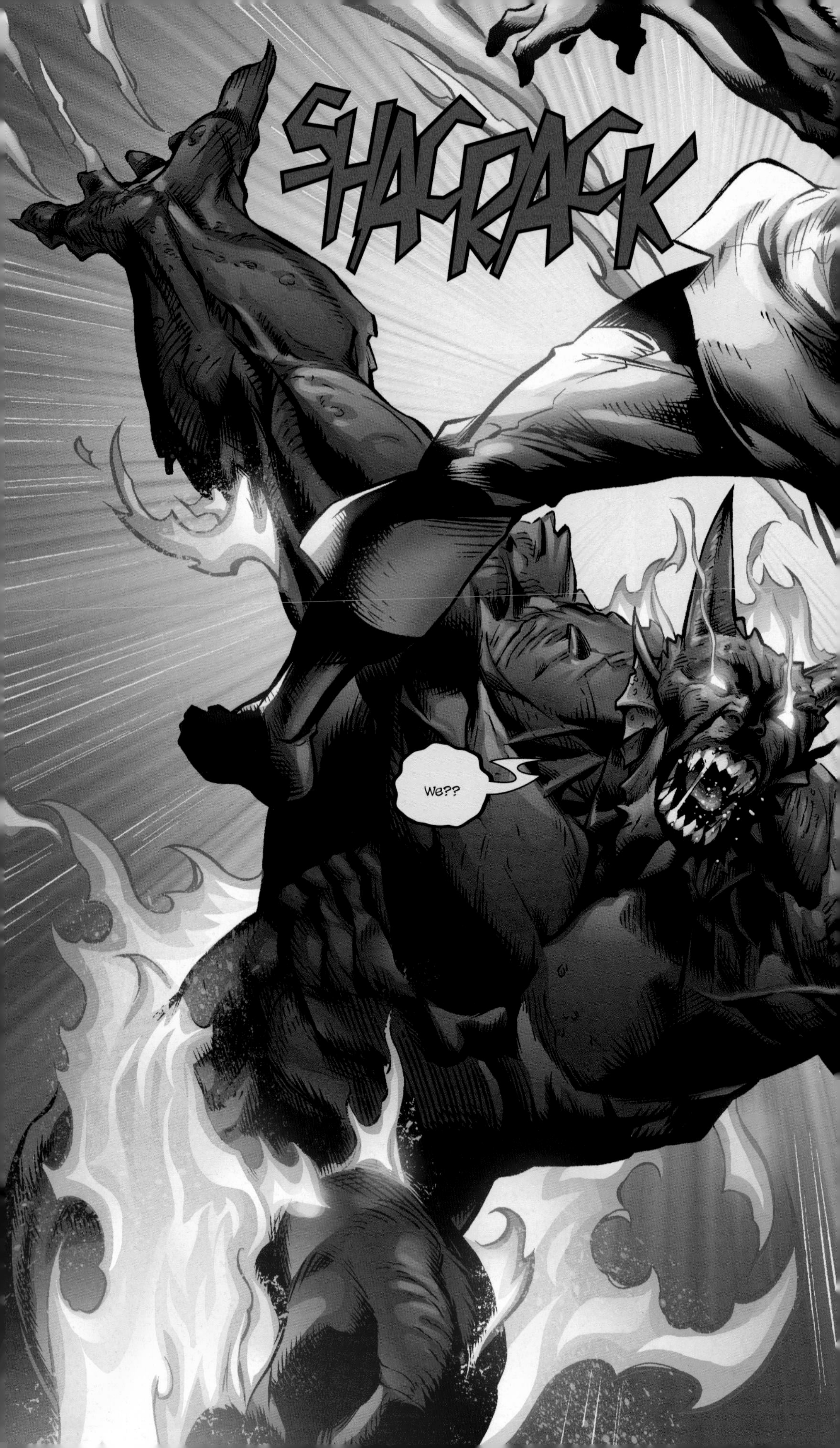
SHACRACK
WE??

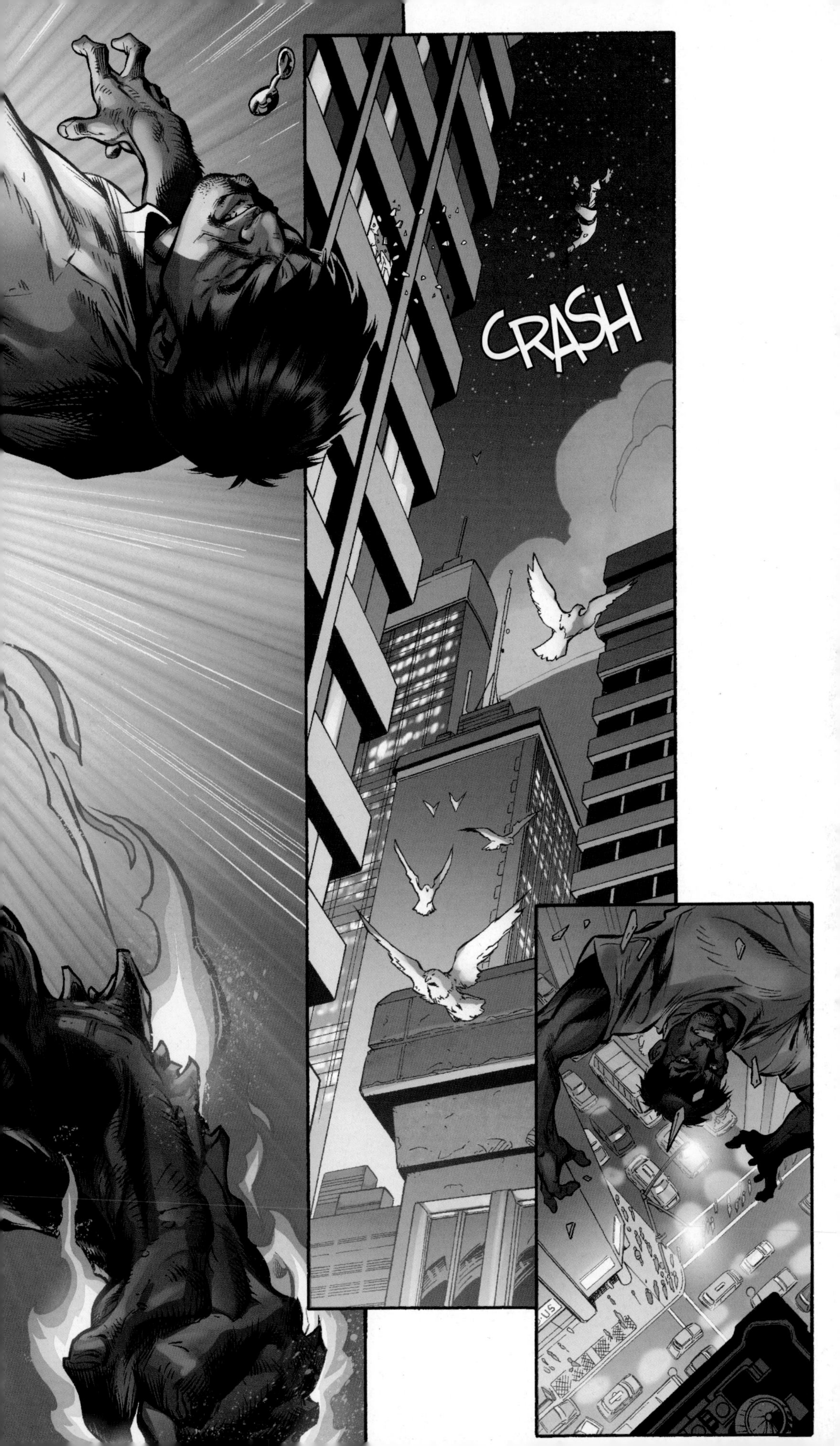
CRASH

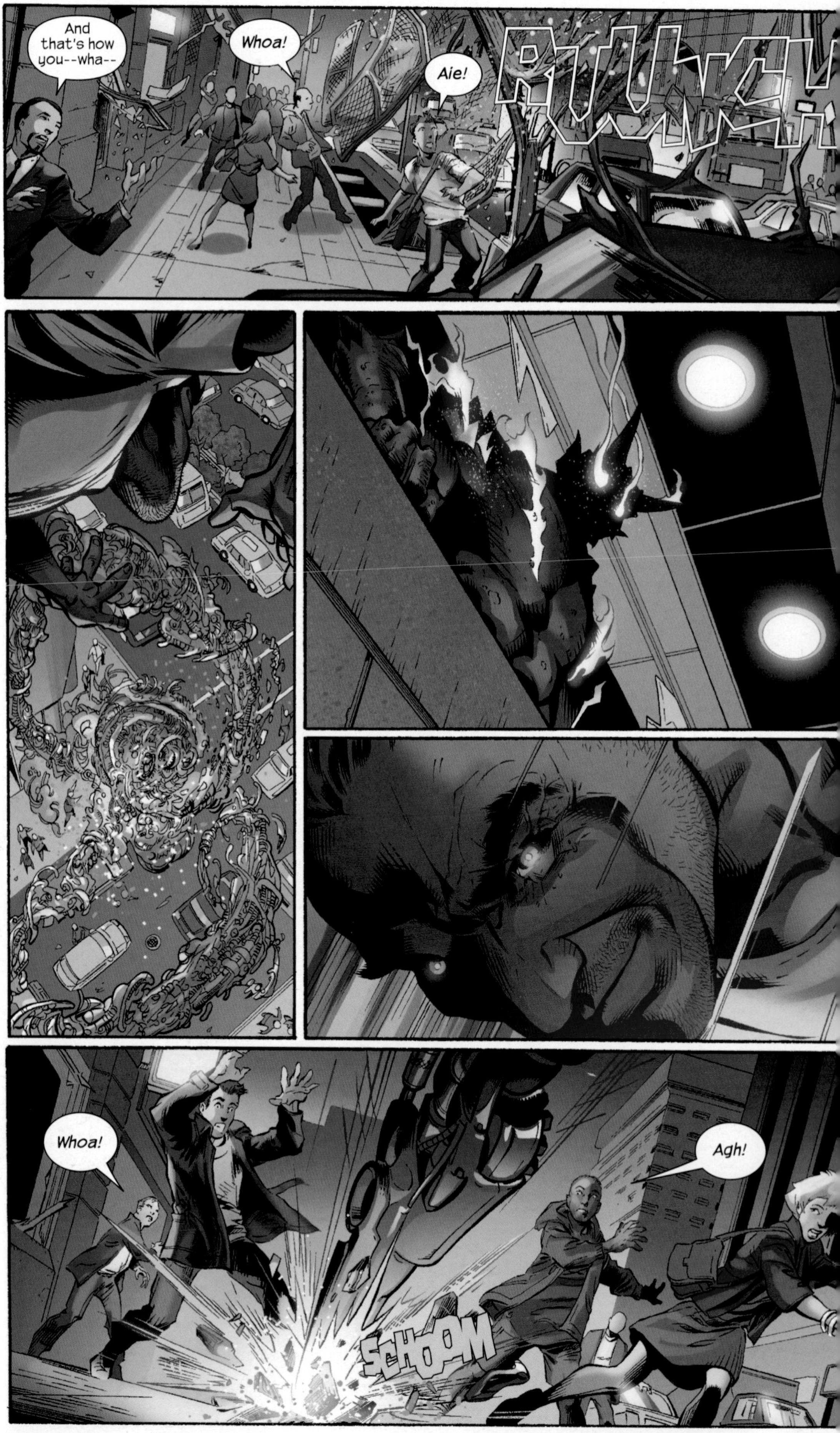
And that's how you--wha--
Whoa!
Aie!
Whoa!
Agh!
SCHOOM

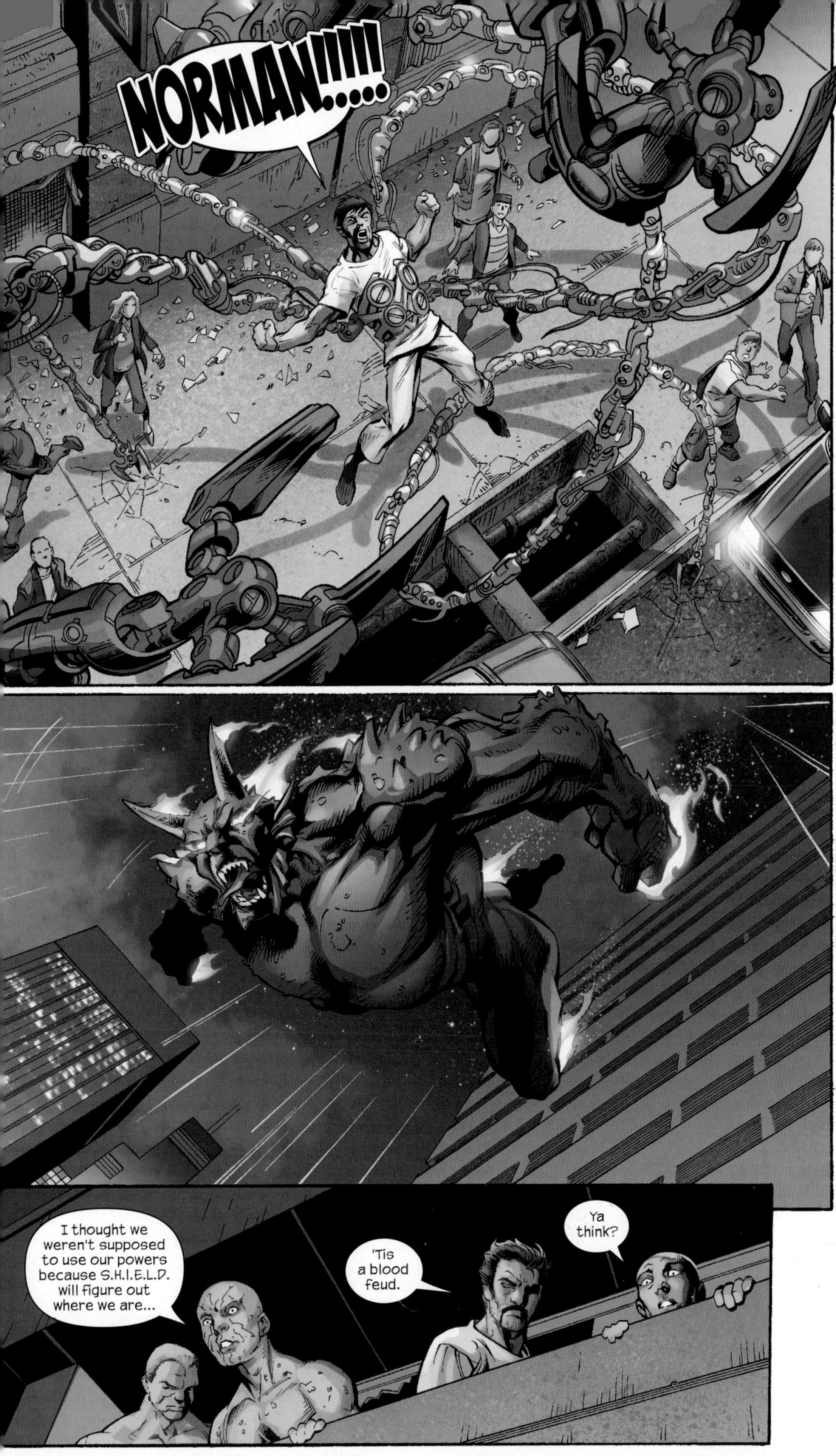
NORMAN!!!!!.....
I thought we weren't supposed to use our powers because S.H.I.E.L.D. will figure out where we are...
'Tis a blood feud.
Ya think?

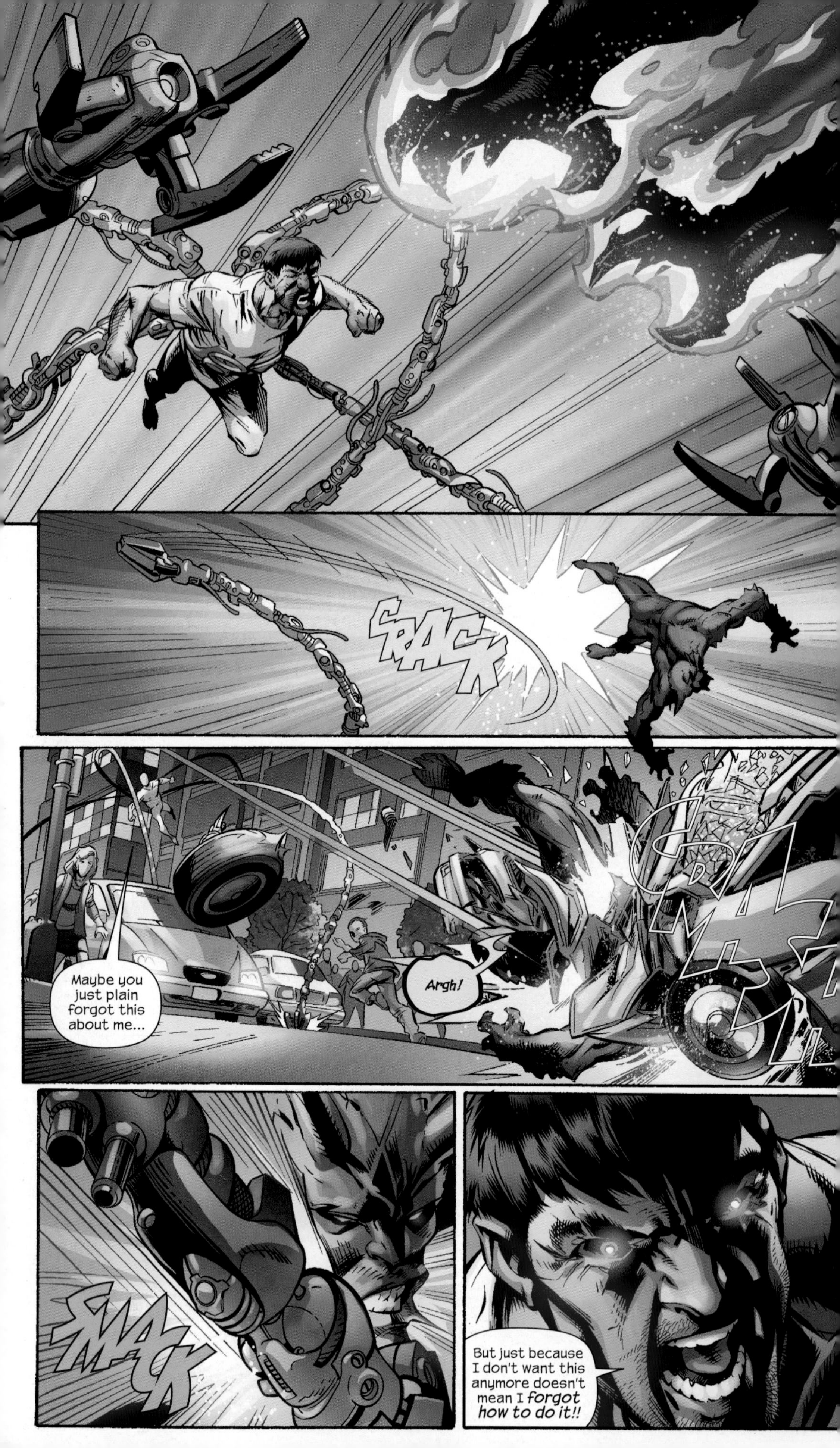
SKRACK
Maybe you just plain forgot this about me...
Argh!
CRUNCH
SMACK
But just because I don't want this anymore doesn't mean I *forgot how to do it!!*

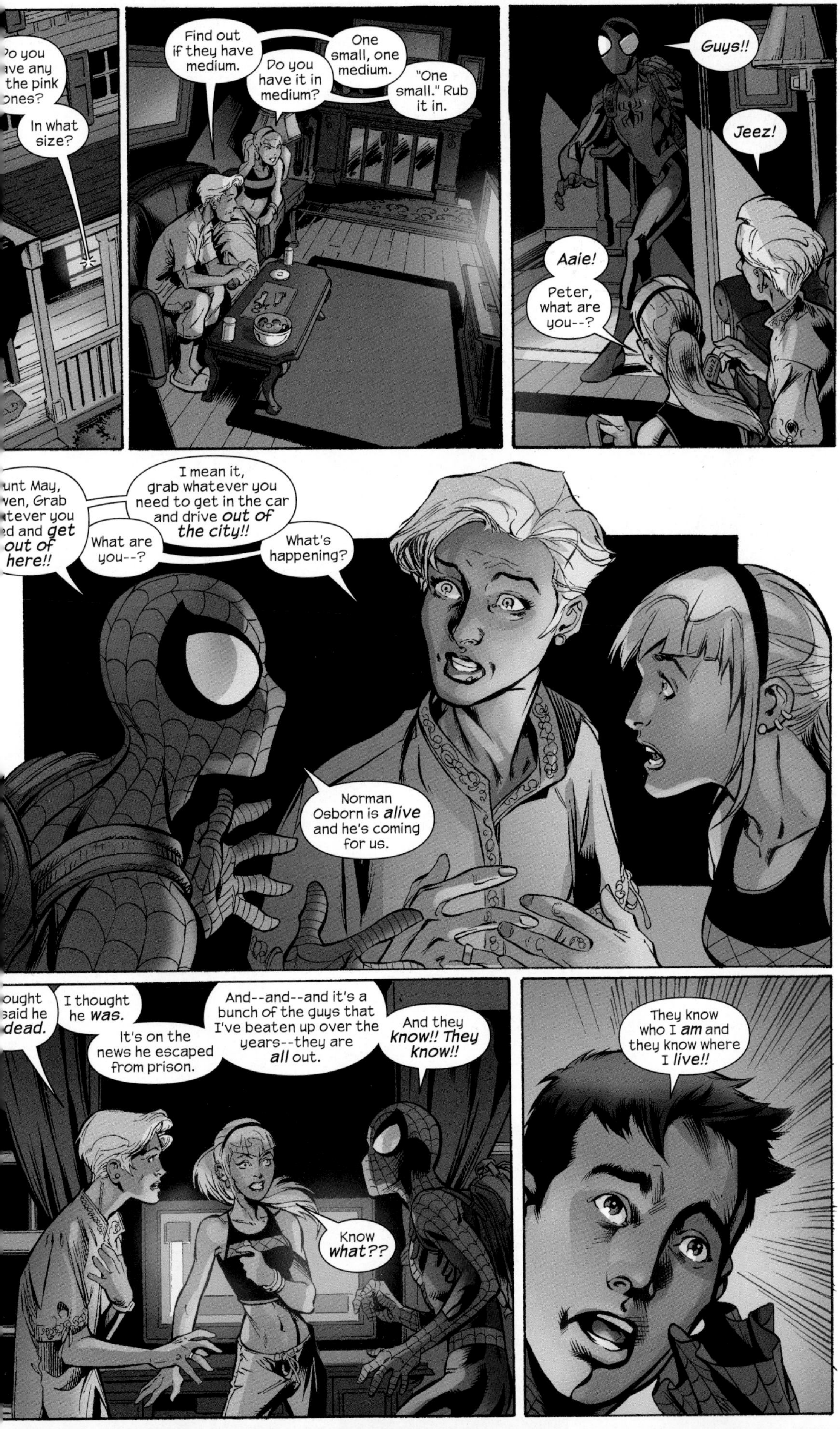

Do you
ave any
the pink
ones?
In what
size?
Find out
if they have
medium.
One
small, one
medium.
Do you
have it in
medium?
"One
small." Rub
it in.
Guys!!
Jeez!
Aaie!
Peter,
what are
you--?
unt May,
wen, Grab
atever you
ed and get
out of
here!!
I mean it,
grab whatever you
need to get in the car
and drive out of
the city!!
What are
you--?
What's
happening?
Norman
Osborn is alive
and he's coming
for us.
ought
said he
dead.
I thought
he was.
It's on the
news he escaped
from prison.
And--and--and it's a
bunch of the guys that
I've beaten up over the
years--they are
all out.
And they
know!! They
know!!
Know
what??
They know
who I am and
they know where
I live!!

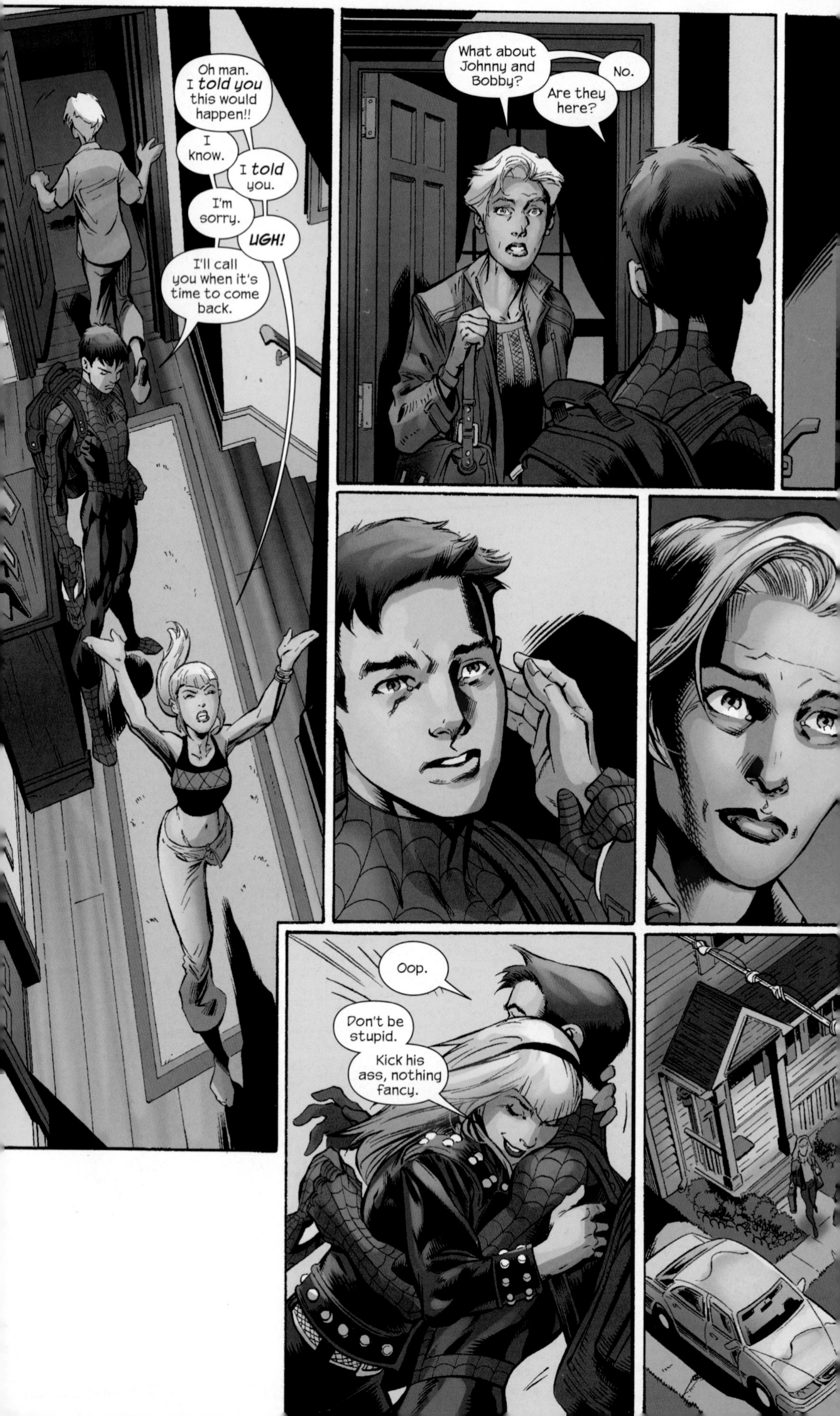
Oh man. I told you this would happen!!
I know.
I told you.
I'm sorry.
UGH!
I'll call you when it's time to come back.
What about Johnny and Bobby?
No.
Are they here?
Oop.
Don't be stupid.
Kick his ass, nothing fancy.

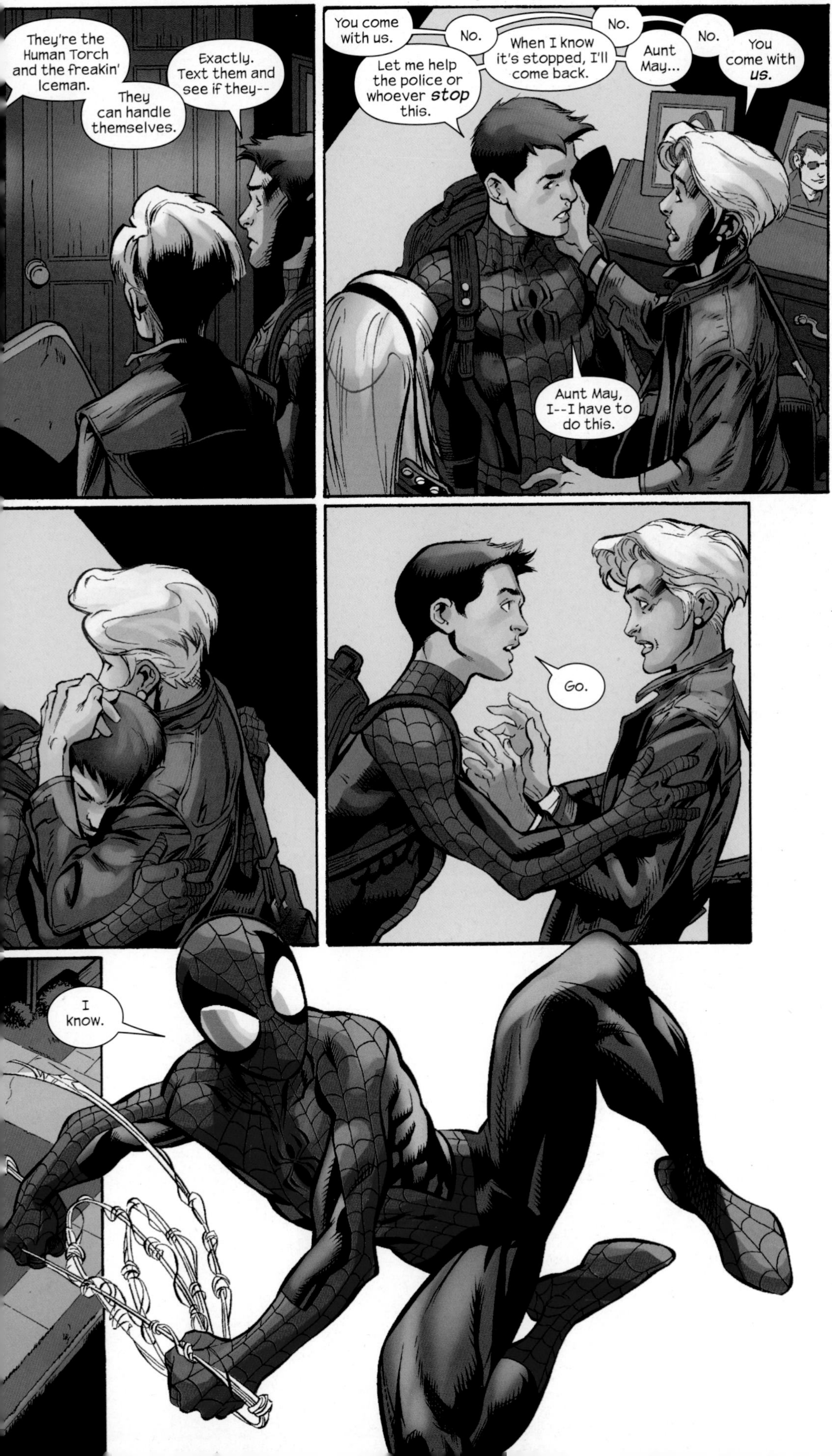

They're the Human Torch and the freakin' Iceman.
They can handle themselves.
Exactly. Text them and see if they--
You come with us.
Let me help the police or whoever stop this.
No.
When I know it's stopped, I'll come back.
No.
Aunt May...
No.
You come with us.
Aunt May, I--I have to do this.
Go.
I know.

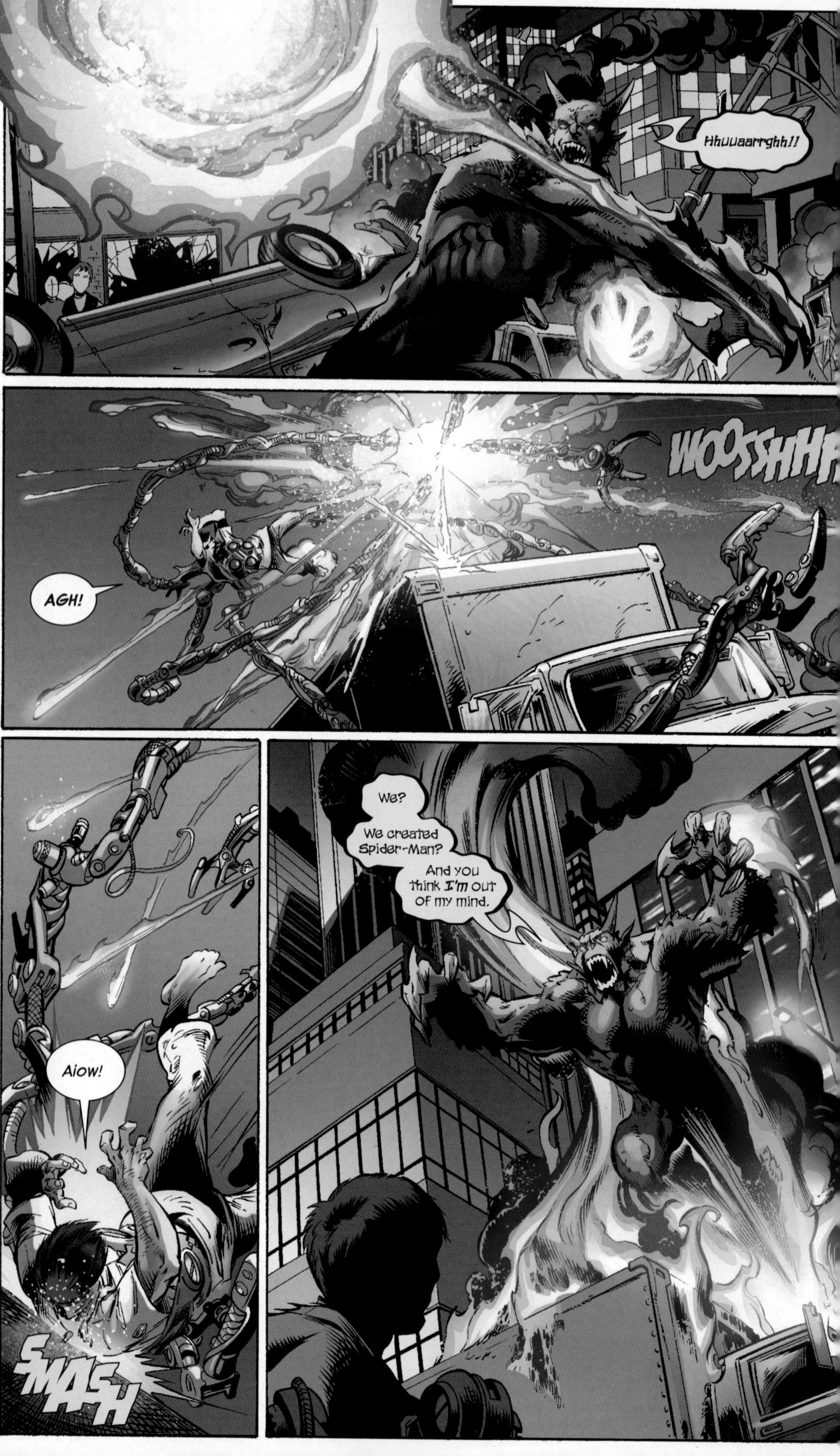
Hhuuaarrghh!!
WOOSSHHH
AGH!
Aiow!
SMASH
We?
We created Spider-Man?
And you think I'm out of my mind.

S-stop it, Norman!!

All I've done for you, and you want to bail on me *now??!!*

All I've done for you!!

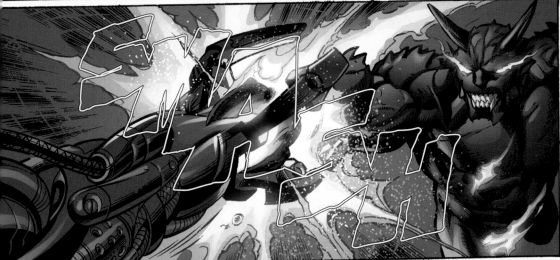

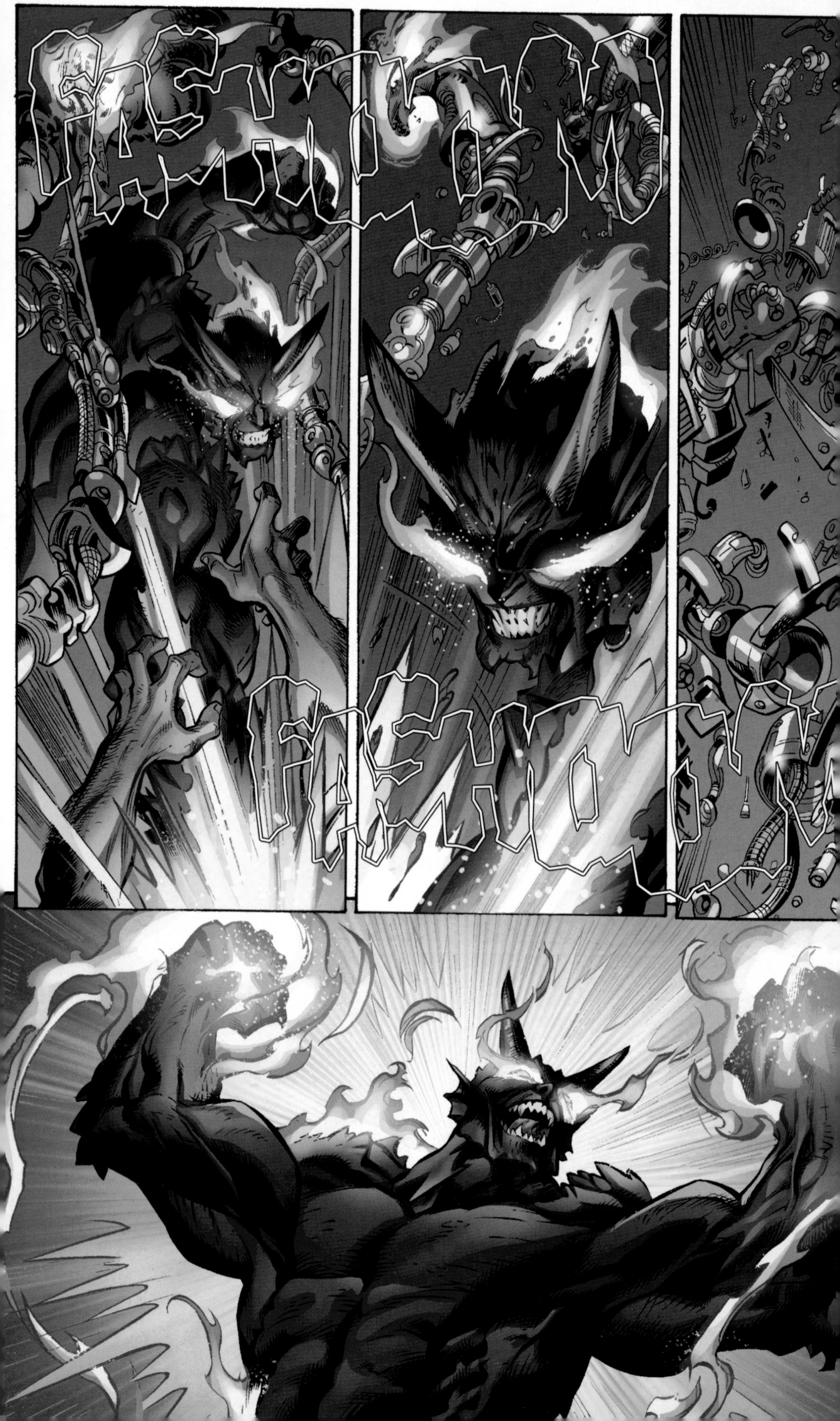
FASHOOOM
FASHOOOS

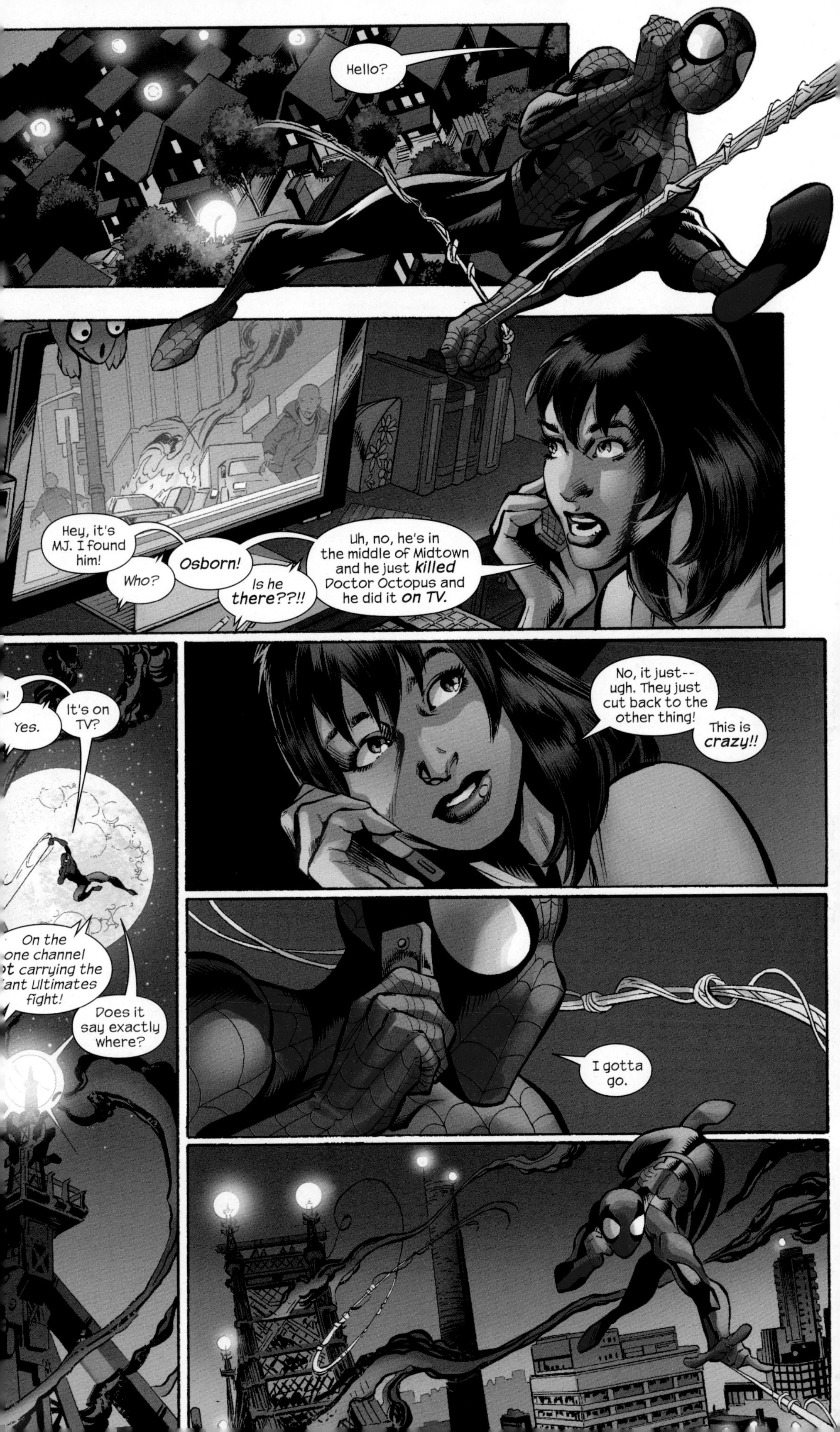
Hello?
Hey, it's MJ. I found him!
Who?
Osborn!
Is he there??!!
Uh, no, he's in the middle of Midtown and he just killed Doctor Octopus and he did it on TV.
Yes.
It's on TV?
No, it just-- ugh. They just cut back to the other thing!
This is crazy!!
fight!
Does it say exactly where?
I gotta go.

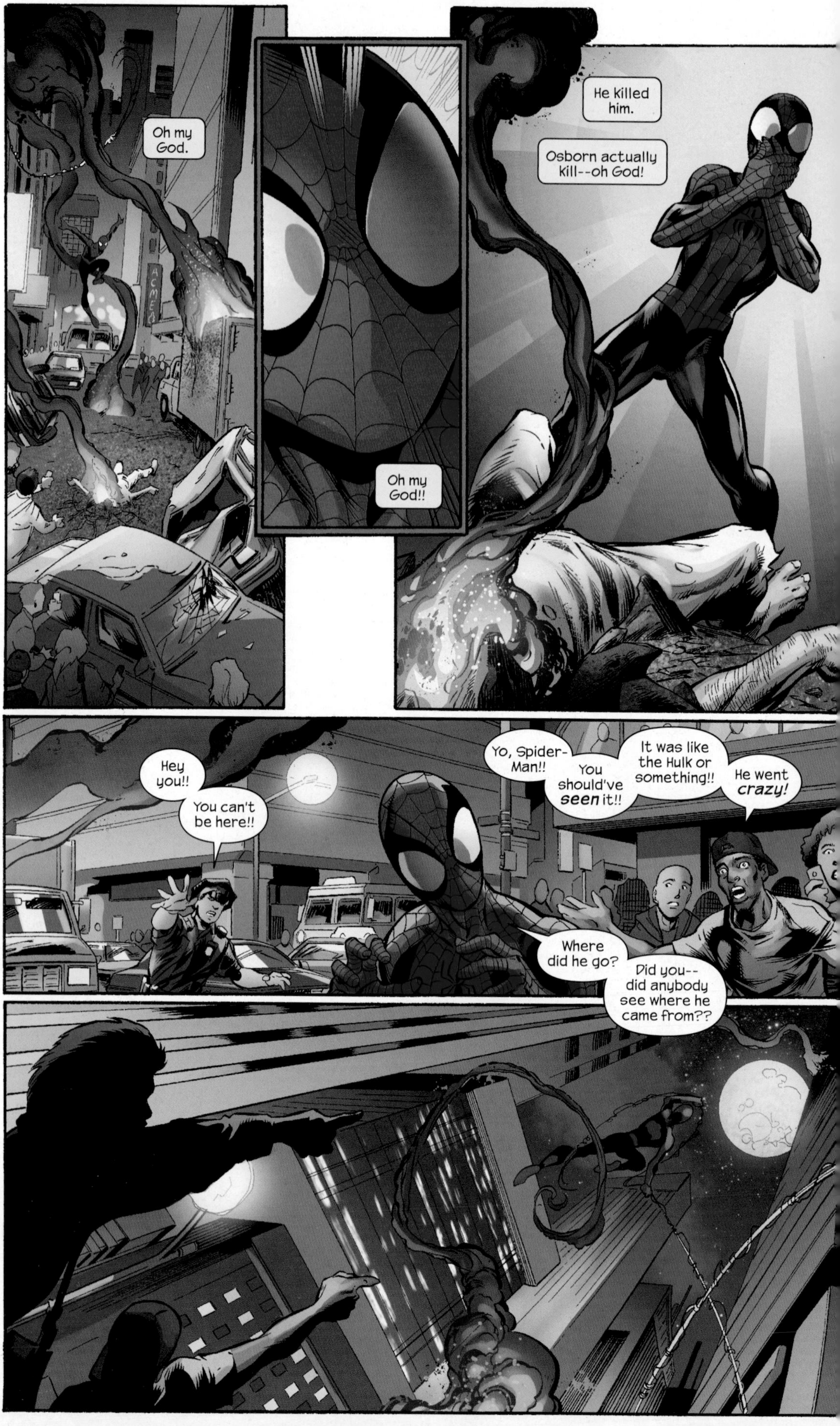
Oh my God.
Oh my God!!
He killed him.
Osborn actually kill--oh God!
Hey you!!
You can't be here!!
Yo, Spider-Man!!
You should've *seen* it!!
It was like the Hulk or something!!
He went *crazy!*
Where did he go?
Did you--did anybody see where he came from??

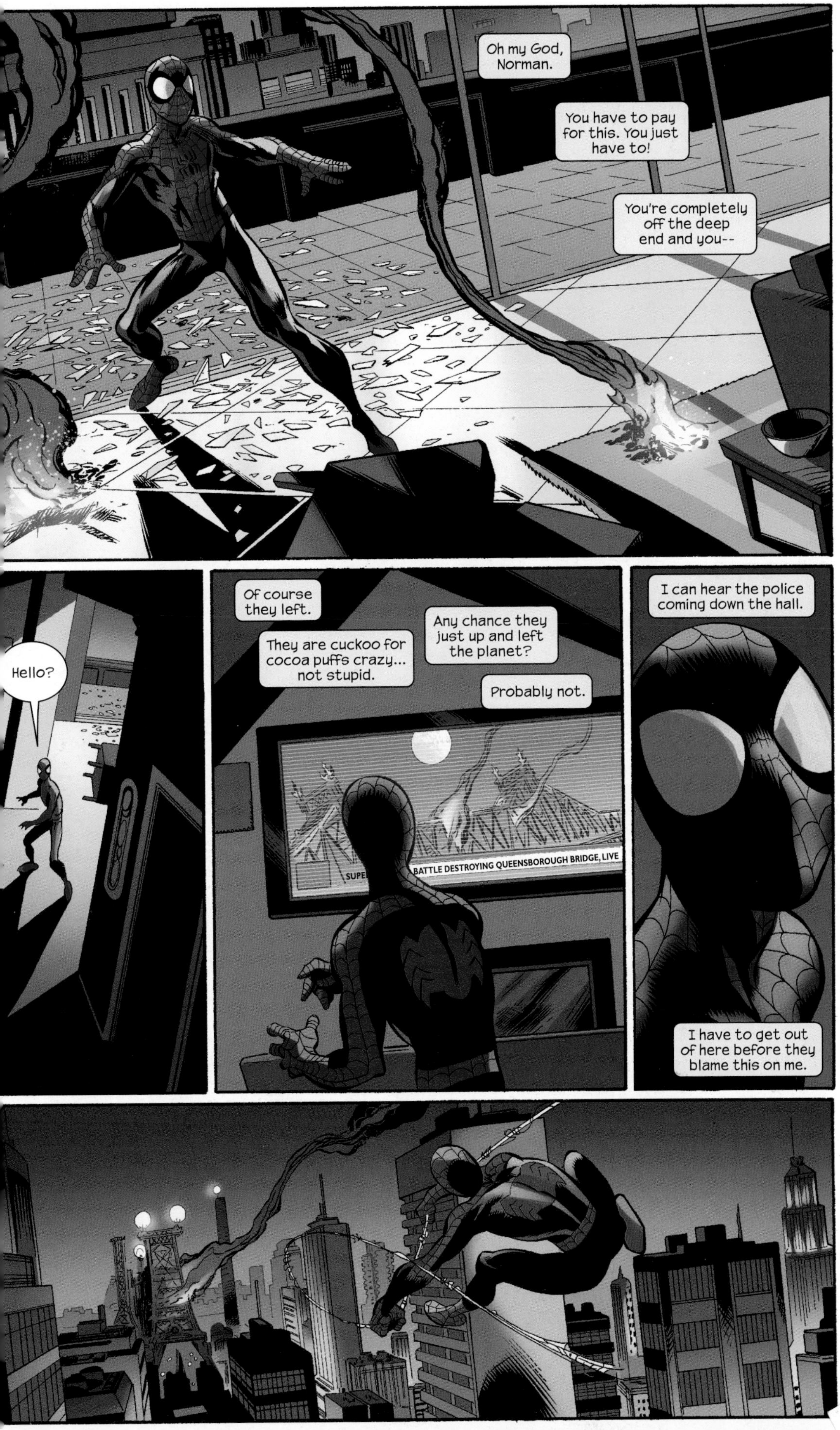
Oh my God, Norman.
You have to pay for this. You just have to!
You're completely off the deep end and you--
Hello?
Of course they left.
They are cuckoo for cocoa puffs crazy... not stupid.
Any chance they just up and left the planet?
Probably not.
SUPE BATTLE DESTROYING QUEENSBOROUGH BRIDGE, LIVE
I can hear the police coming down the hall.
I have to get out of here before they blame this on me.

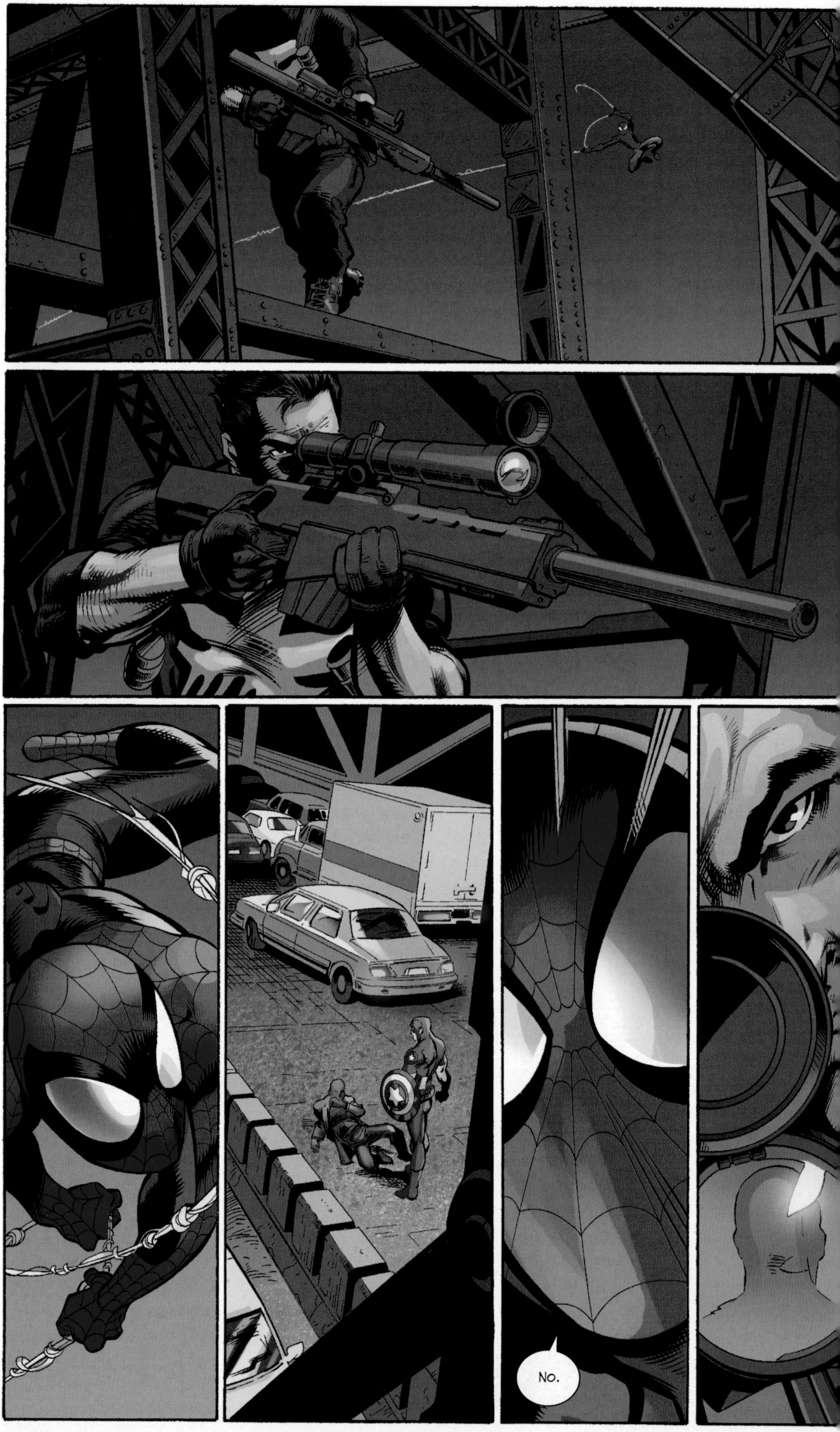
NO.

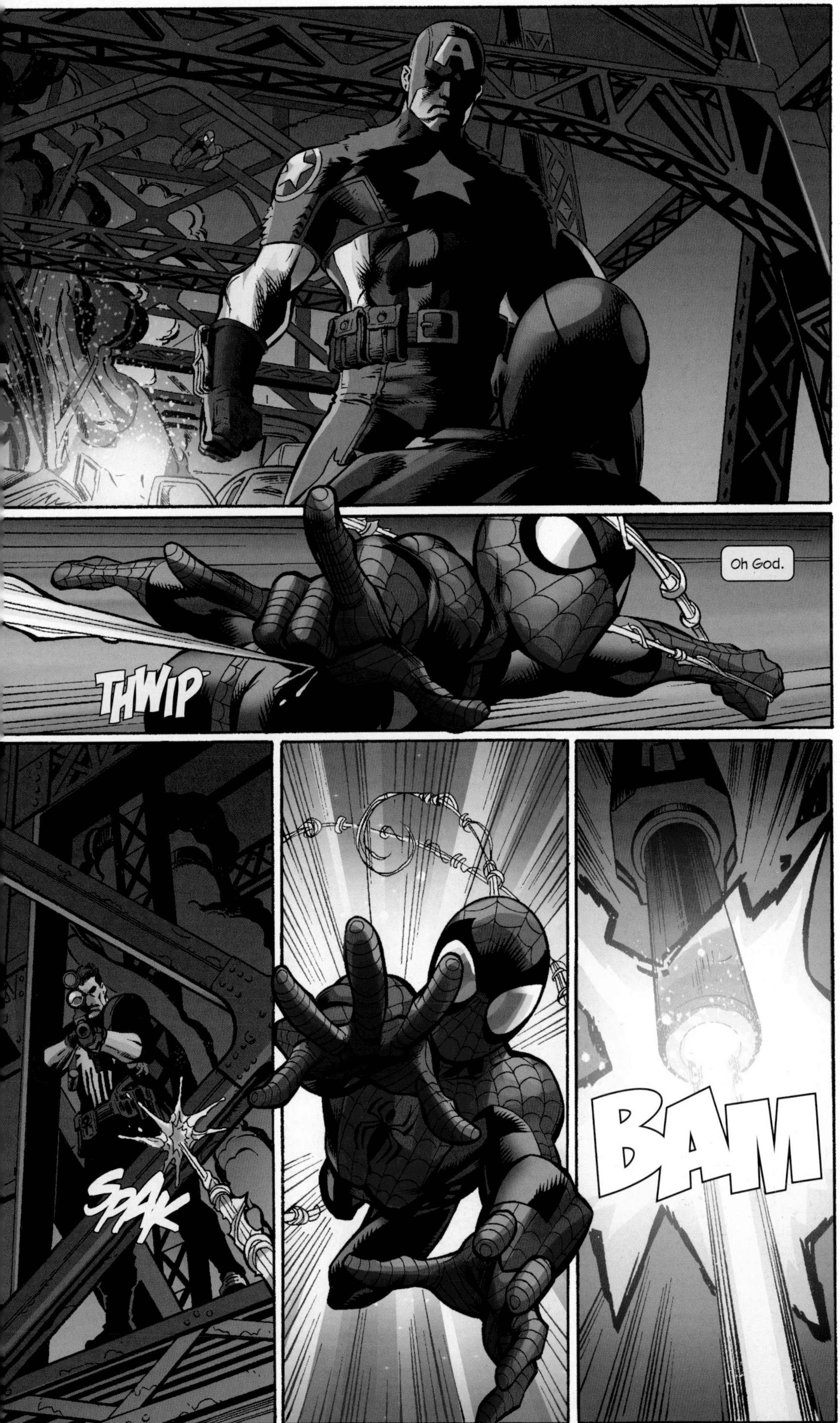
Oh God.
THWIP
SPAK
BAM

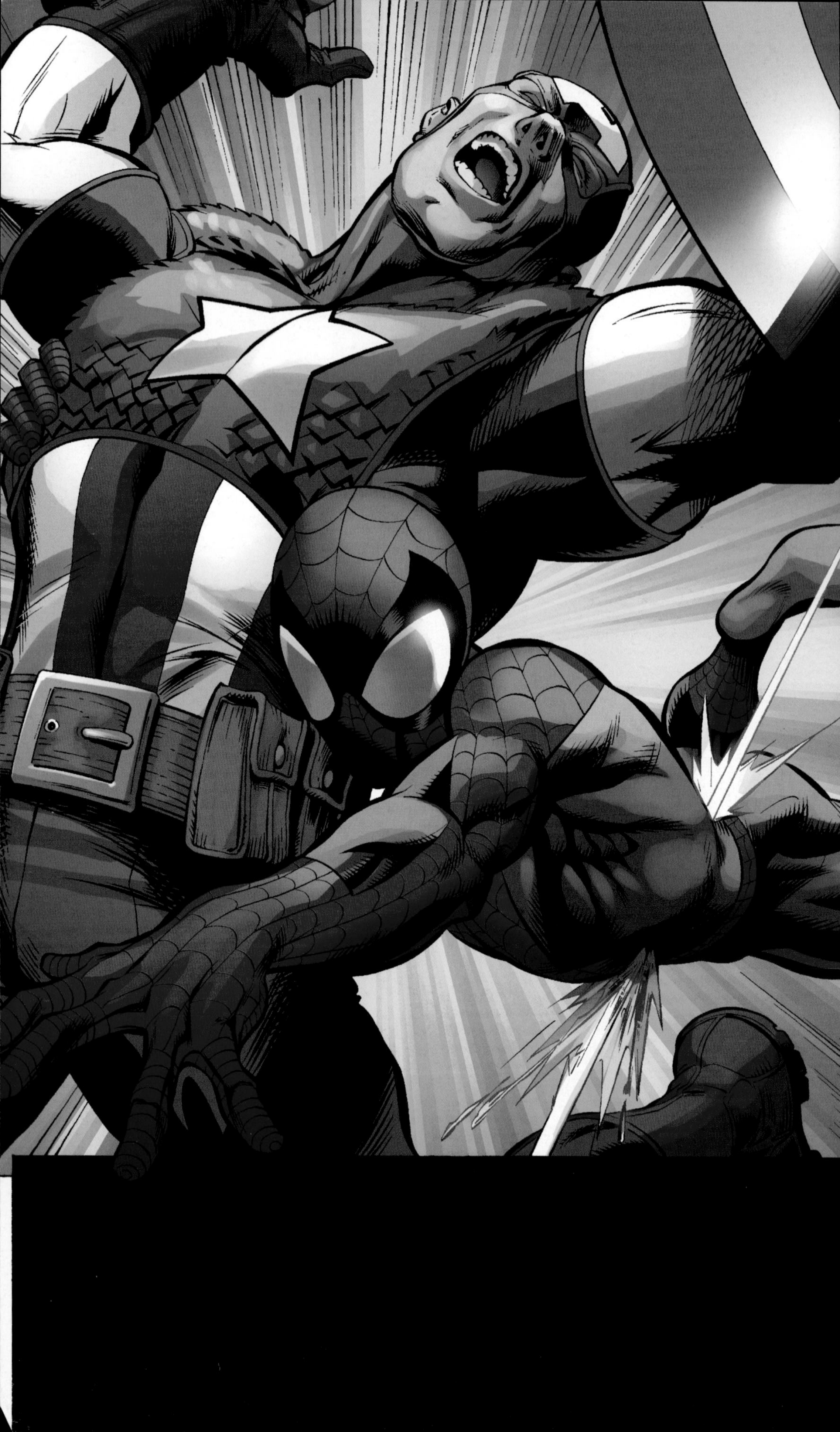

158

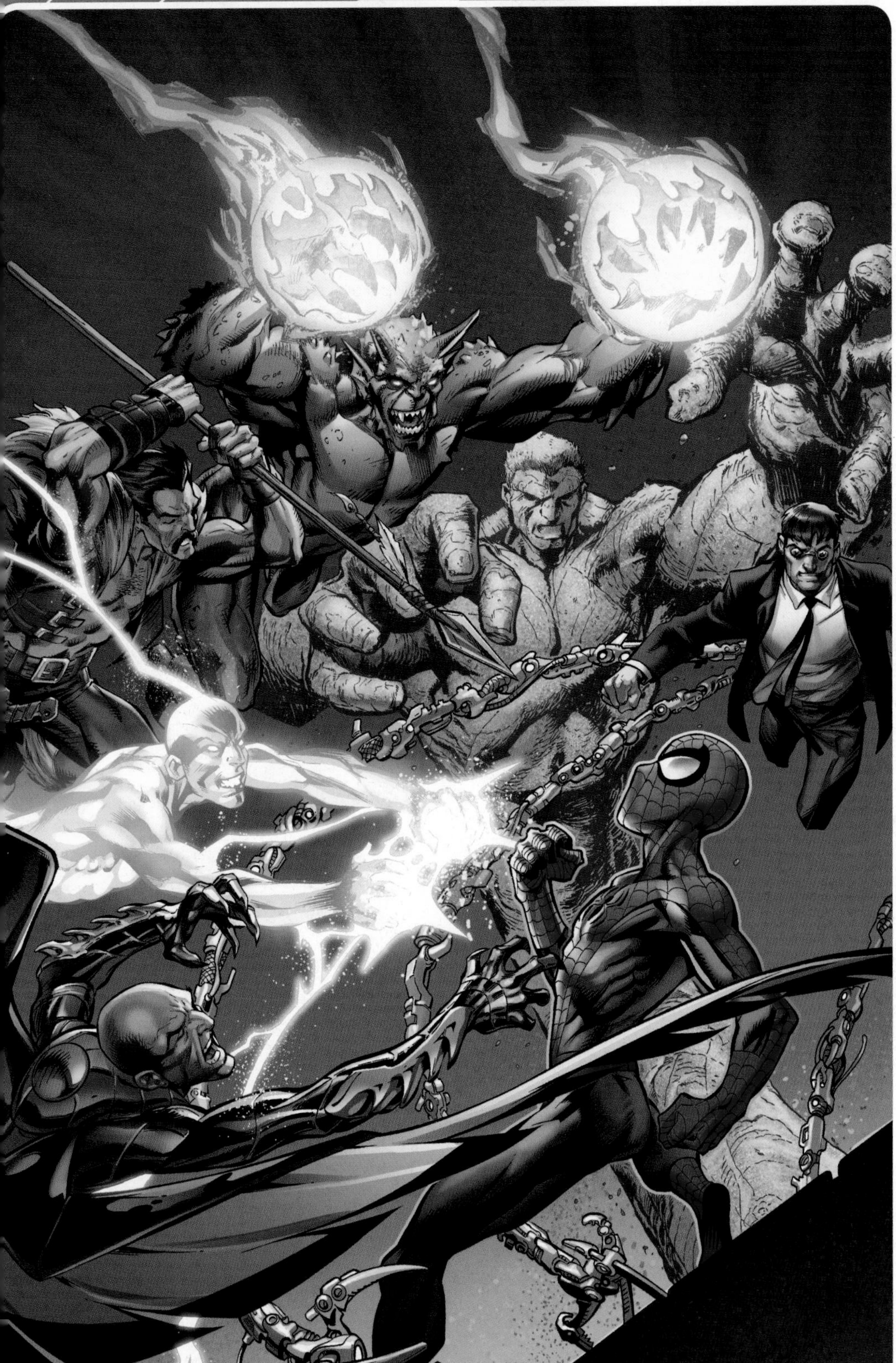

Hey, Tinkerer!

The Vulture.

And he brought friends.

I don't suppose any of your friends have my money.

Well, no.

We--we don't have money for you *today* but--

We had a *deal*.

And the last time I he[ard] your song and dance, [I] ended up leading S.H.I.E.[LD] right to *my* door.

The last time w[e] did business...And [I use] the term business as [loosely] as possible because [...] when two people do bu[siness] there is a busine[ss] *transaction*..

Not som[e] bald-hea[ded] fart rippin[g] someone [ten] times th[e] intelle[ct...]

Man, you suck.

Listen--

No, *you* listen!

Give the man what he asked for.

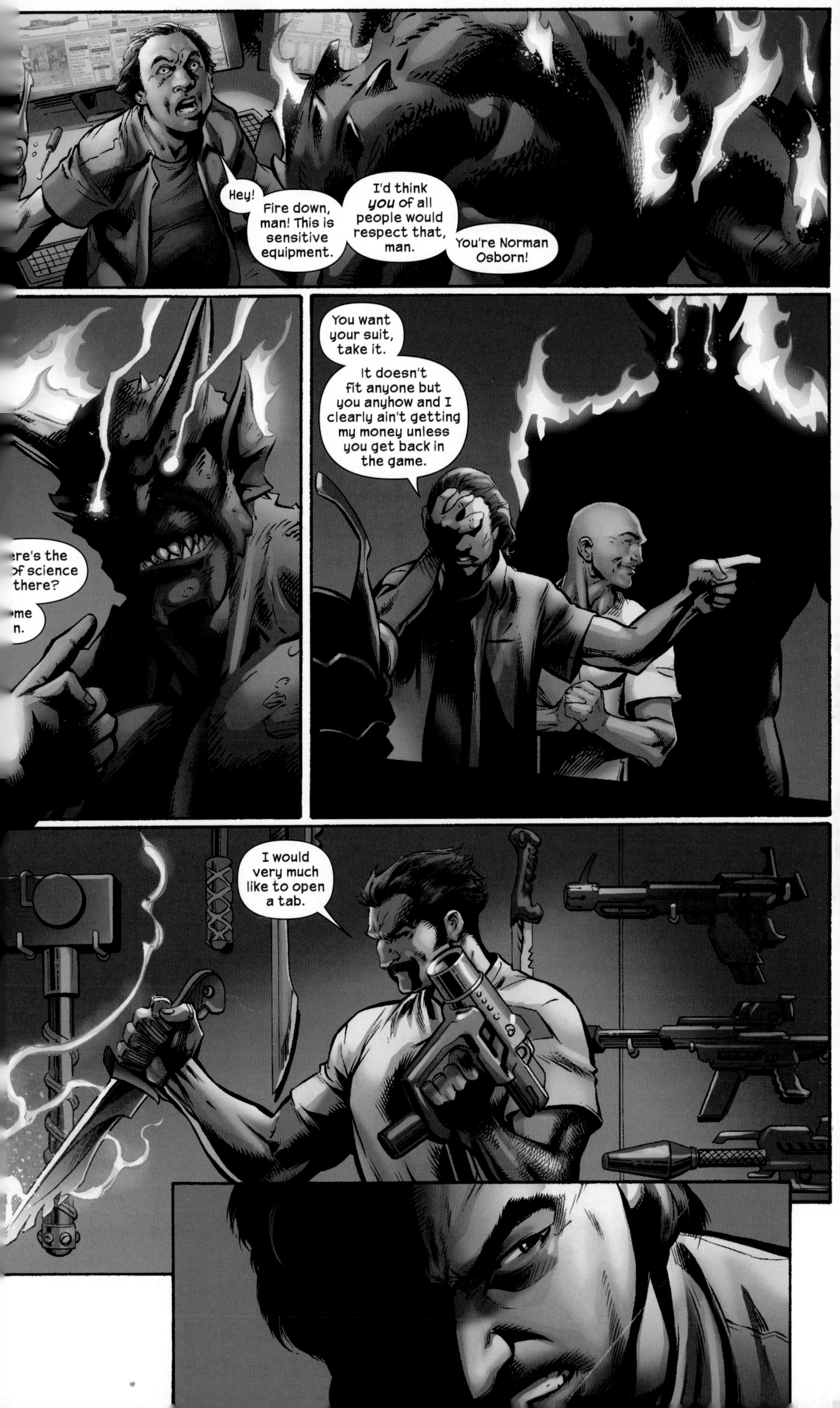
Hey!
Fire down, man! This is sensitive equipment.
I'd think *you* of all people would respect that, man.
You're Norman Osborn!
ere's the
of science
there?
me
n.
You want your suit, take it.
It doesn't fit anyone but you anyhow and I clearly ain't getting my money unless you get back in the game.
I would very much like to open a tab.

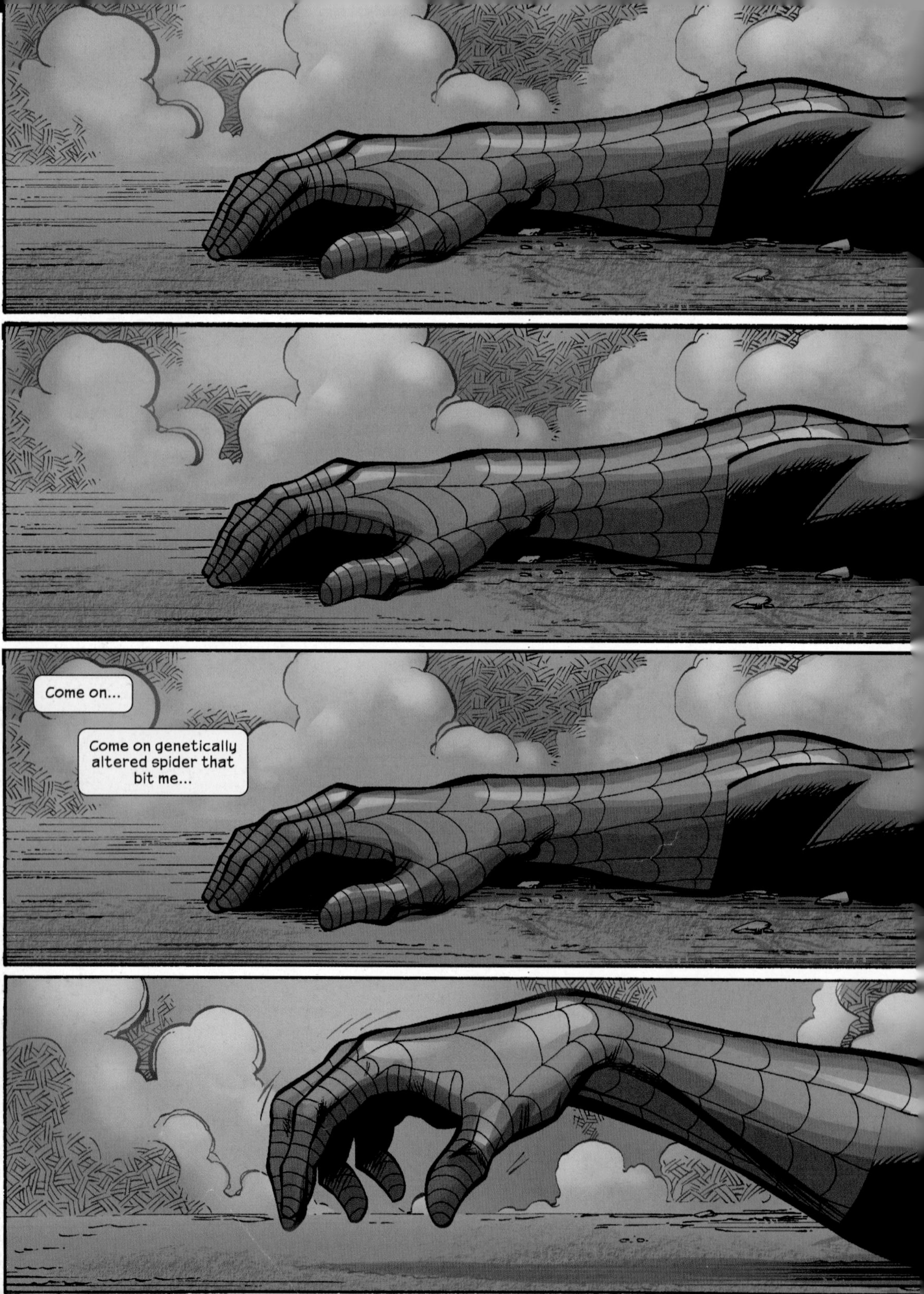
Come on...
Come on genetically altered spider that bit me...

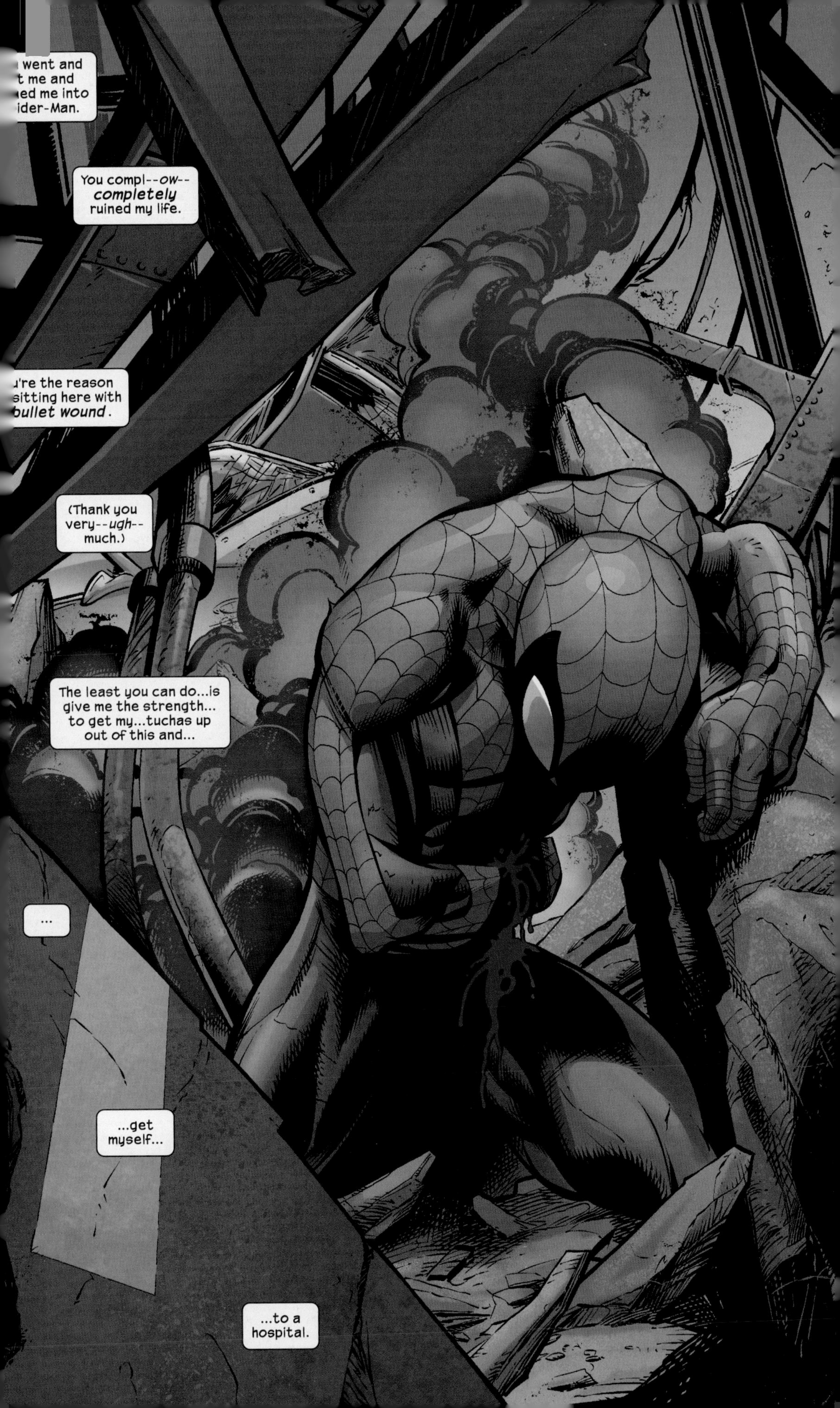
went and t me and ed me into ider-Man.
You compl--ow-- *completely* ruined my life.
're the reason sitting here with *bullet wound*.
(Thank you very--*ugh*-- much.)
The least you can do...is give me the strength... to get my...tuchas up out of this and...
...
...get myself...
...to a hospital.

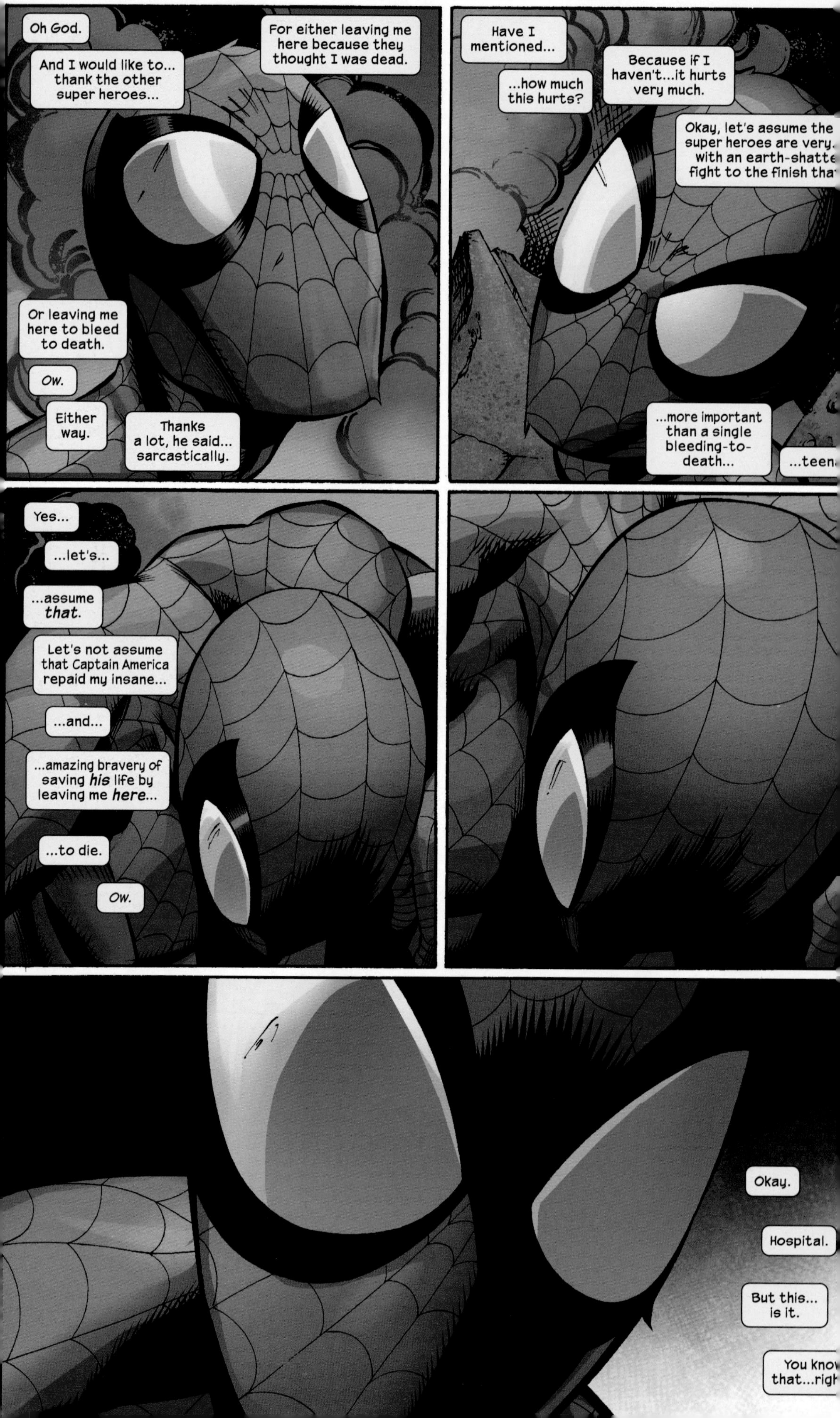
Oh God.
And I would like to... thank the other super heroes...
For either leaving me here because they thought I was dead.
Or leaving me here to bleed to death.
Ow.
Either way.
Thanks a lot, he said... sarcastically.
Have I mentioned...
...how much this hurts?
Because if I haven't...it hurts very much.
Okay, let's assume the super heroes are very. with an earth-shatte fight to the finish tha
...more important than a single bleeding-to-death...
...teen
Yes...
...let's...
...assume *that*.
Let's not assume that Captain America repaid my insane...
...and...
...amazing bravery of saving *his* life by leaving me *here*...
...to die.
Ow.
Okay.
Hospital.
But this... is it.
You kno that...rig

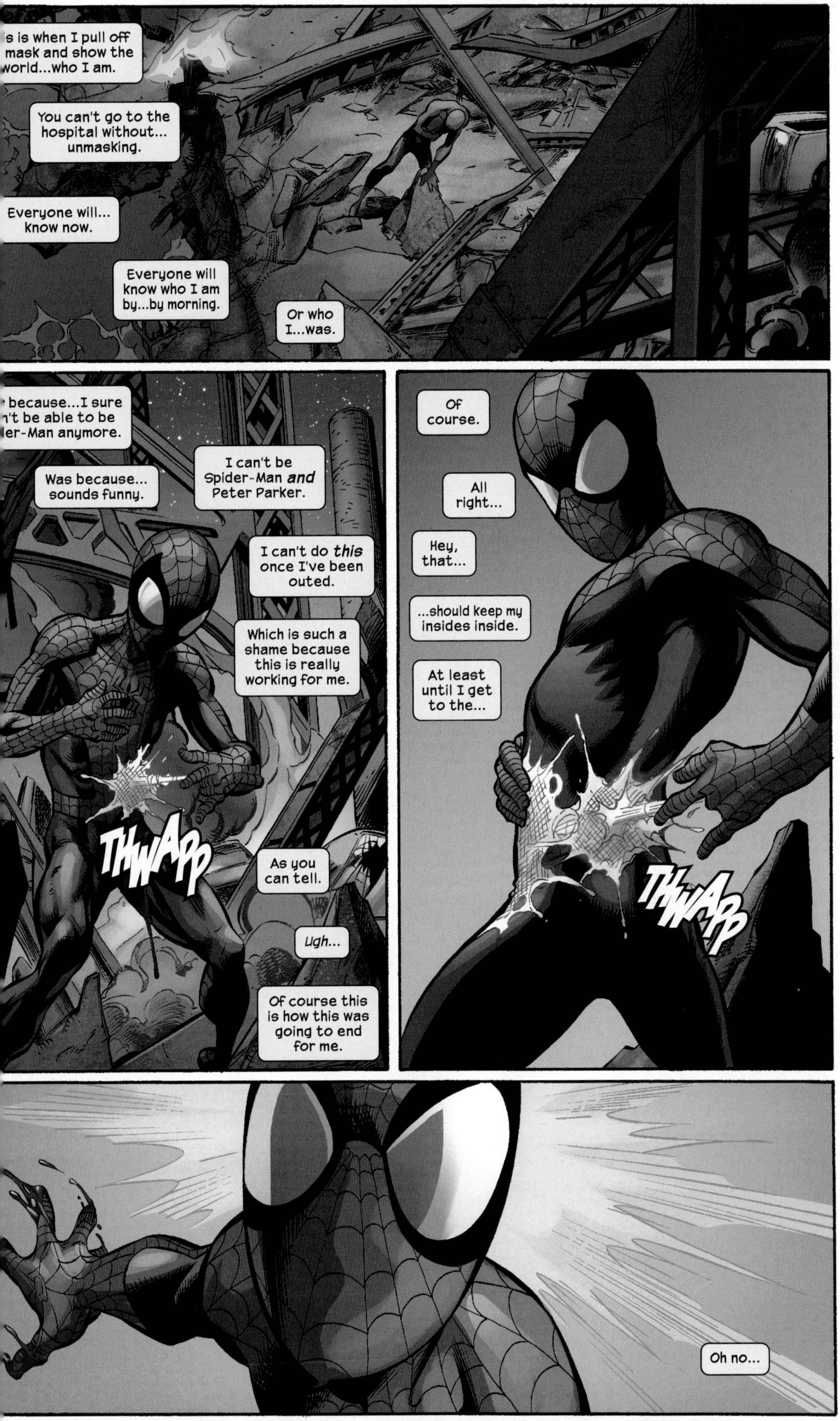
s is when I pull off mask and show the world...who I am.
You can't go to the hospital without... unmasking.
Everyone will... know now.
Everyone will know who I am by...by morning.
Or who I...was.
because...I sure n't be able to be ler-Man anymore.
Was because... sounds funny.
I can't be Spider-Man *and* Peter Parker.
I can't do *this* once I've been outed.
Which is such a shame because this is really working for me.
THWAPP
As you can tell.
Ugh...
Of course this is how this was going to end for me.
Of course.
All right...
Hey, that...
...should keep my insides inside.
At least until I get to the...
THWAPP
Oh no...

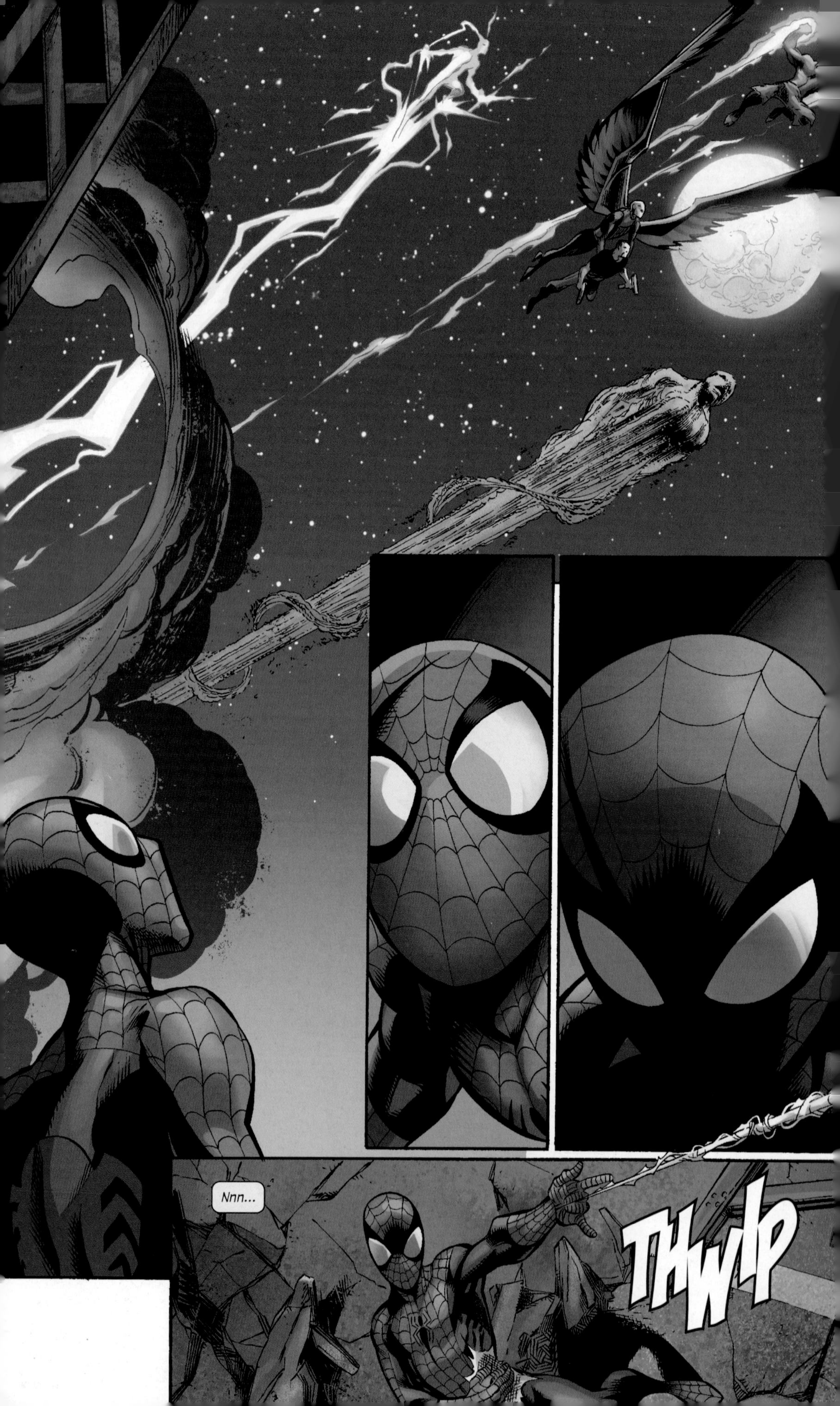
Nnn...
THWIP

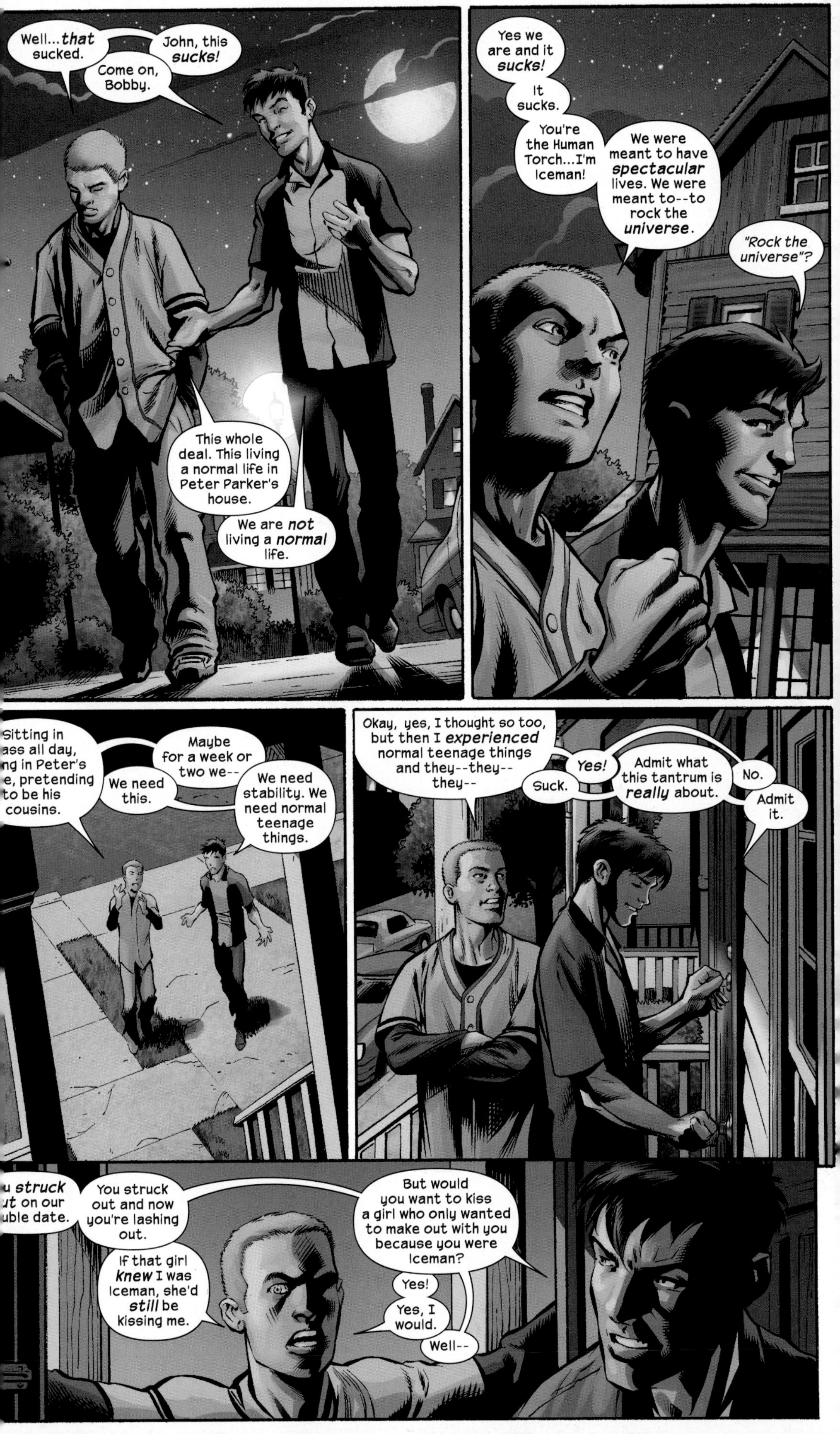
Well...*that* sucked.
John, this *sucks!*
Come on, Bobby.
This whole deal. This living a normal life in Peter Parker's house.
We are *not* living a *normal* life.
Yes we are and it *sucks!*
It sucks.
You're the Human Torch...I'm Iceman!
We were meant to have *spectacular* lives. We were meant to--to rock the *universe*.
"Rock the universe"?
Sitting in
ass all day,
ng in Peter's
e, pretending
to be his
cousins.
Maybe for a week or two we--
We need this.
We need stability. We need normal teenage things.
Okay, yes, I thought so too, but then I *experienced* normal teenage things and they--they--they--
Suck.
Yes!
Admit what this tantrum is *really* about.
No.
Admit it.
u *struck*
ut on our
uble date.
You struck out and now you're lashing out.
If that girl *knew* I was Iceman, she'd *still* be kissing me.
But would you want to kiss a girl who only wanted to make out with you because you were Iceman?
Yes!
Yes, I would.
Well--

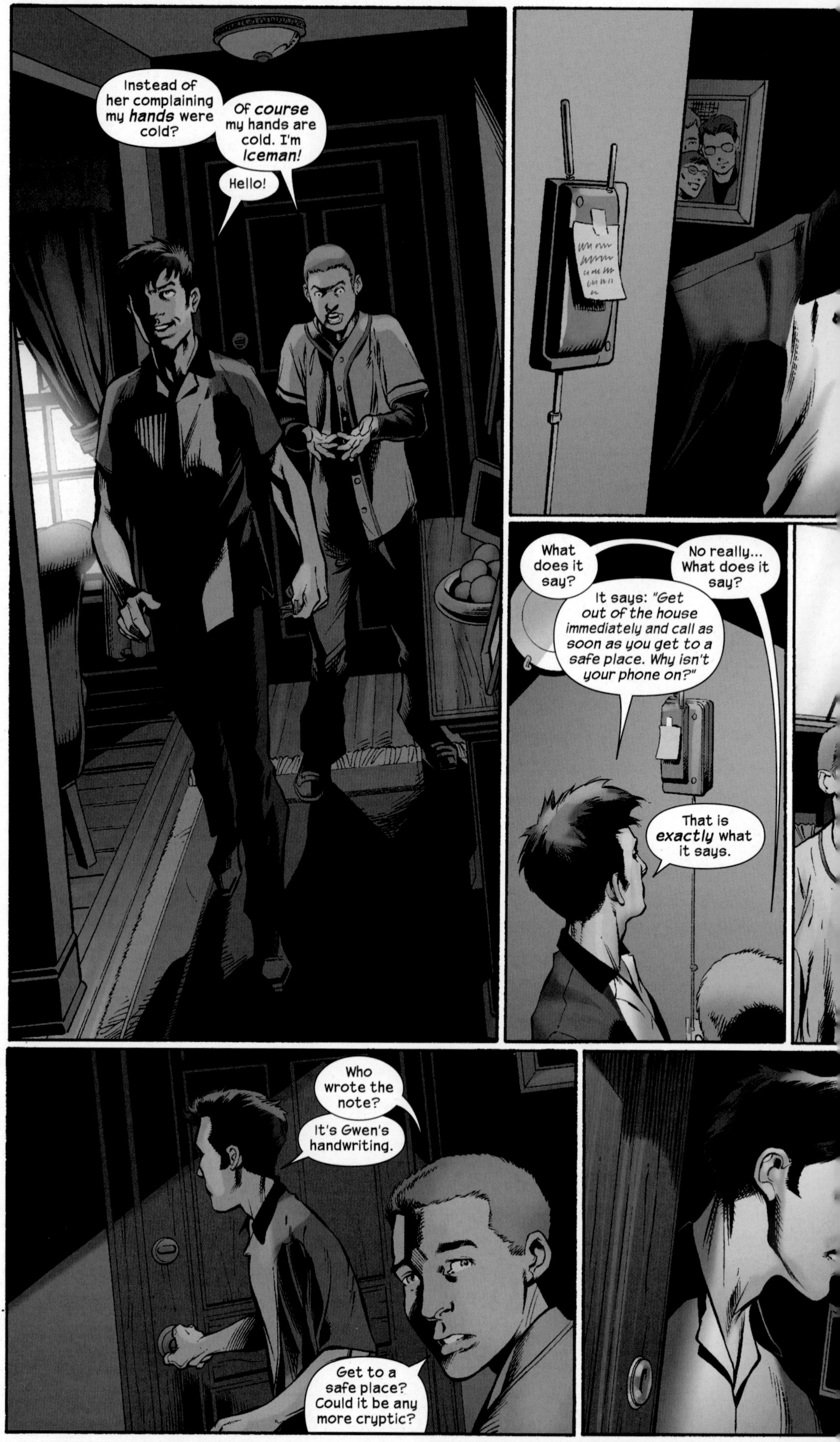
Instead of her complaining my *hands* were cold?
Of *course* my hands are cold. I'm *Iceman!*
Hello!
What does it say?
No really... What does it say?
It says: *"Get out of the house immediately and call as soon as you get to a safe place. Why isn't your phone on?"*
That is *exactly* what it says.
Who wrote the note?
It's Gwen's handwriting.
Get to a safe place? Could it be any more cryptic?

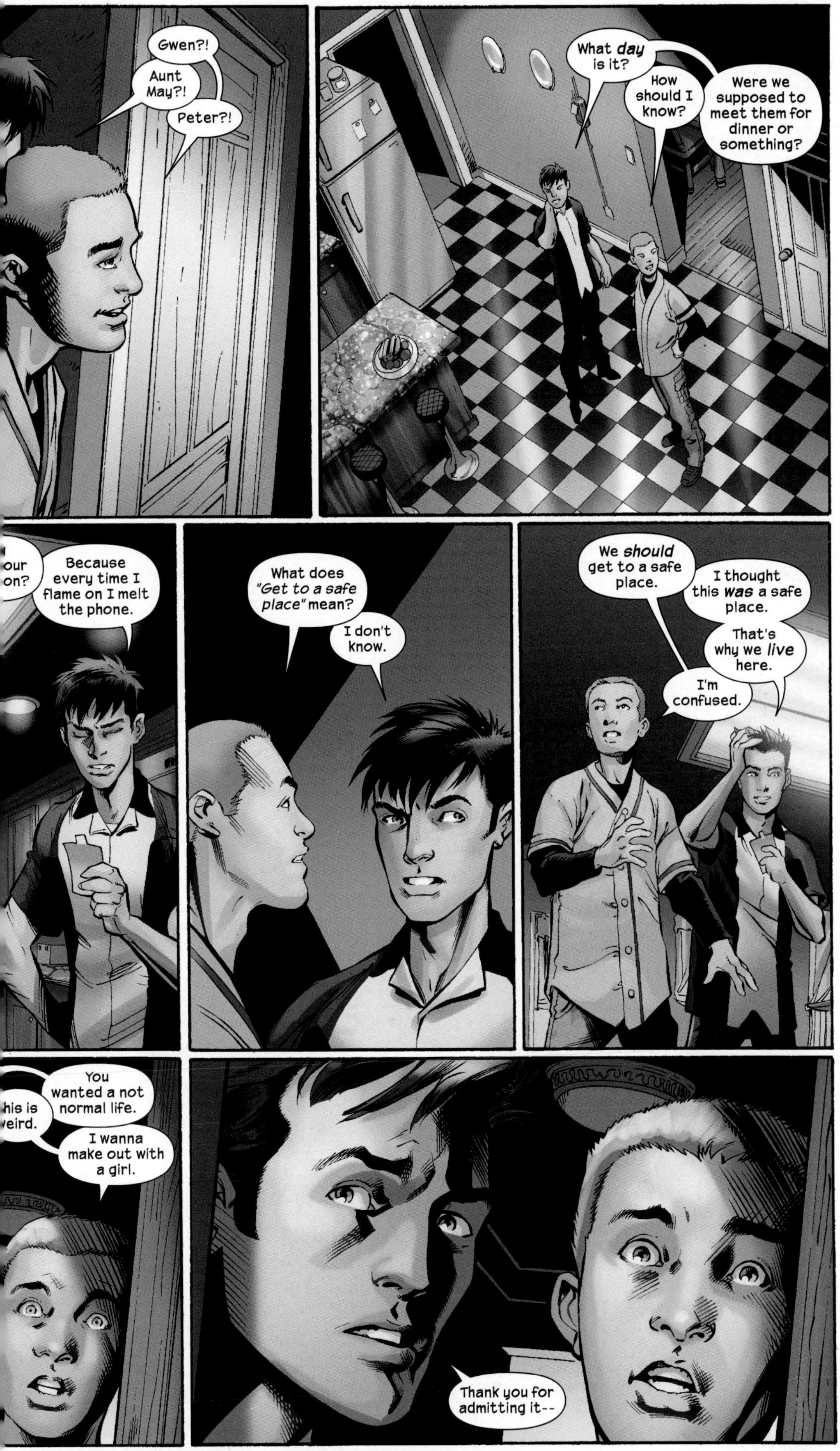
Gwen?!
Aunt May?!
Peter?!
What day is it?
How should I know?
Were we supposed to meet them for dinner or something?
our on?
Because every time I flame on I melt the phone.
What does "Get to a safe place" mean?
I don't know.
We should get to a safe place.
I thought this was a safe place.
That's why we live here.
I'm confused.
his is eird.
You wanted a not normal life.
I wanna make out with a girl.
Thank you for admitting it--

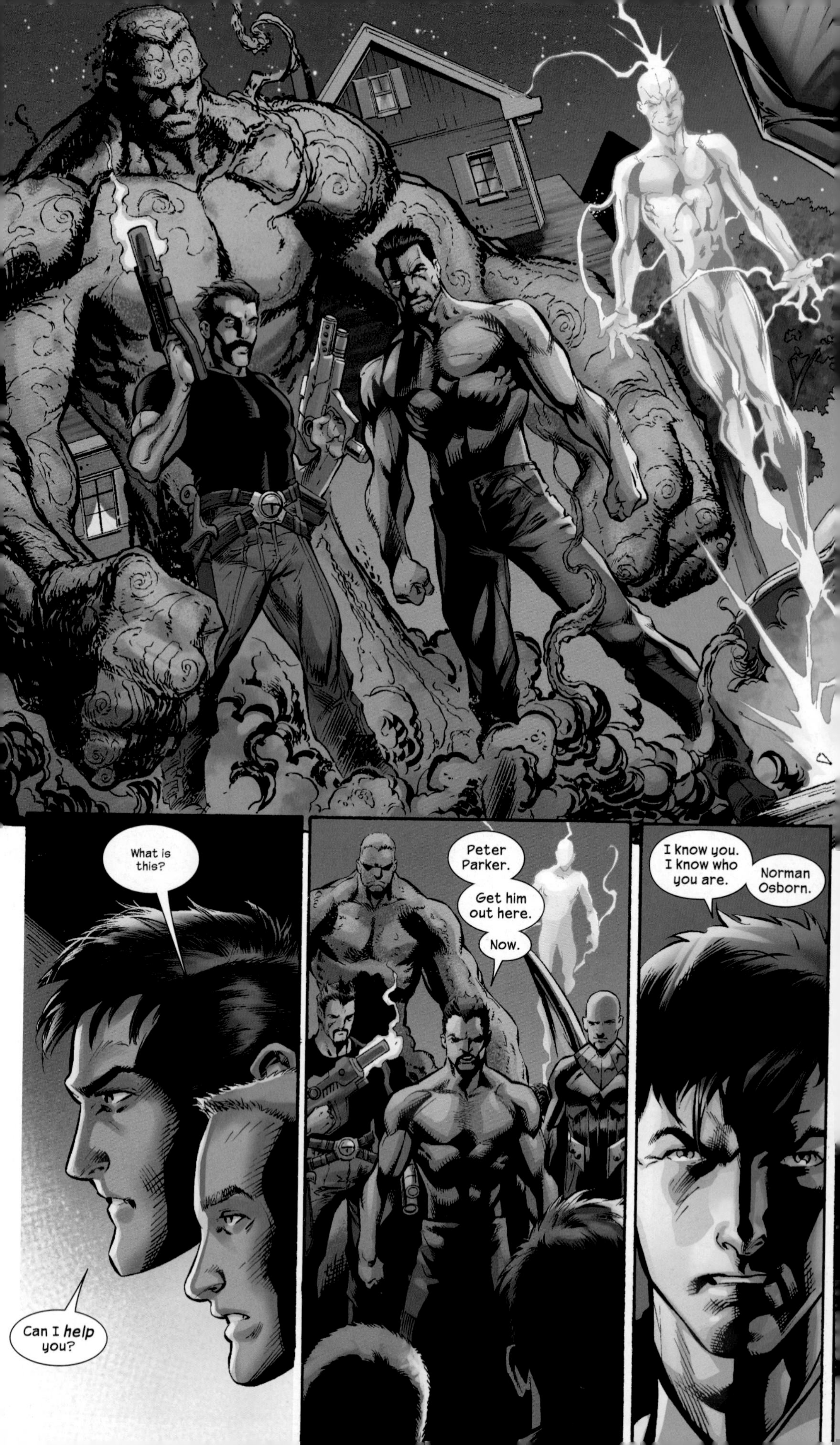
What is this?
Can I help you?
Peter Parker.
Get him out here.
Now.
I know you. I know who you are.
Norman Osborn.

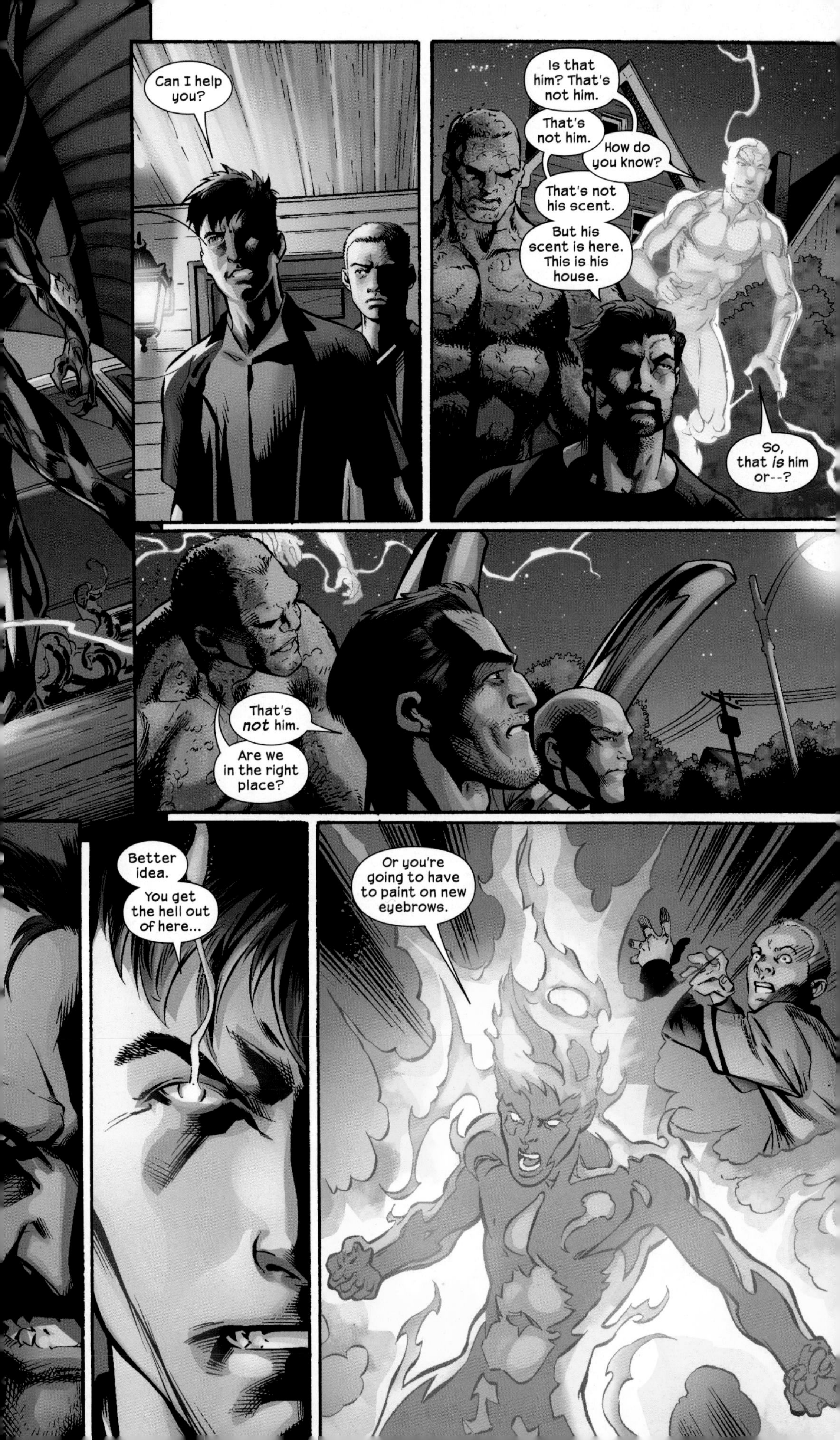
Can I help you?
Is that him? That's not him.
That's not him.
How do you know?
That's not his scent.
But his scent is here. This is his house.
So, that *is* him or--?
That's *not* him.
Are we in the right place?
Better idea.
You get the hell out of here...
Or you're going to have to paint on new eyebrows.

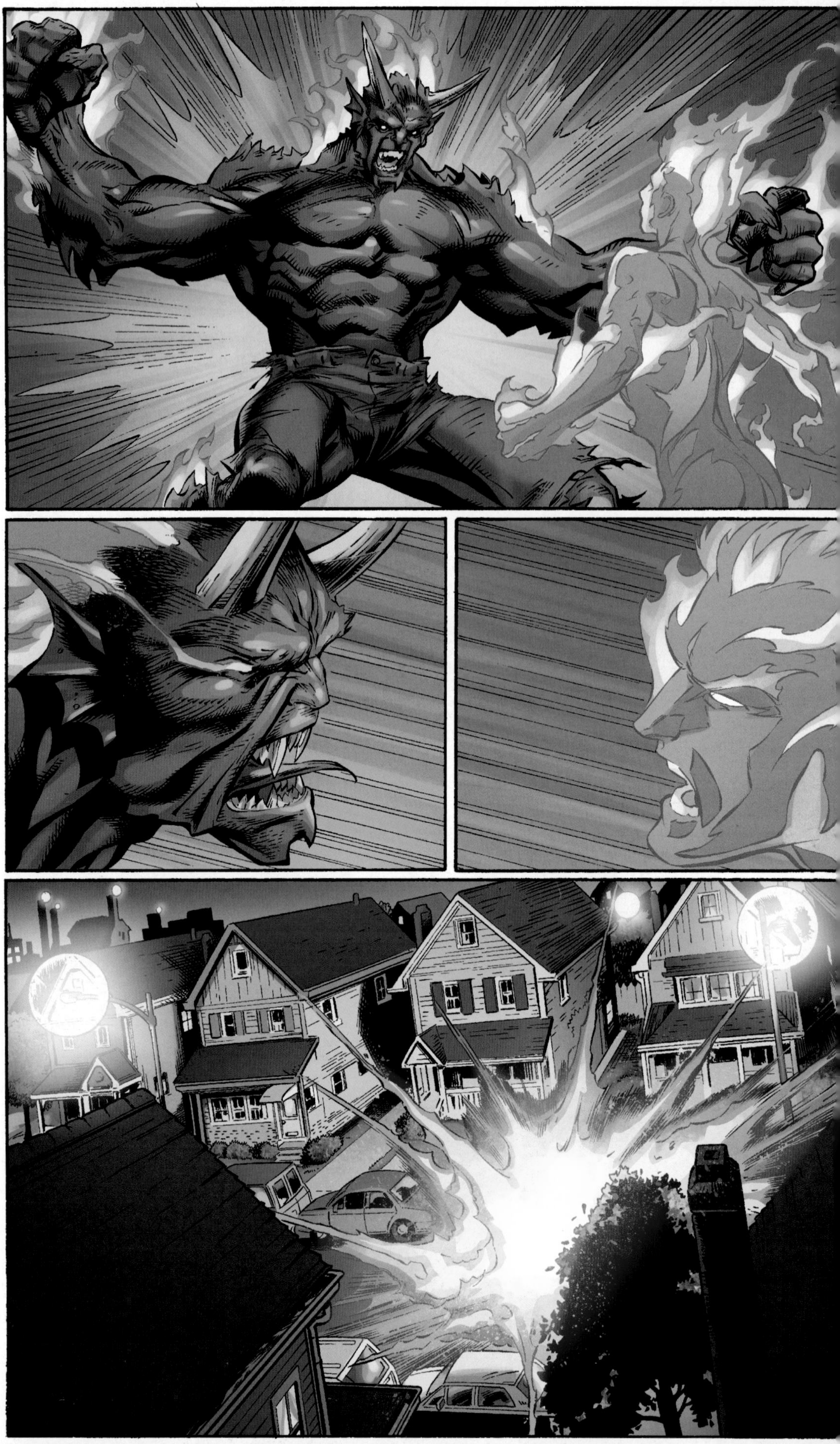

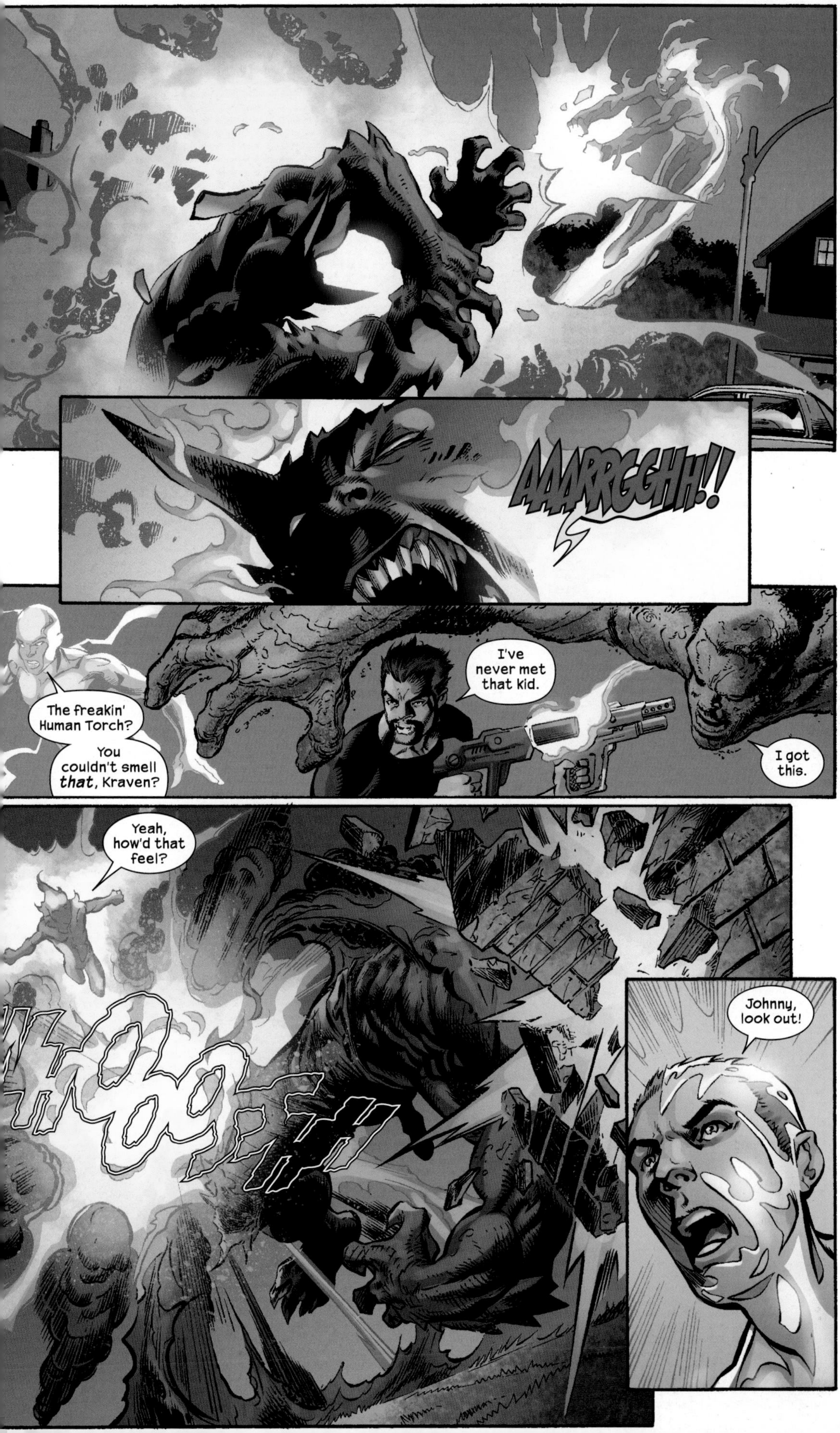
AAAARRGGHH!!
The freakin' Human Torch?
You couldn't smell *that*, Kraven?
I've never met that kid.
I got this.
Yeah, how'd that feel?
Johnny, look out!

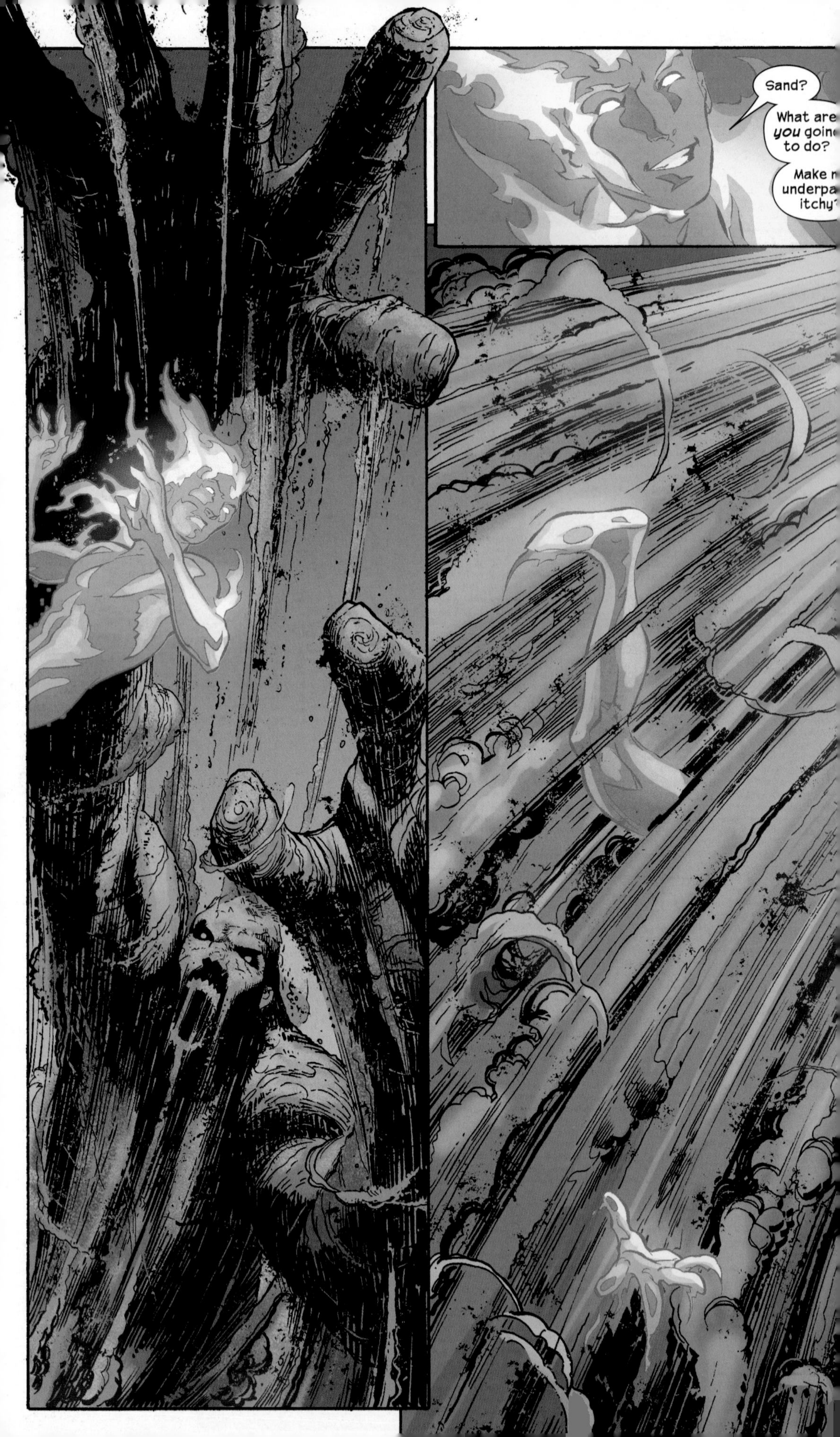
Sand?
What are you goin to do?
Make m underpa itchy

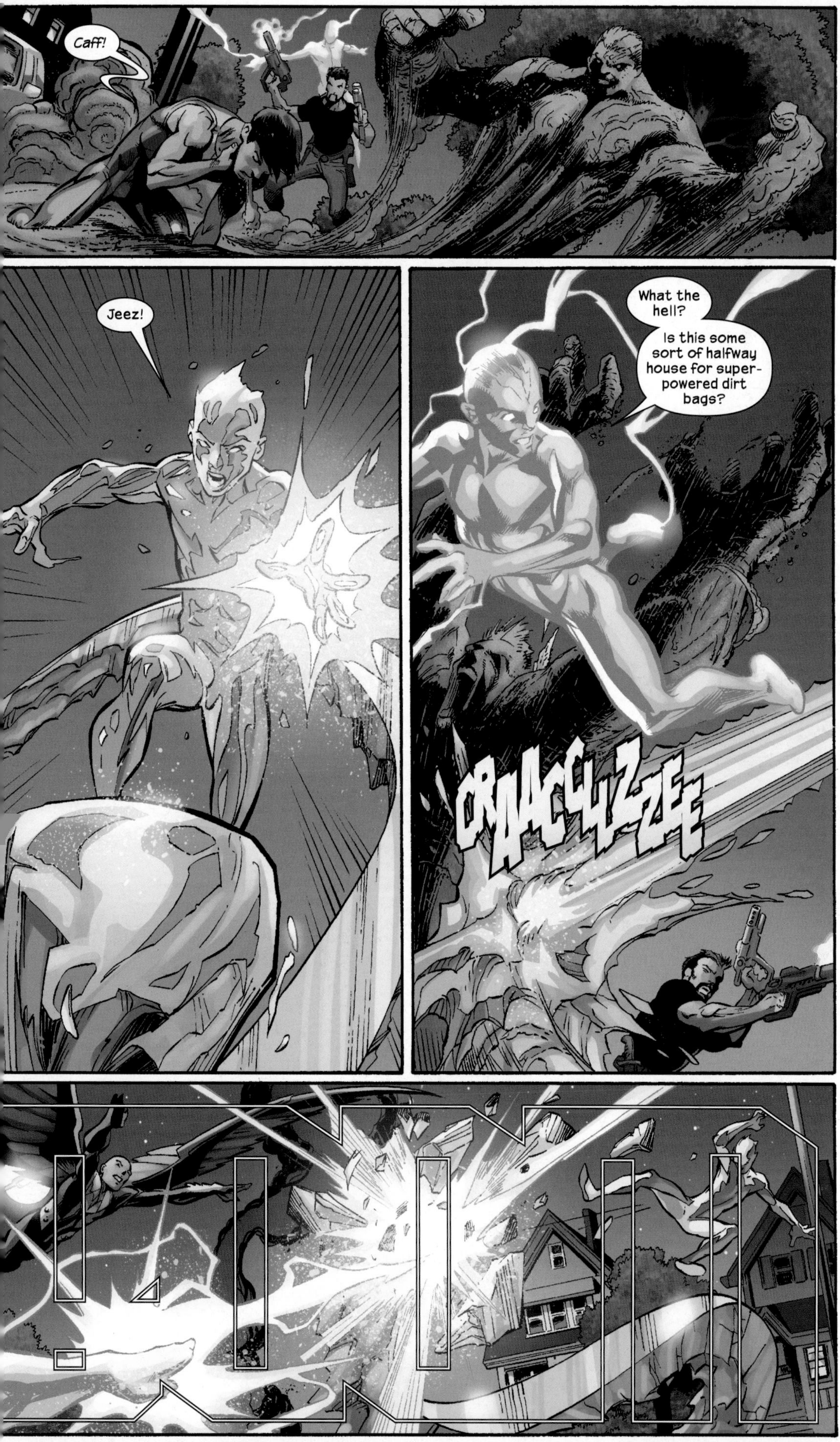
Caff!
Jeez!
What the hell?
Is this some sort of halfway house for super-powered dirt bags?

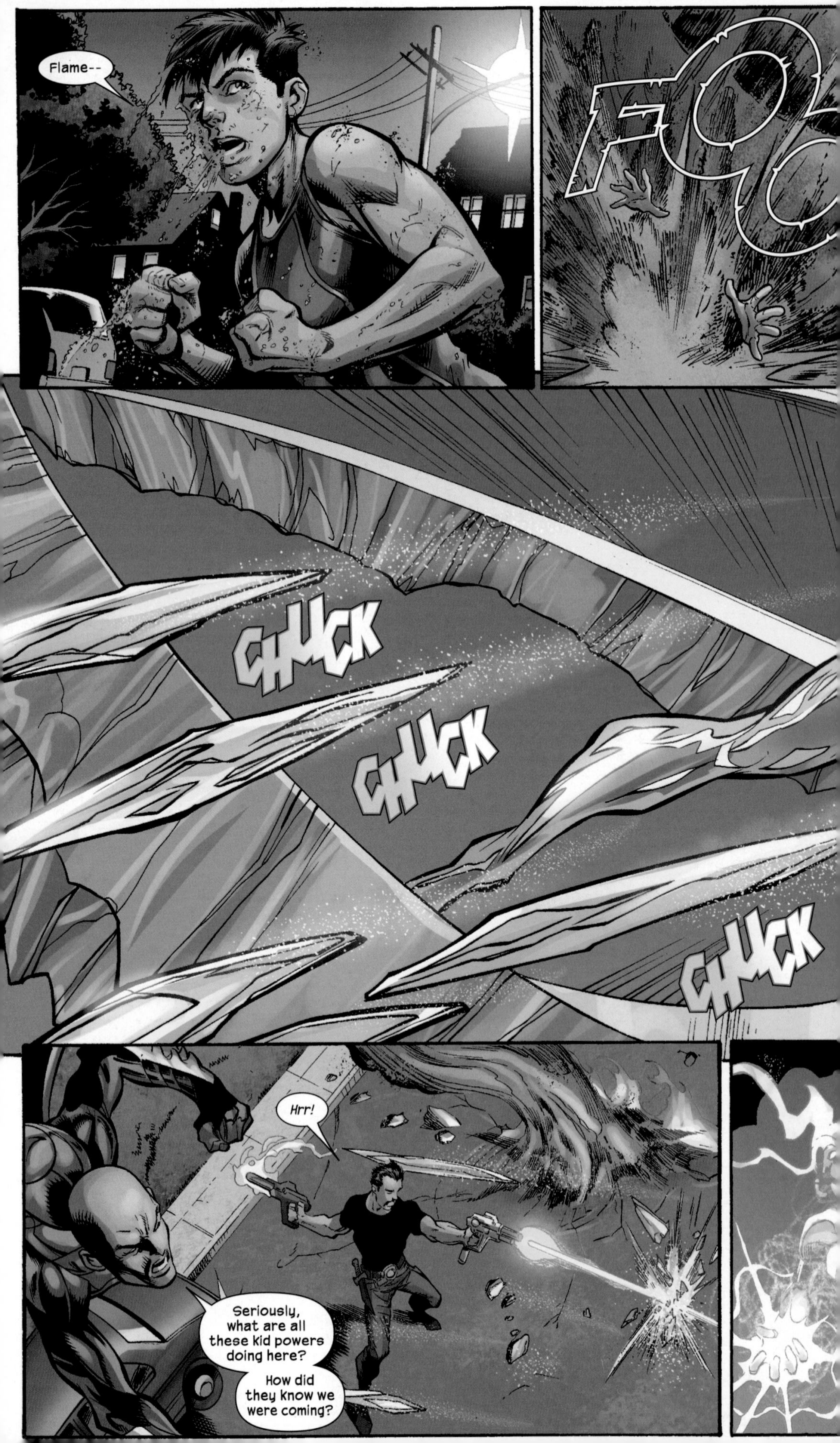

Flame--
FOOO
CHUCK
CHUCK
CHUCK
Hrr!
Seriously, what are all these kid powers doing here?
How did they know we were coming?

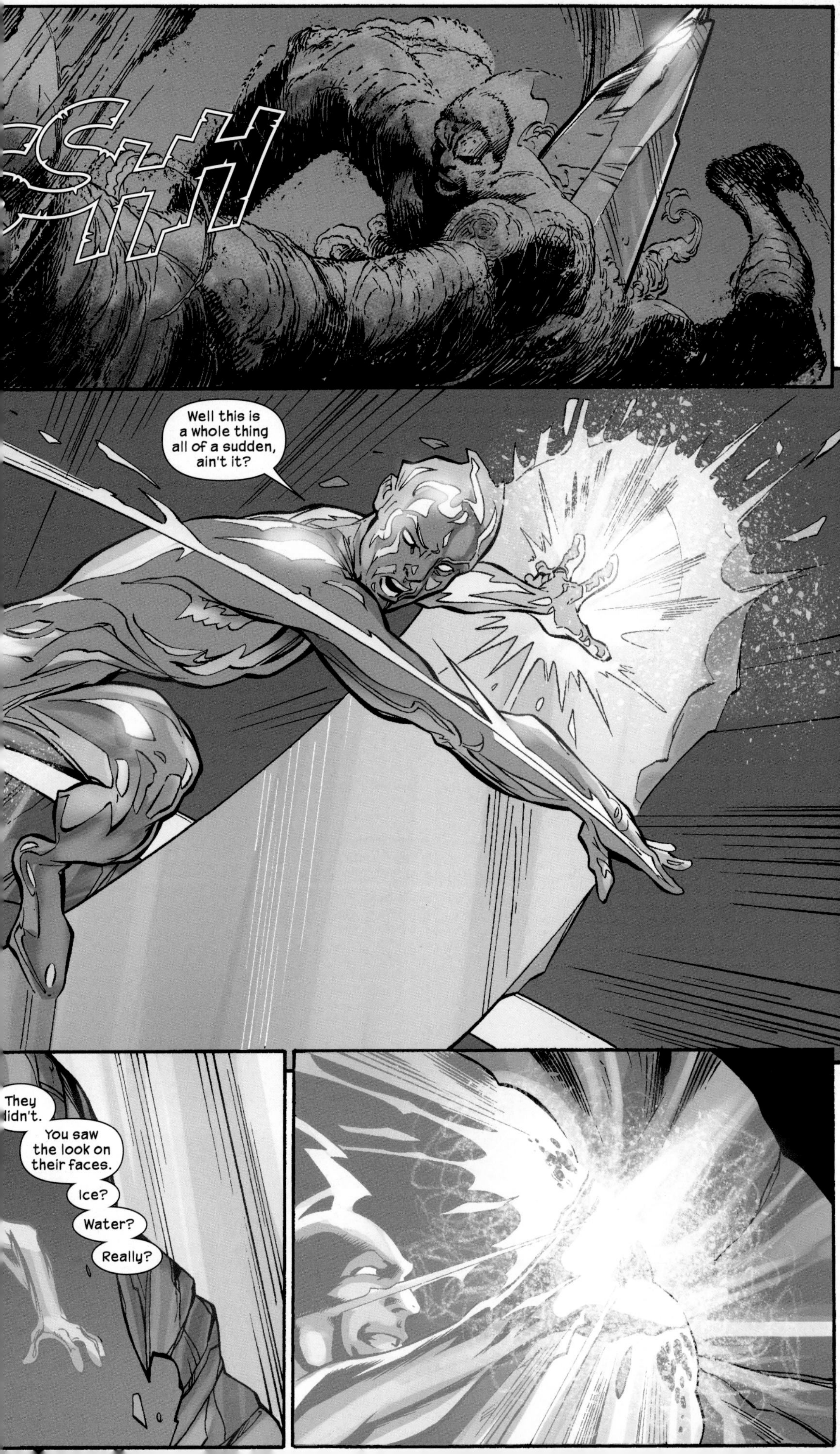
Well this is a whole thing all of a sudden, ain't it?
They
You saw the look on their faces.
Ice?
Water?
Really?

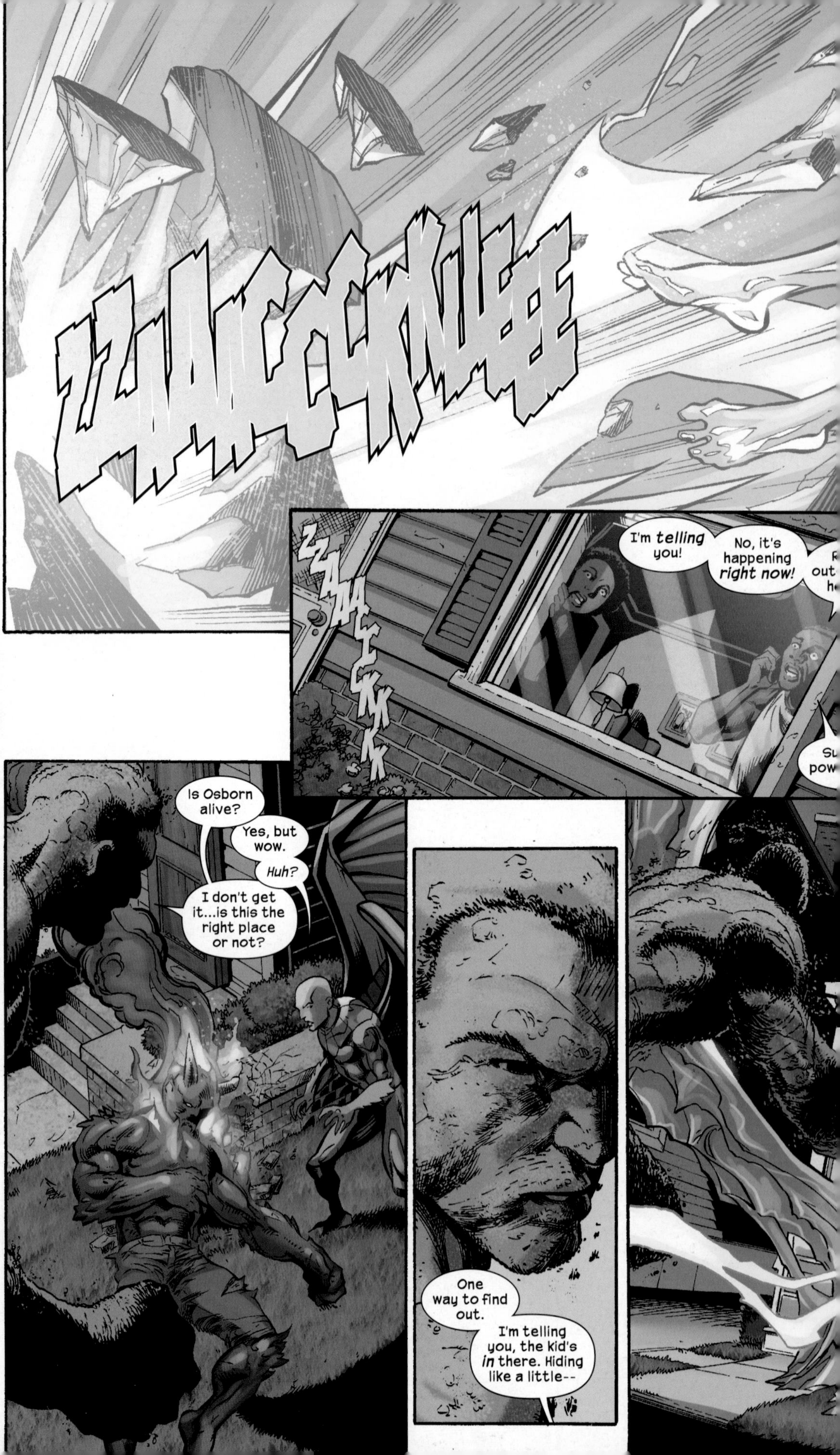

ZZAAKCCKKKLLEE
ZZAAACKKKK
I'm *telling* you!
No, it's happening *right now!*
Is Osborn alive?
Yes, but wow.
Huh?
I don't get it...is this the right place or not?
One way to find out.
I'm telling you, the kid's *in* there. Hiding like a little--

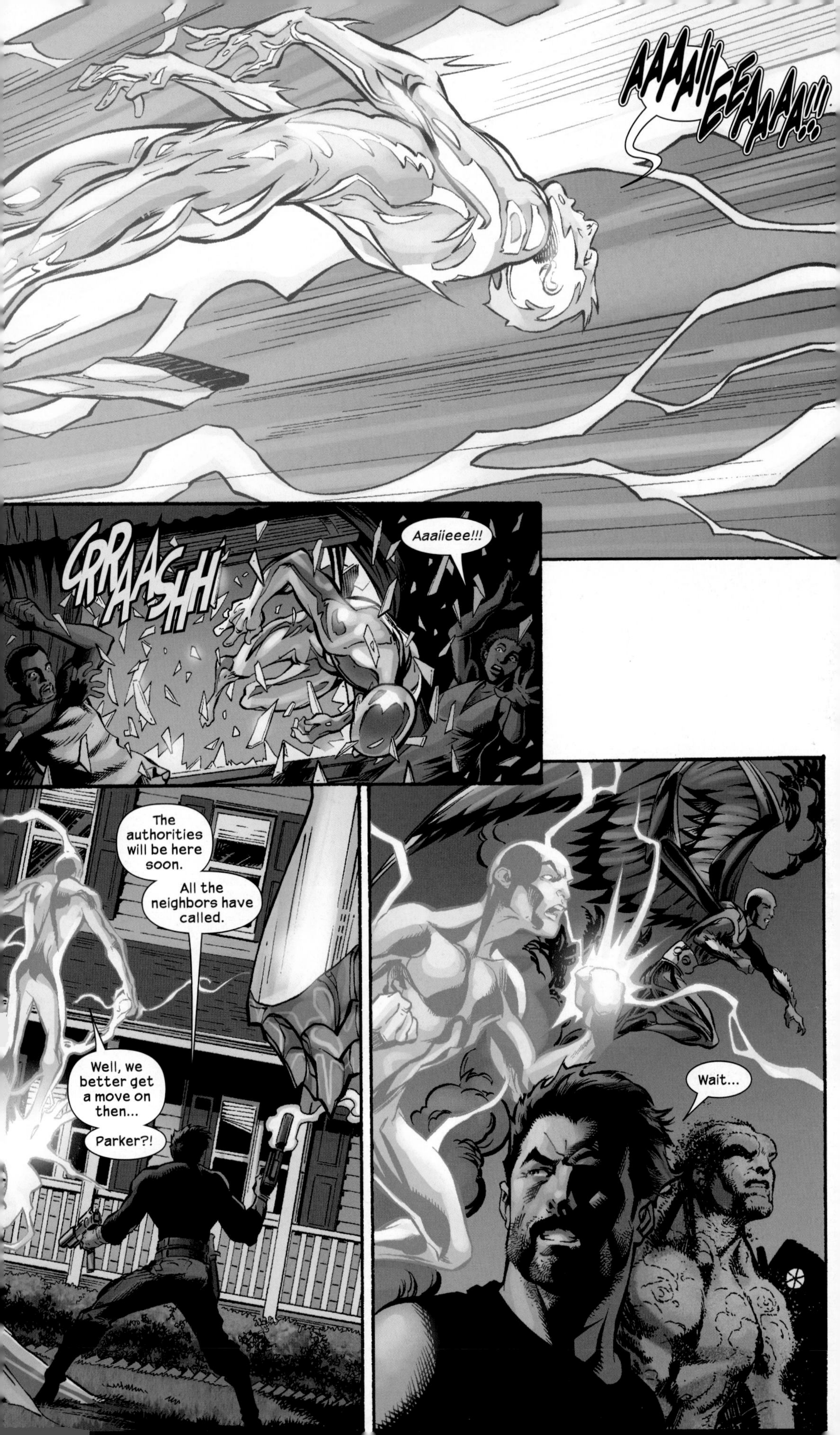
AAAAIIIEEAAAA!!!
CRRAASHH
Aaaiieee!!!
The authorities will be here soon.
All the neighbors have called.
Well, we better get a move on then...
Parker?!
Wait...

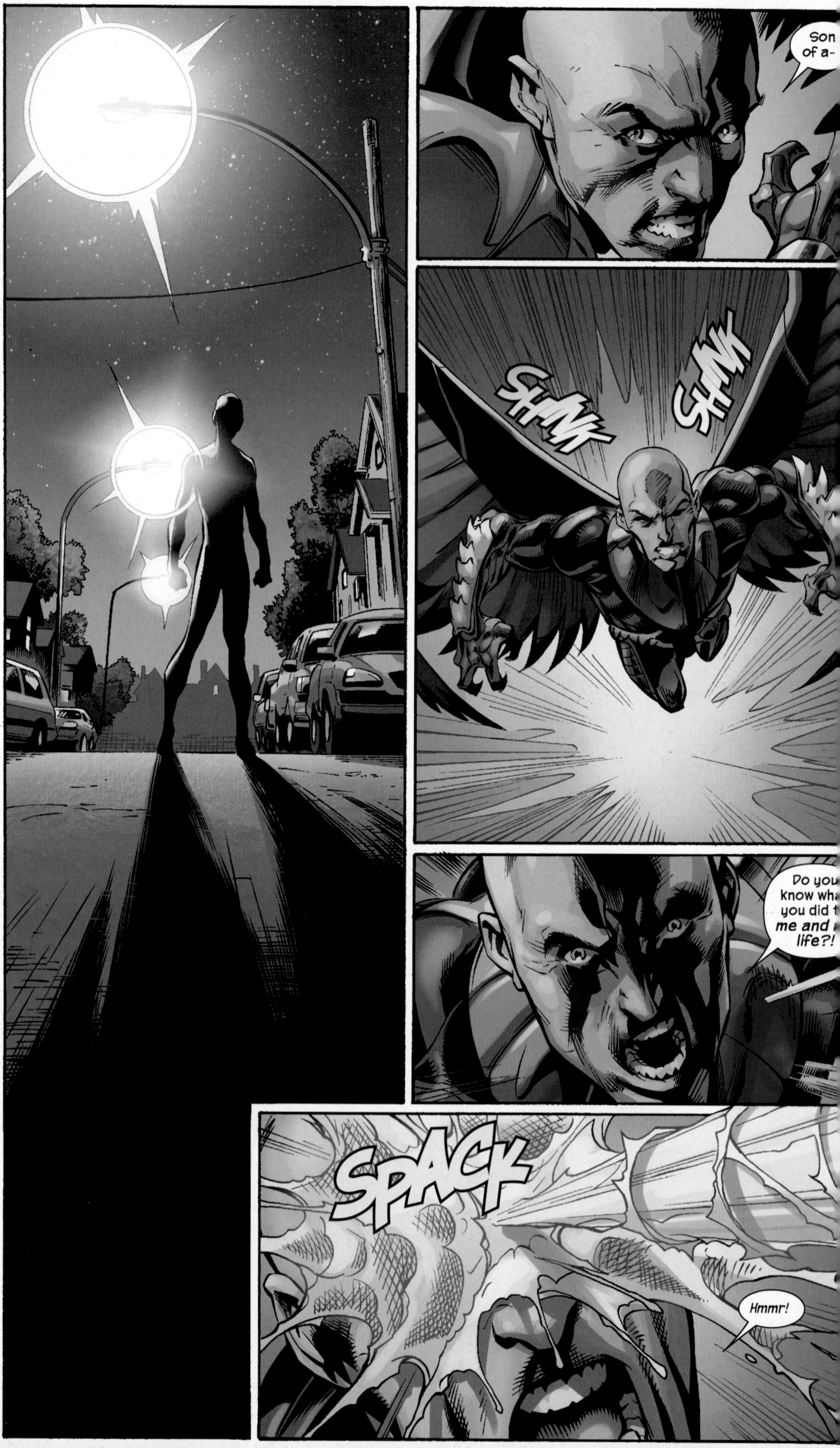
Son of a-
SHNK
SHNK
Do you know wha you did t me and life?!
SPACK
Hmmr!

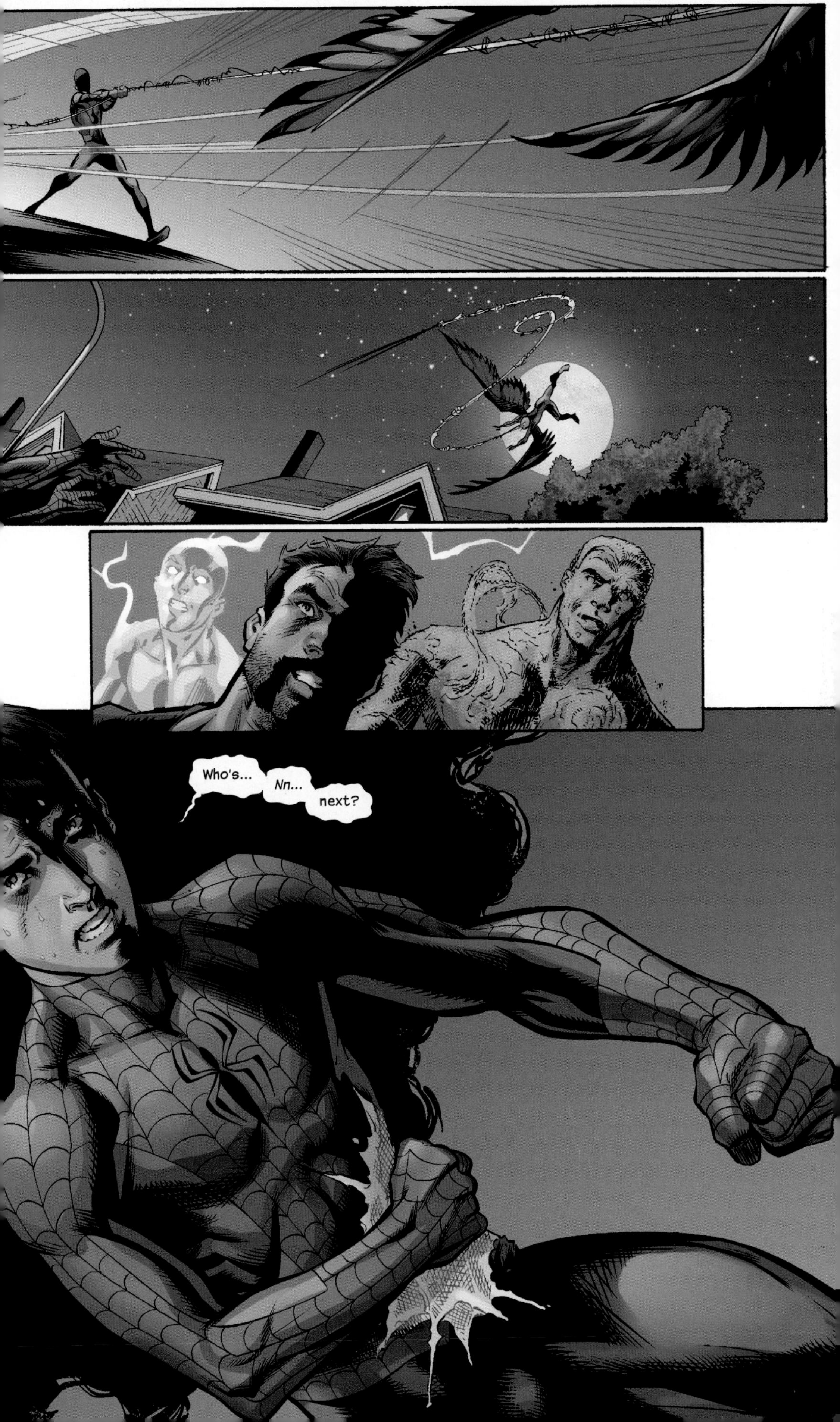
Who's...
Nn...
next?

#157 VARIANT
BY ED McGUINNESS & MORRY HOLLOWELL

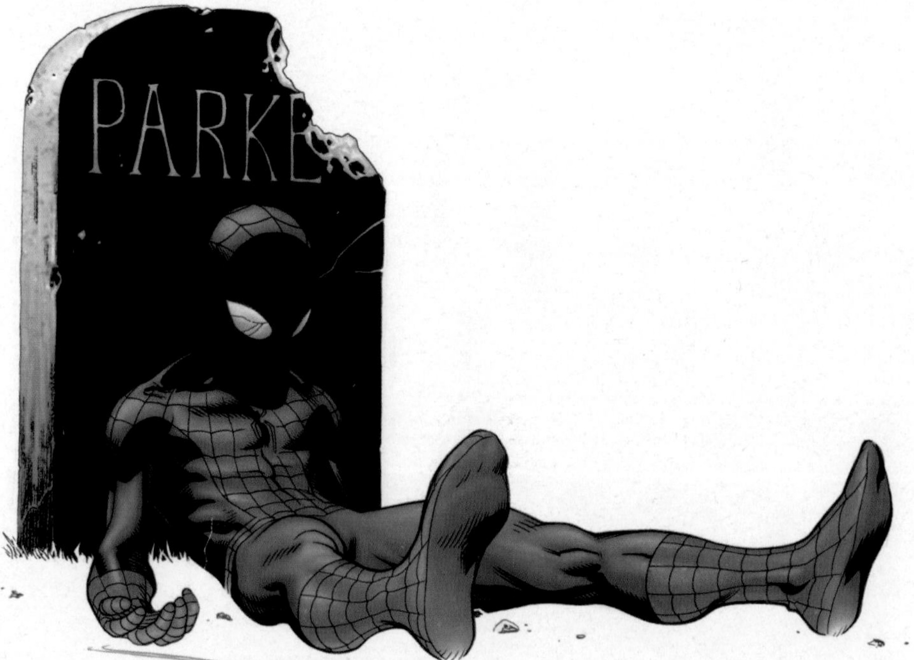
PARKE

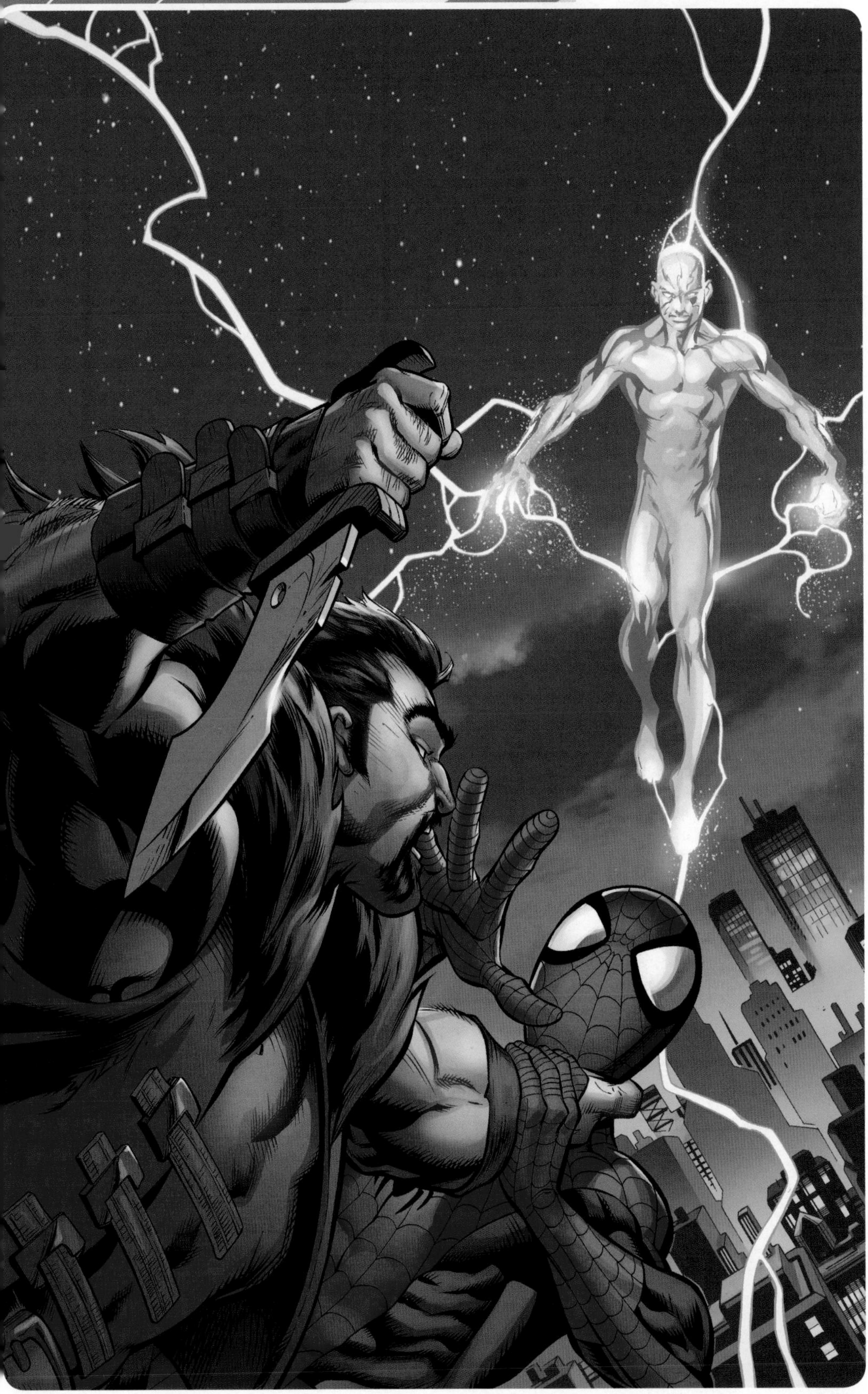

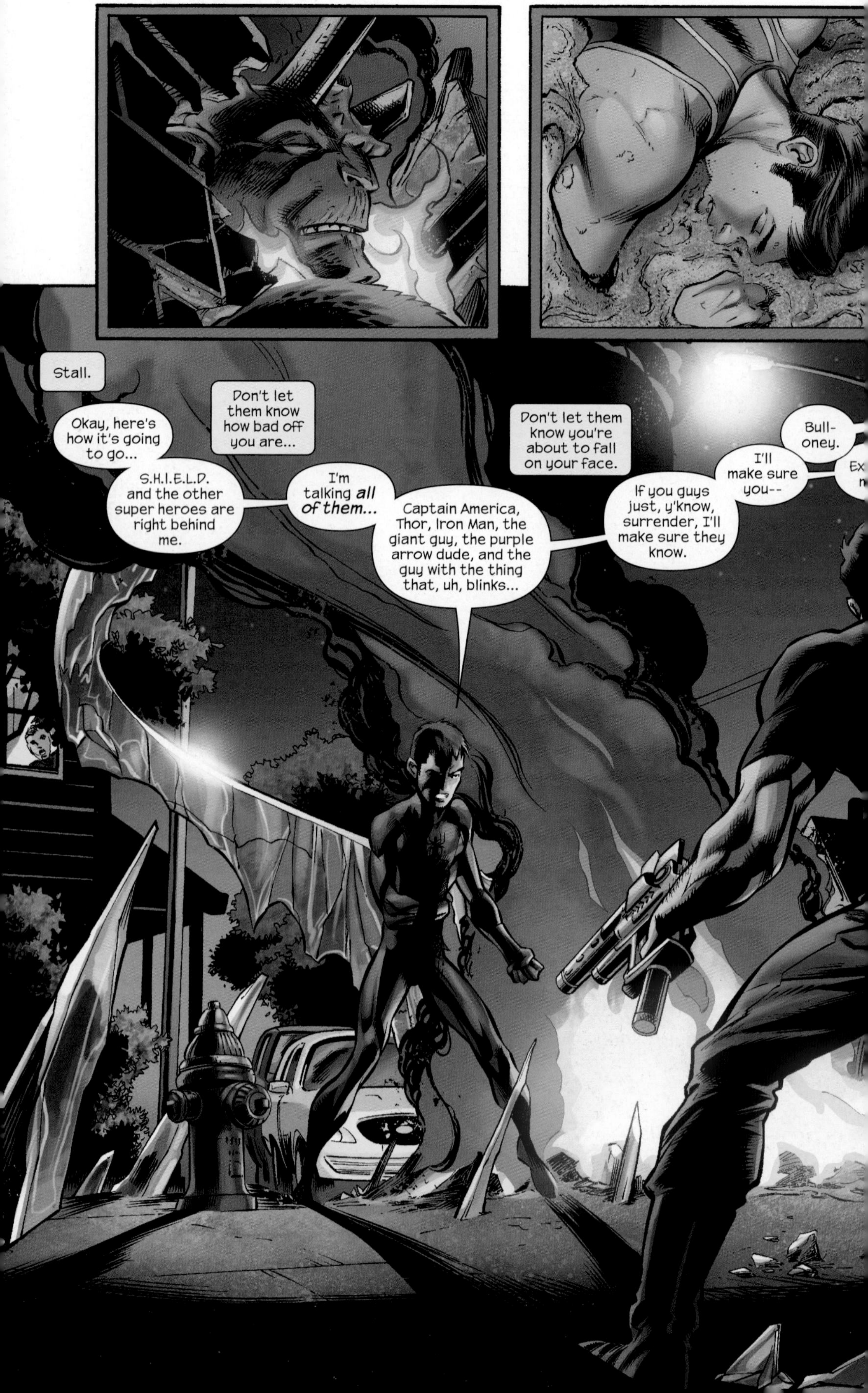

Stall.
Okay, here's how it's going to go...
Don't let them know how bad off you are...
S.H.I.E.L.D. and the other super heroes are right behind me.
I'm talking *all of them...*
Captain America, Thor, Iron Man, the giant guy, the purple arrow dude, and the guy with the thing that, uh, blinks...
Don't let them know you're about to fall on your face.
If you guys just, y'know, surrender, I'll make sure they know.
I'll make sure you--
Bull-oney.

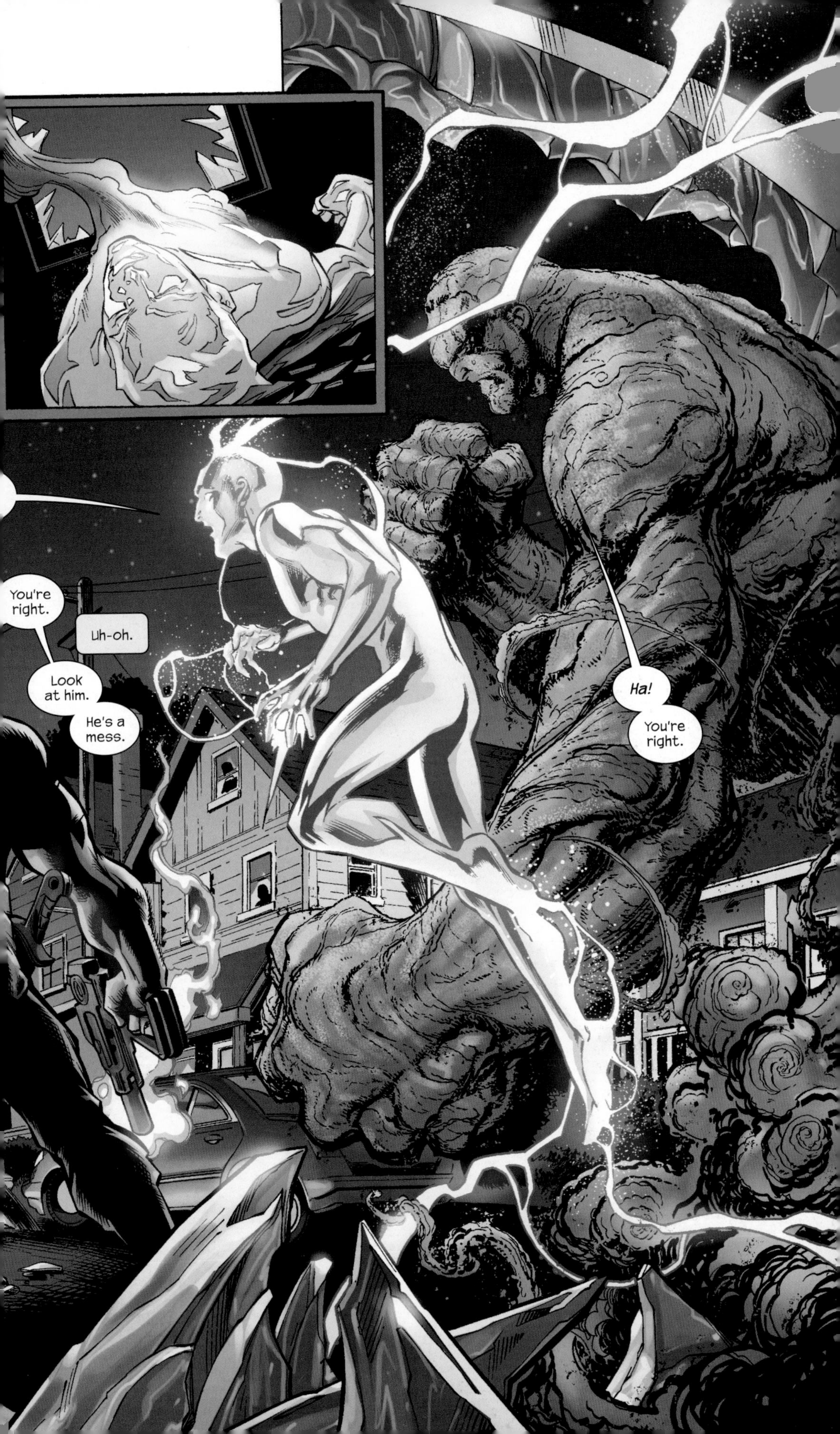
You're right.
Uh-oh.
Look at him.
He's a mess.
Ha!
You're right.

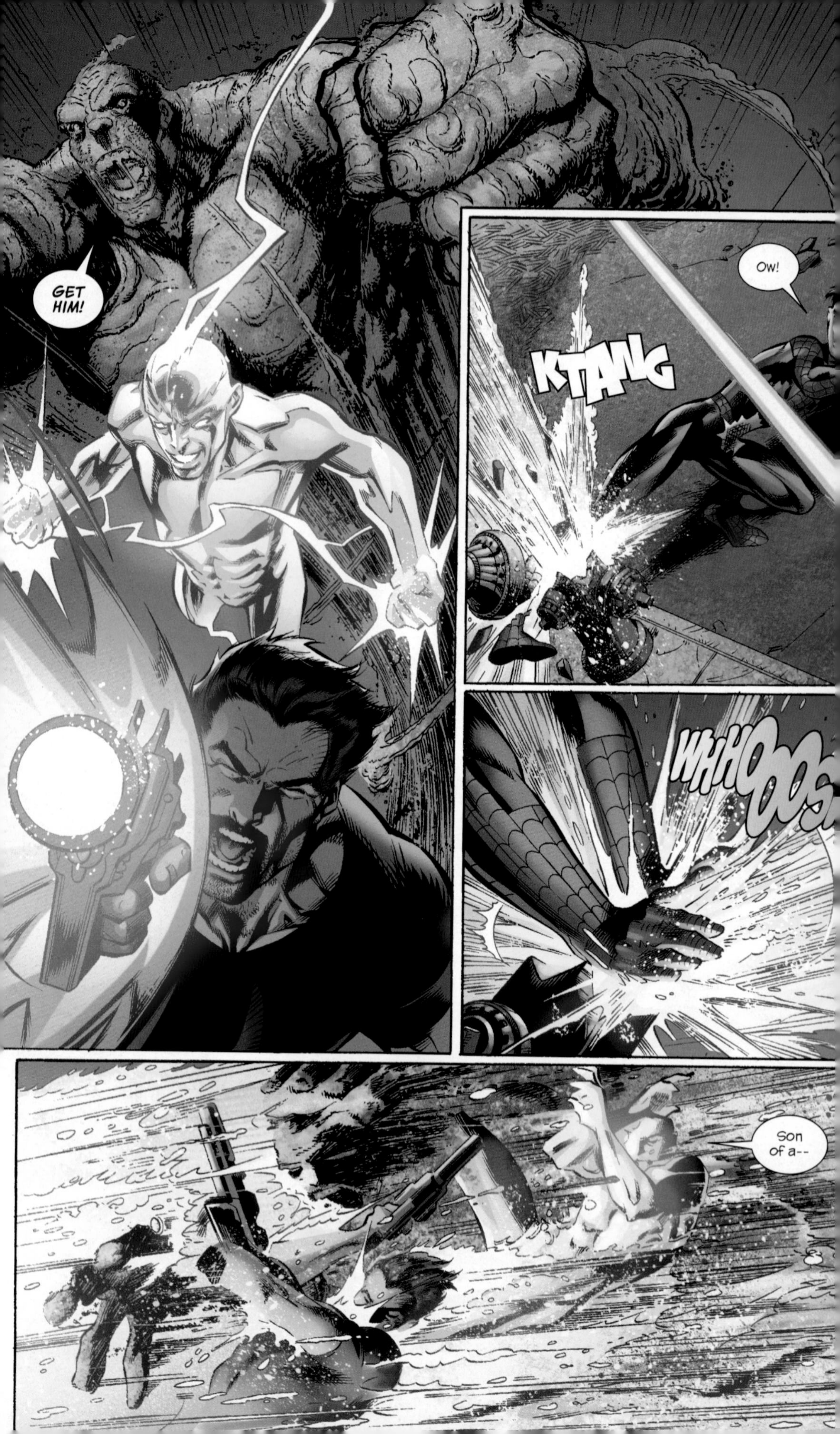
GET HIM!
OW!
KTANG
WHHOOOSH
Son of a--

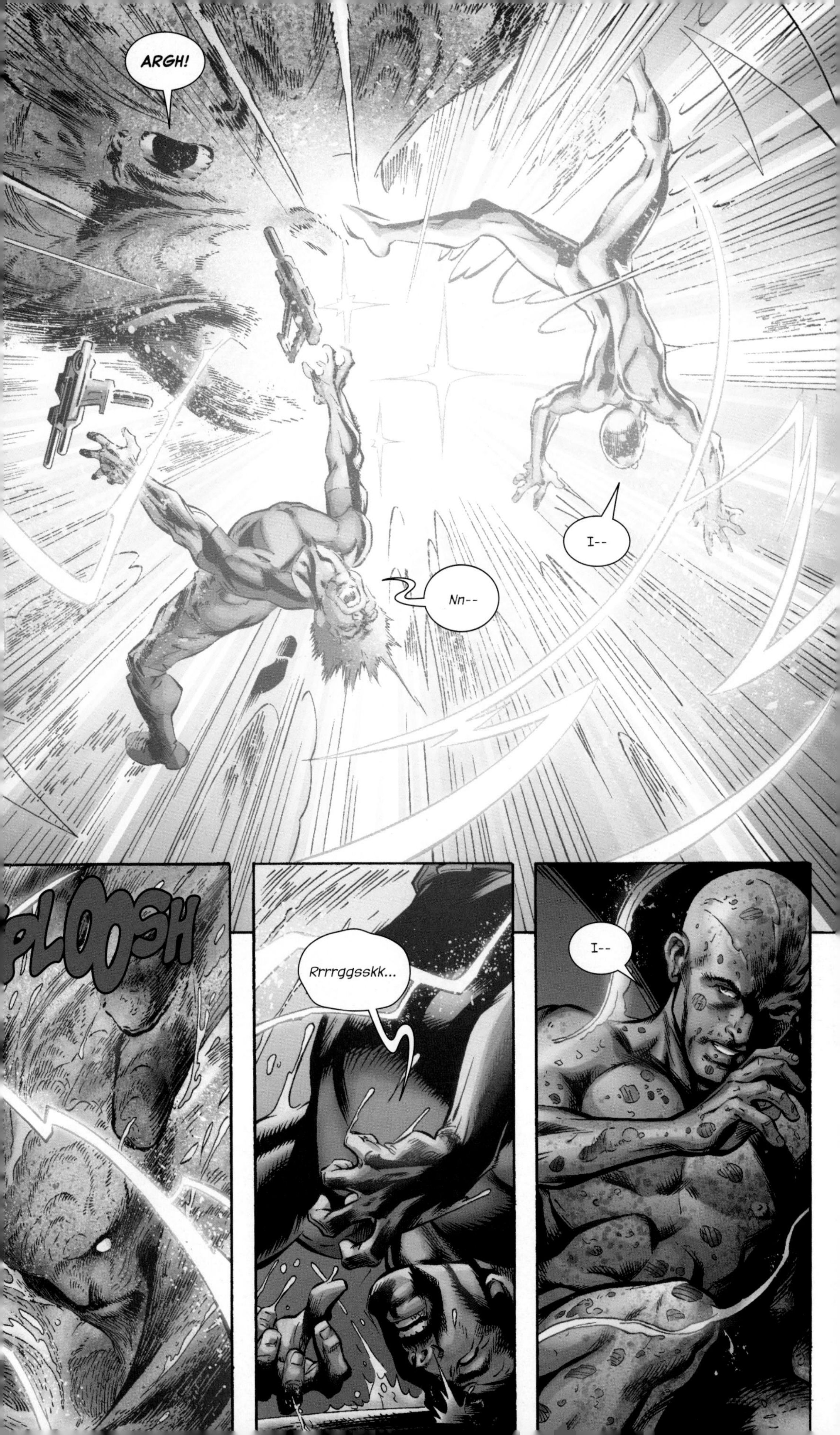
ARGH!
I--
Nn--
PLOOSH
Rrrrggsskk...
I--

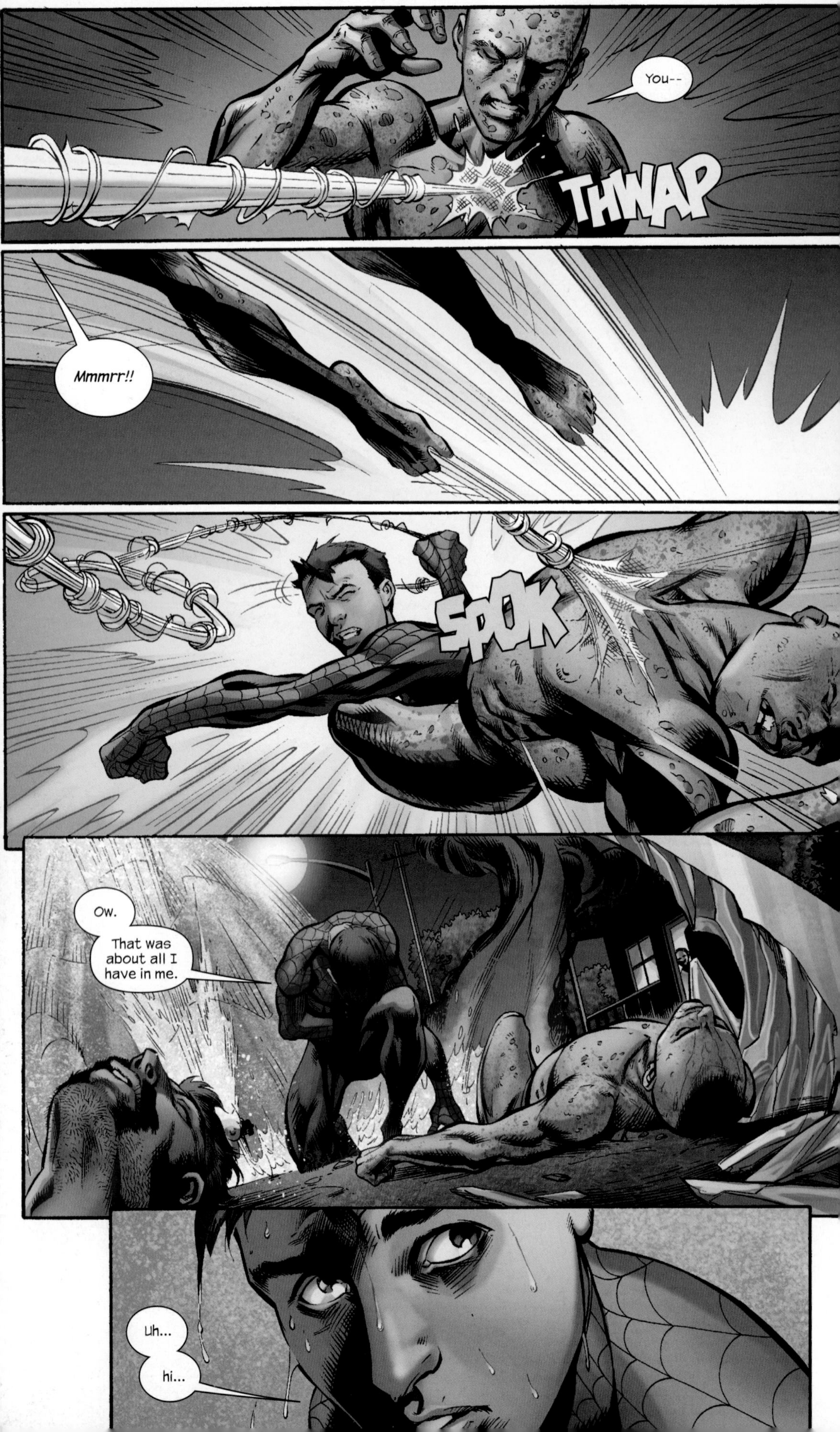
You--
THWAP
Mmmrr!!
SPOK
Ow.
That was about all I have in me.
Uh...
hi...

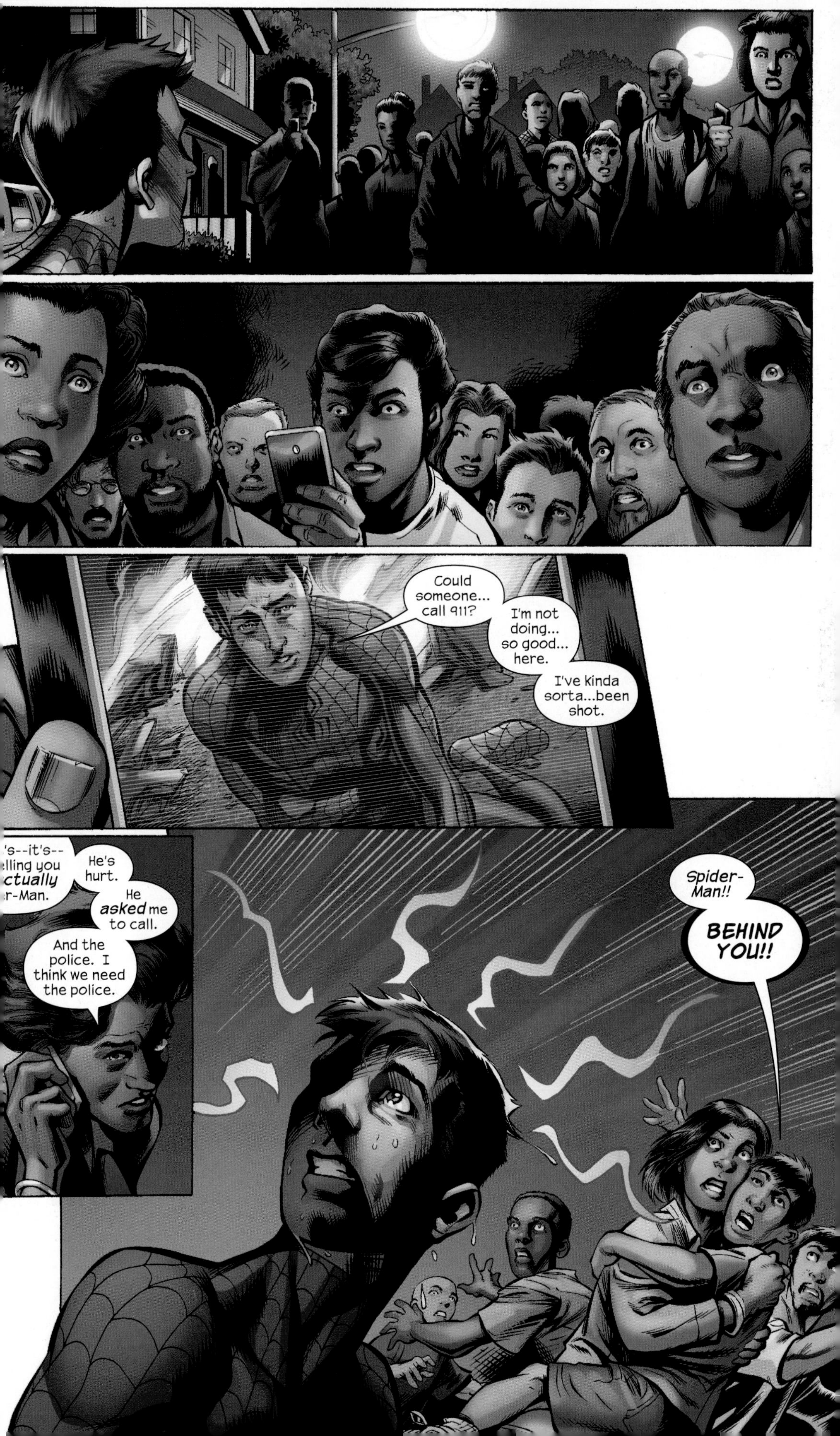
Could someone... call 911?
I'm not doing... so good... here.
I've kinda sorta...been shot.
's--it's-- elling you ctually r-Man.
He's hurt.
He asked me to call.
And the police. I think we need the police.
Spider-Man!!
BEHIND YOU!!

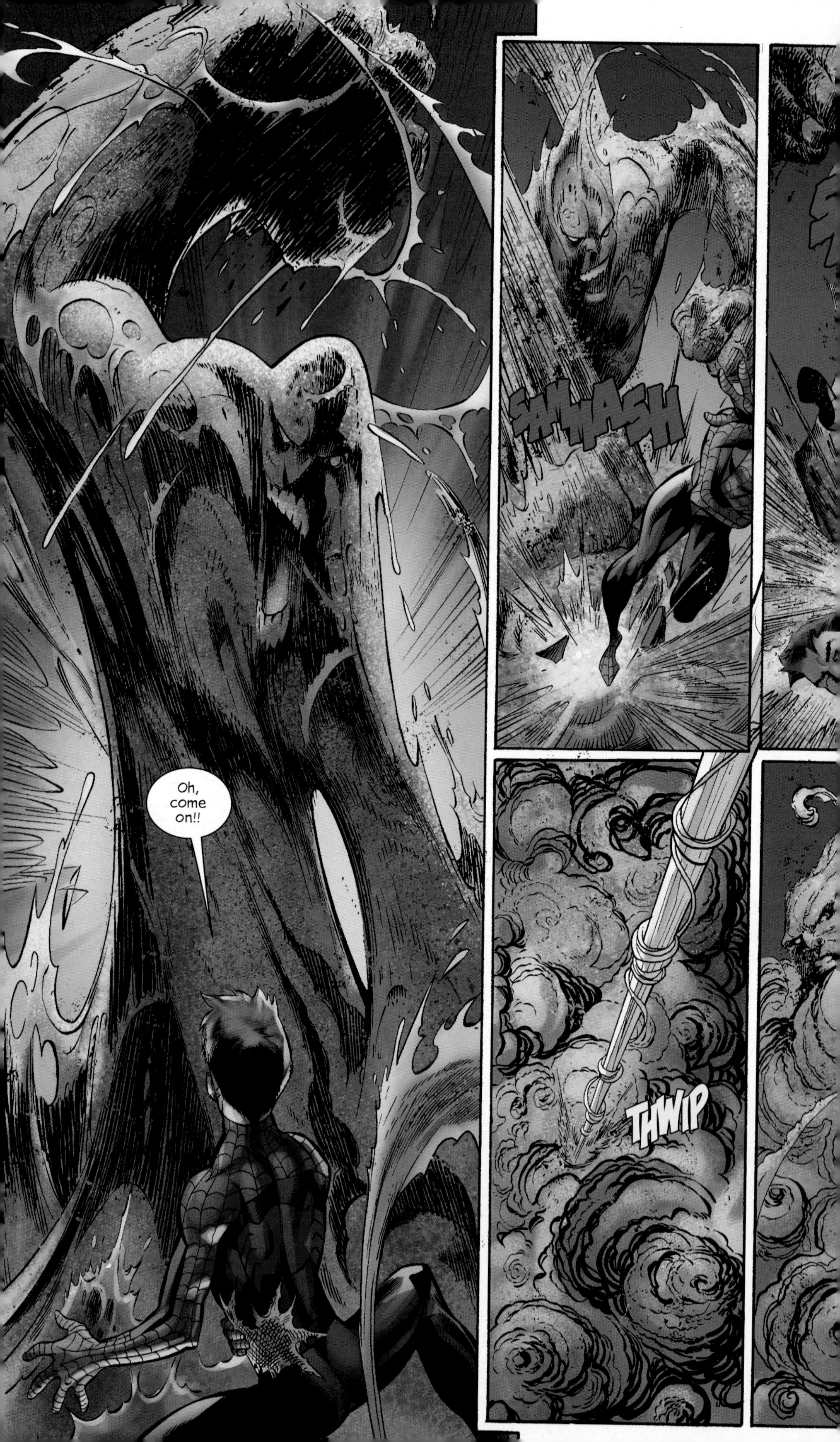
Oh, come on!!
SMMASH
THWIP

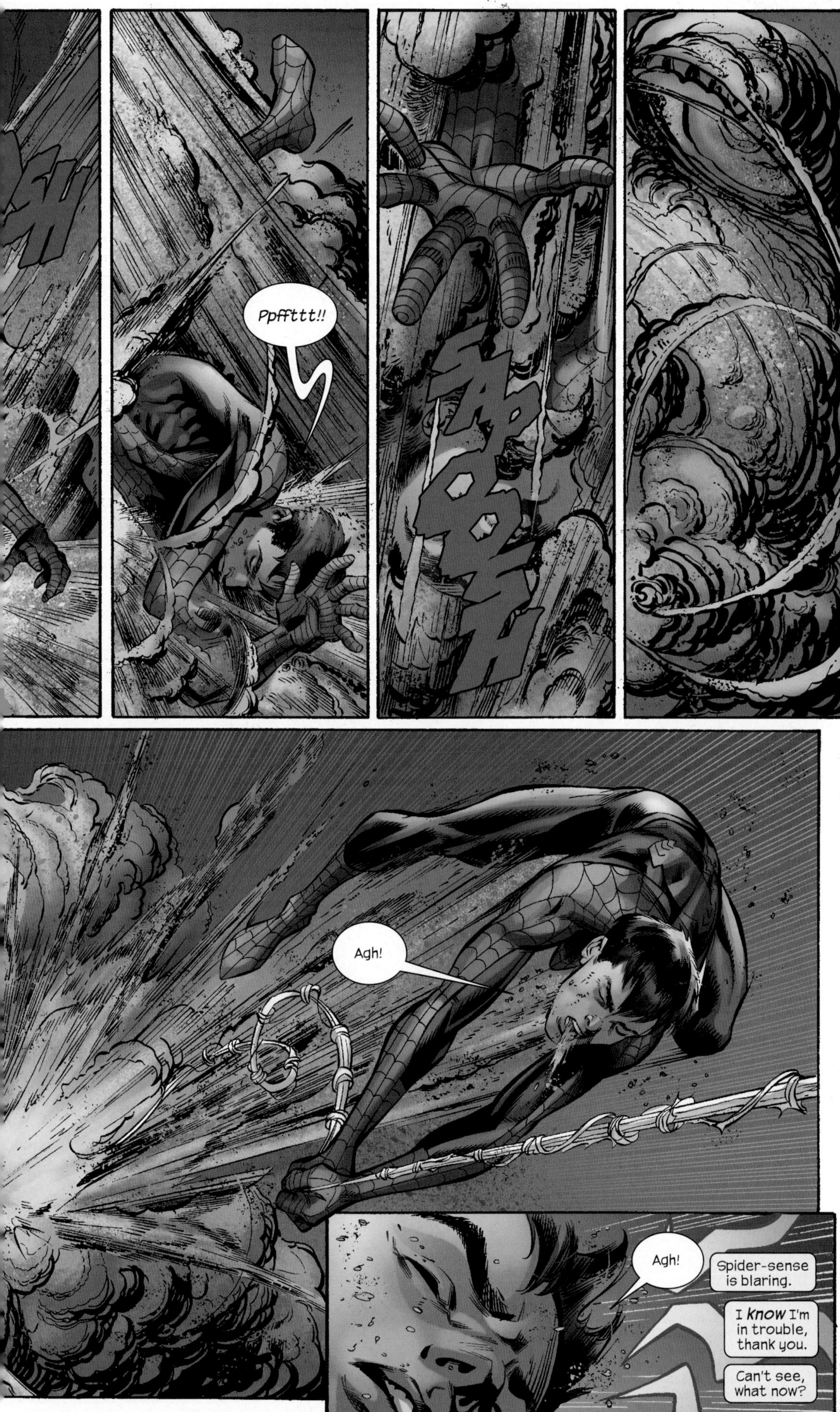
Ppffttt!!
Agh!
Agh!
Spider-sense is blaring.
I *know* I'm in trouble, thank you.
Can't see, what now?

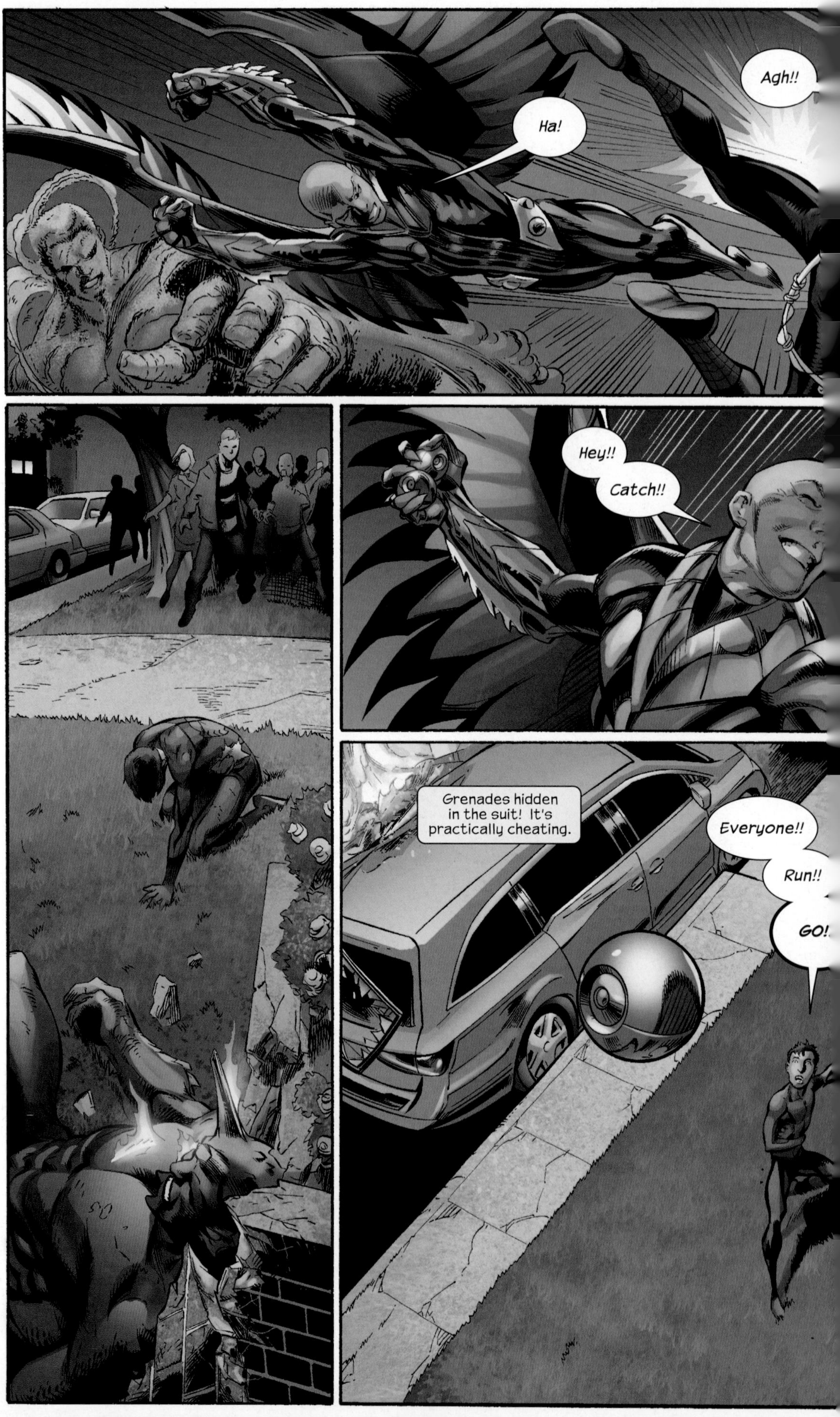
Ha!
Agh!!
Hey!!
Catch!!
Grenades hidden in the suit! It's practically cheating.
Everyone!!
Run!!
GO!!

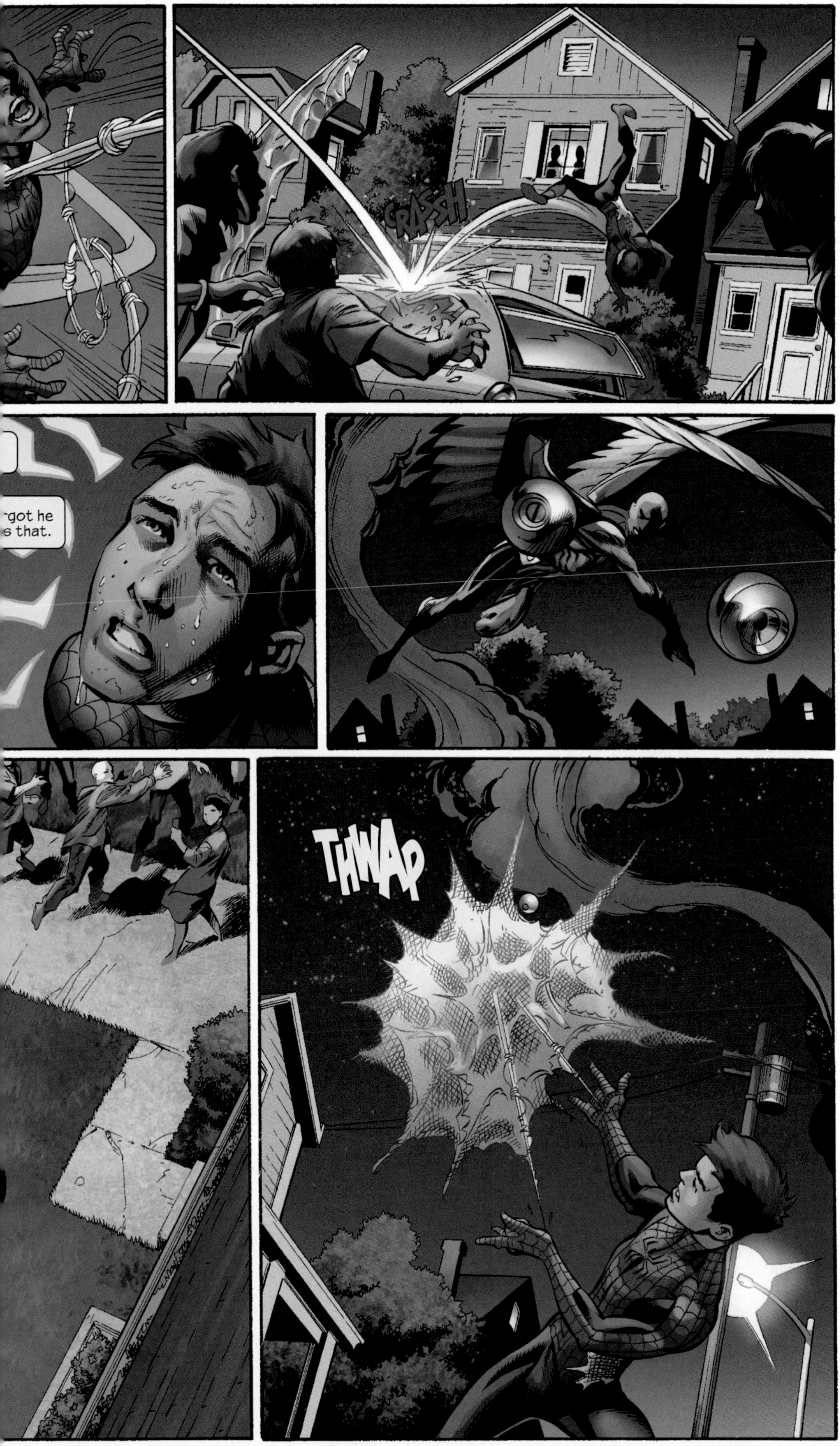
CRASSH
rgot he
s that.
THWAP

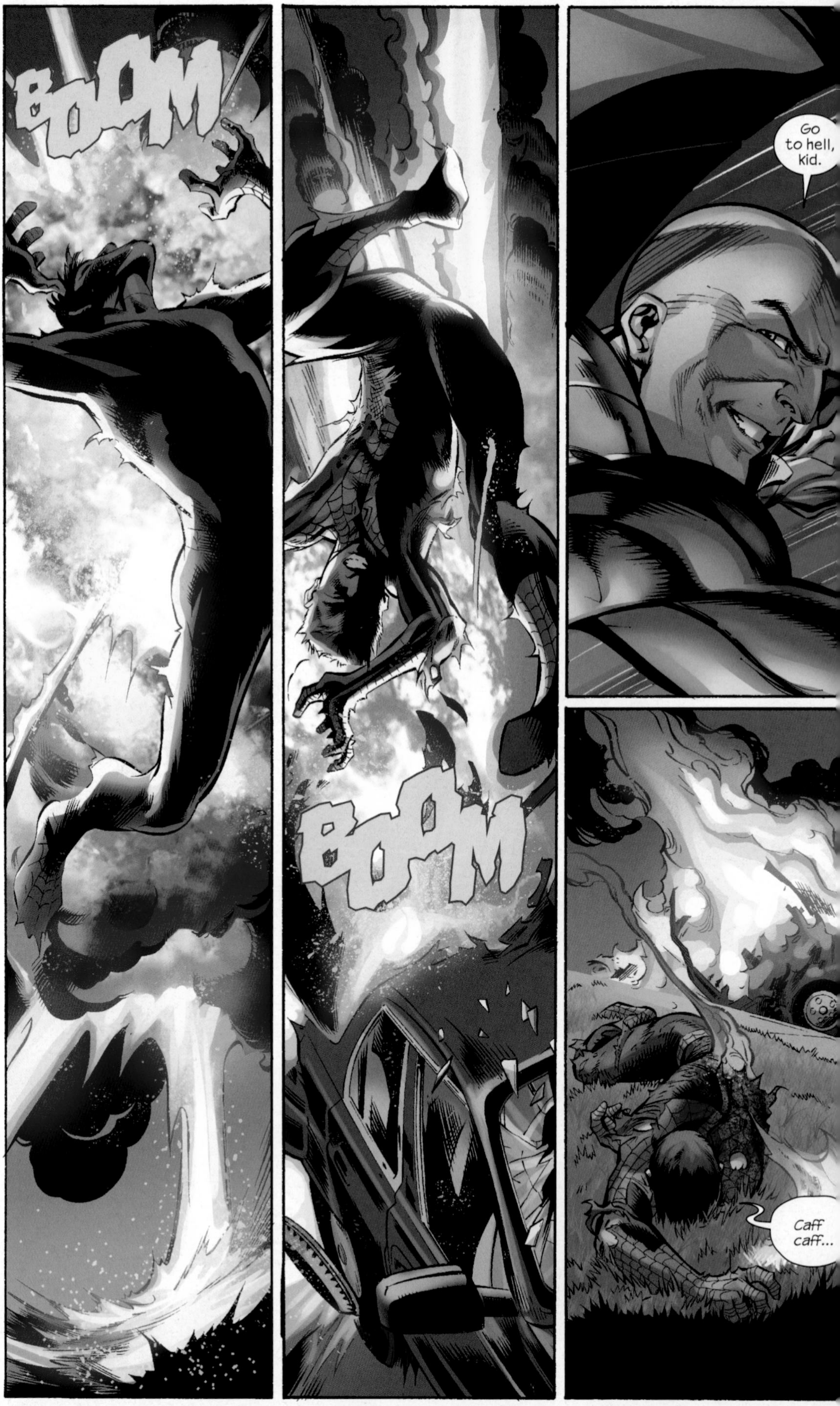
BOOM
BOOM
Go to hell, kid.
Caff caff...

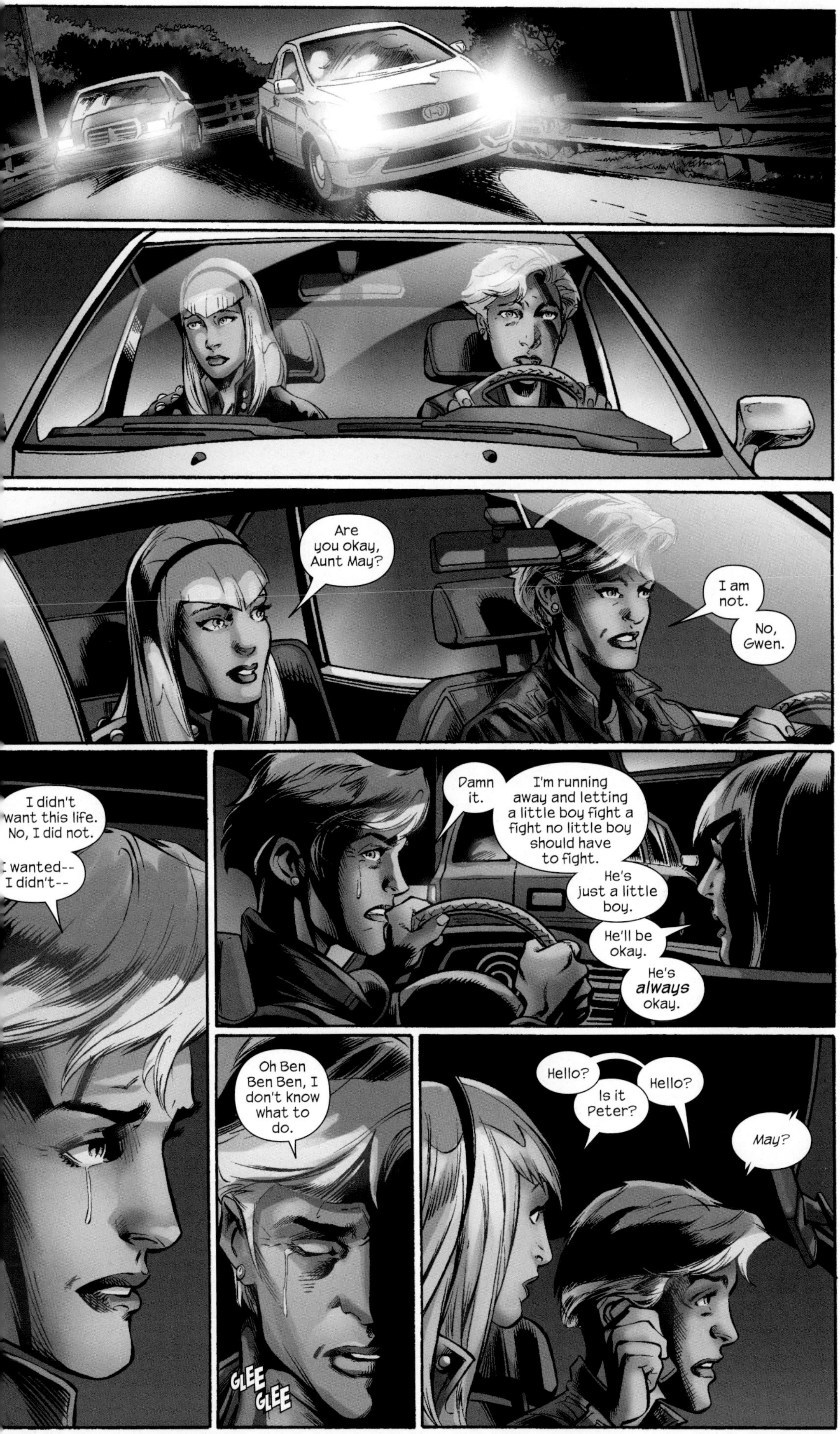
Are you okay, Aunt May?
I am not.
No, Gwen.
I didn't want this life. No, I did not.
I wanted-- I didn't--
Damn it.
I'm running away and letting a little boy fight a fight no little boy should have to fight.
He's just a little boy.
He'll be okay.
He's *always* okay.
Oh Ben Ben Ben, I don't know what to do.
GLEE GLEE
Hello?
Is it Peter?
Hello?
May?

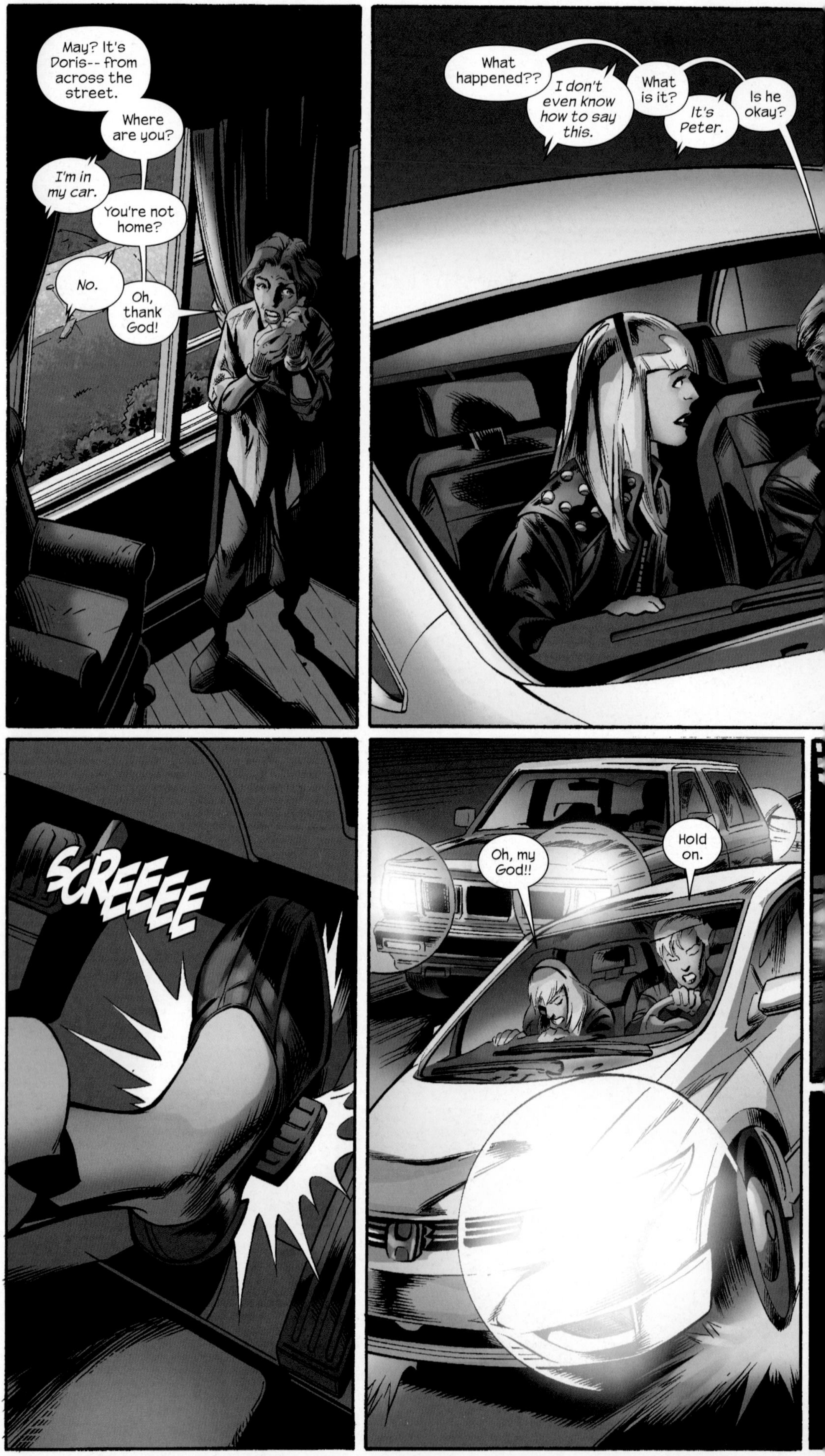
May? It's Doris-- from across the street.
Where are you?
I'm in my car.
You're not home?
No.
Oh, thank God!
What happened??
I don't even know how to say this.
What is it?
It's Peter.
Is he okay?
SCREEEEE
Oh, my God!!
Hold on.

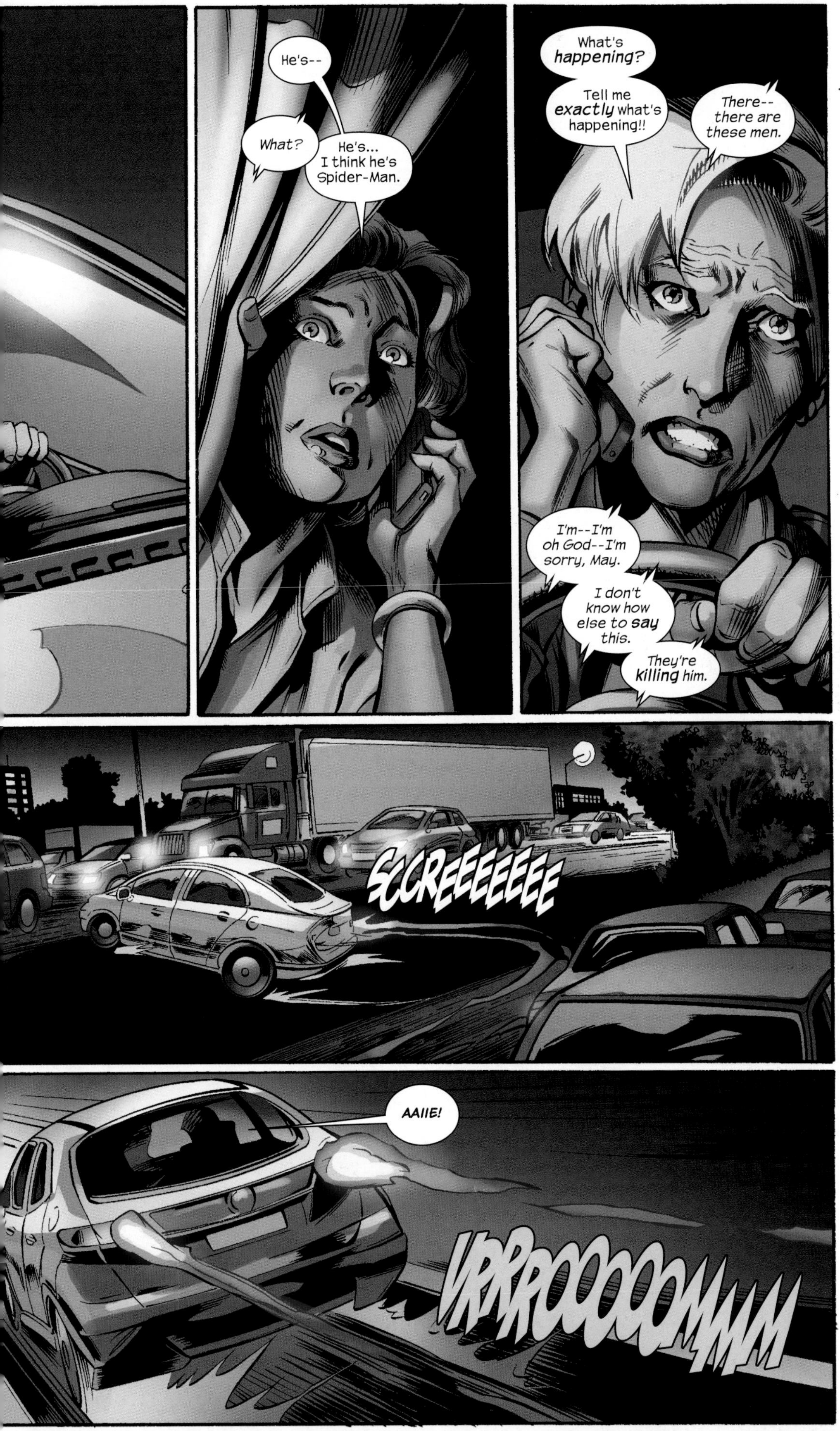
He's--
What?
He's... I think he's Spider-Man.
What's happening?
Tell me exactly what's happening!!
There--there are these men.
I'm--I'm oh God--I'm sorry, May.
I don't know how else to say this.
They're killing him.
SCCREEEEEEEE
AAIIE!
VRRROOOOOMMM

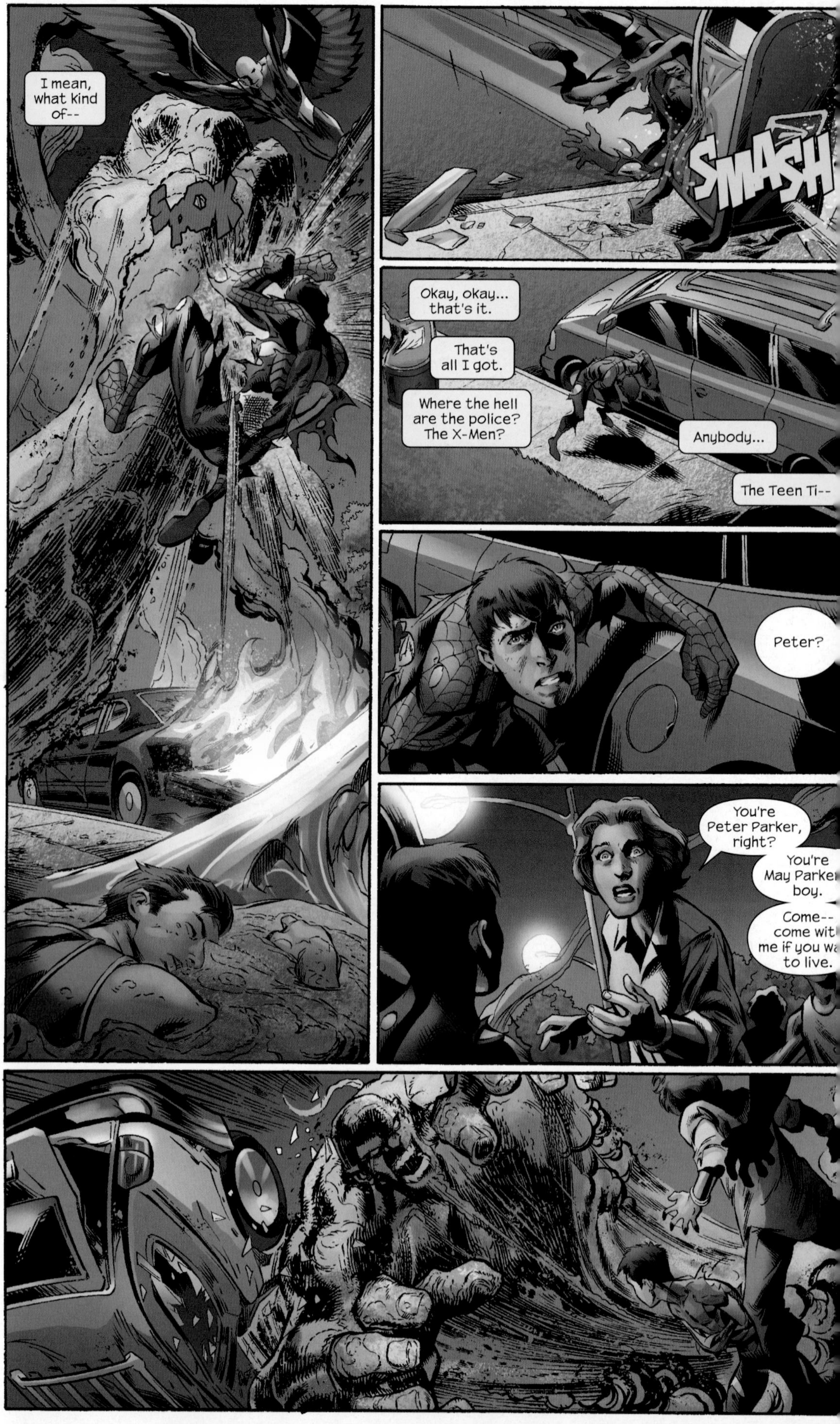
I mean, what kind of--
SMASH
Okay, okay... that's it.
That's all I got.
Where the hell are the police? The X-Men?
Anybody...
The Teen Ti--
Peter?
You're Peter Parker, right?
You're May Parke boy.
Come-- come wit me if you w to live.

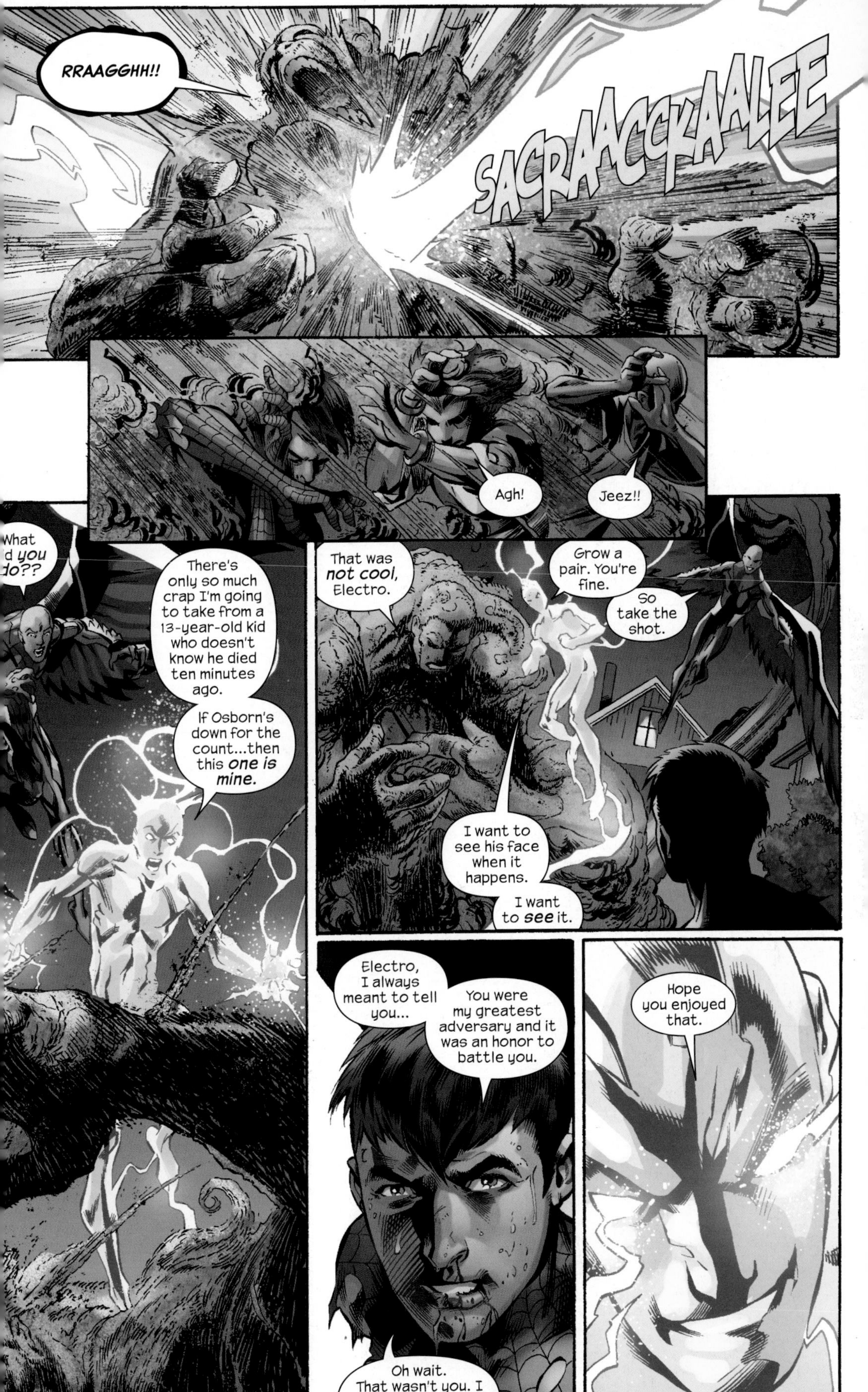
RRAAGGHH!!
SACRAACCKAALEE
Agh!
Jeez!!
What d you do??
There's only so much crap I'm going to take from a 13-year-old kid who doesn't know he died ten minutes ago.
If Osborn's down for the count...then this one is mine.
That was not cool, Electro.
Grow a pair. You're fine.
So take the shot.
I want to see his face when it happens.
I want to see it.
Electro, I always meant to tell you...
You were my greatest adversary and it was an honor to battle you.
Oh wait. That wasn't you. I barely ever gave you a second's thought.
Hope you enjoyed that.

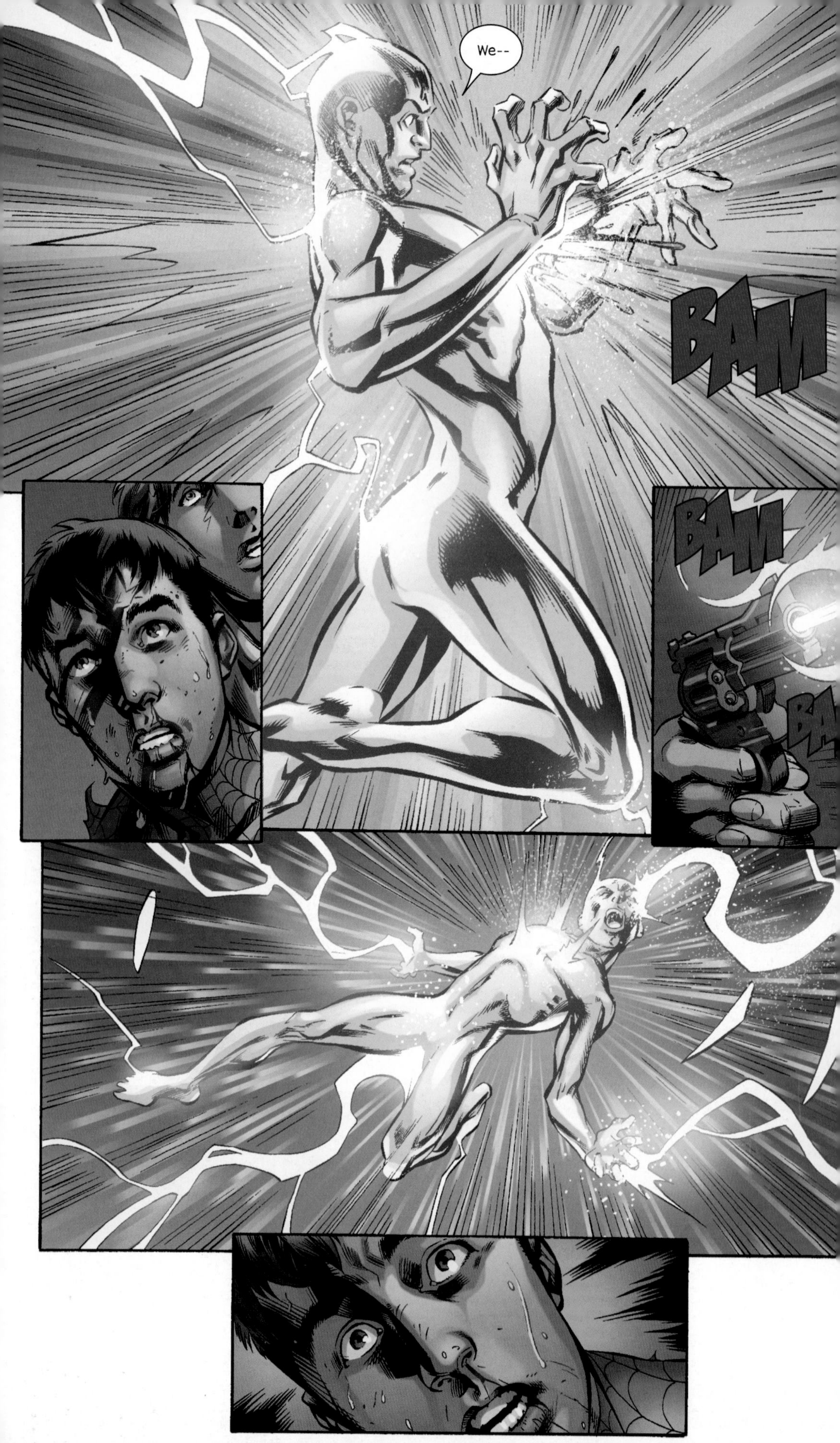
We--
BAM
BAM

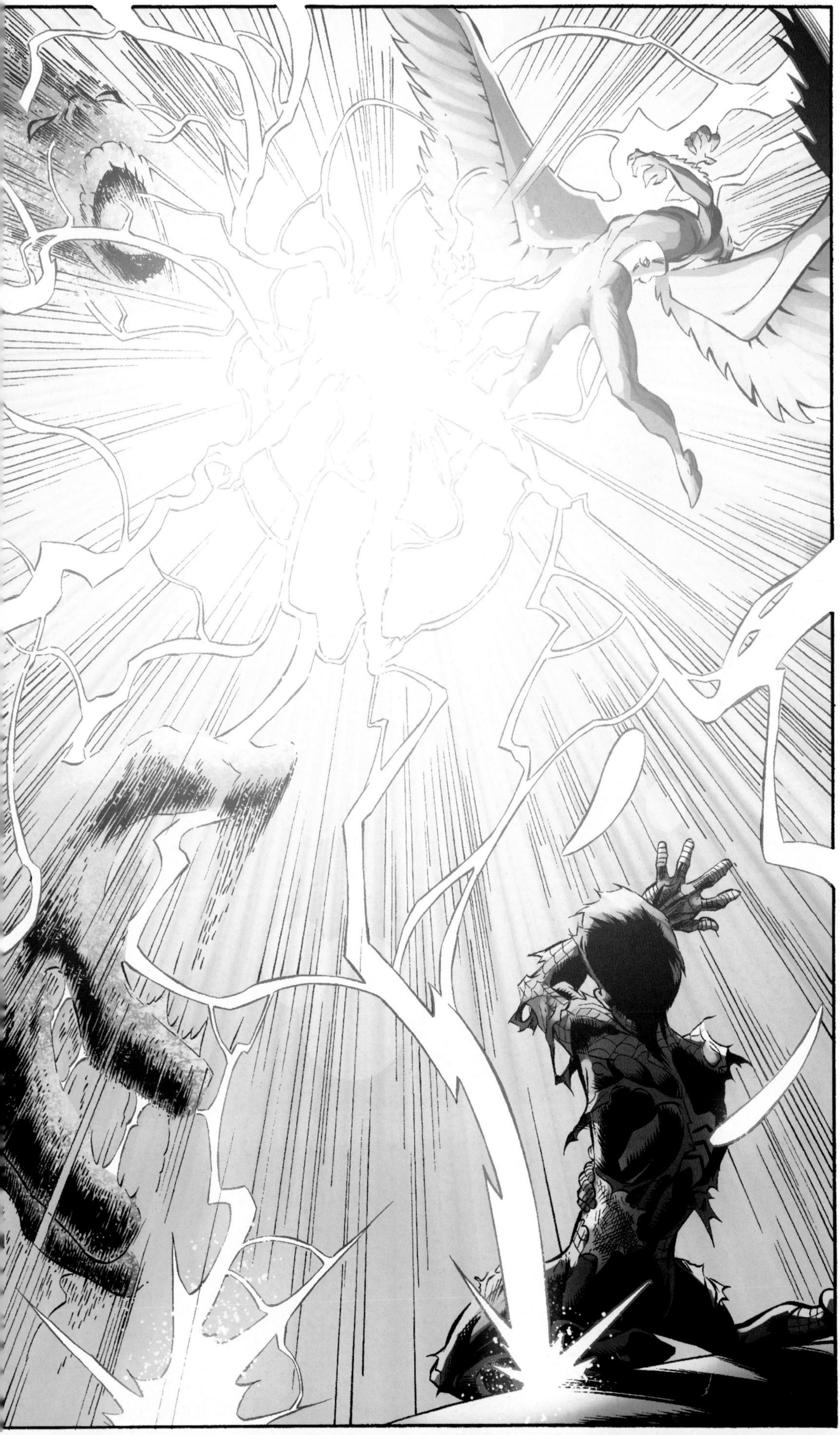

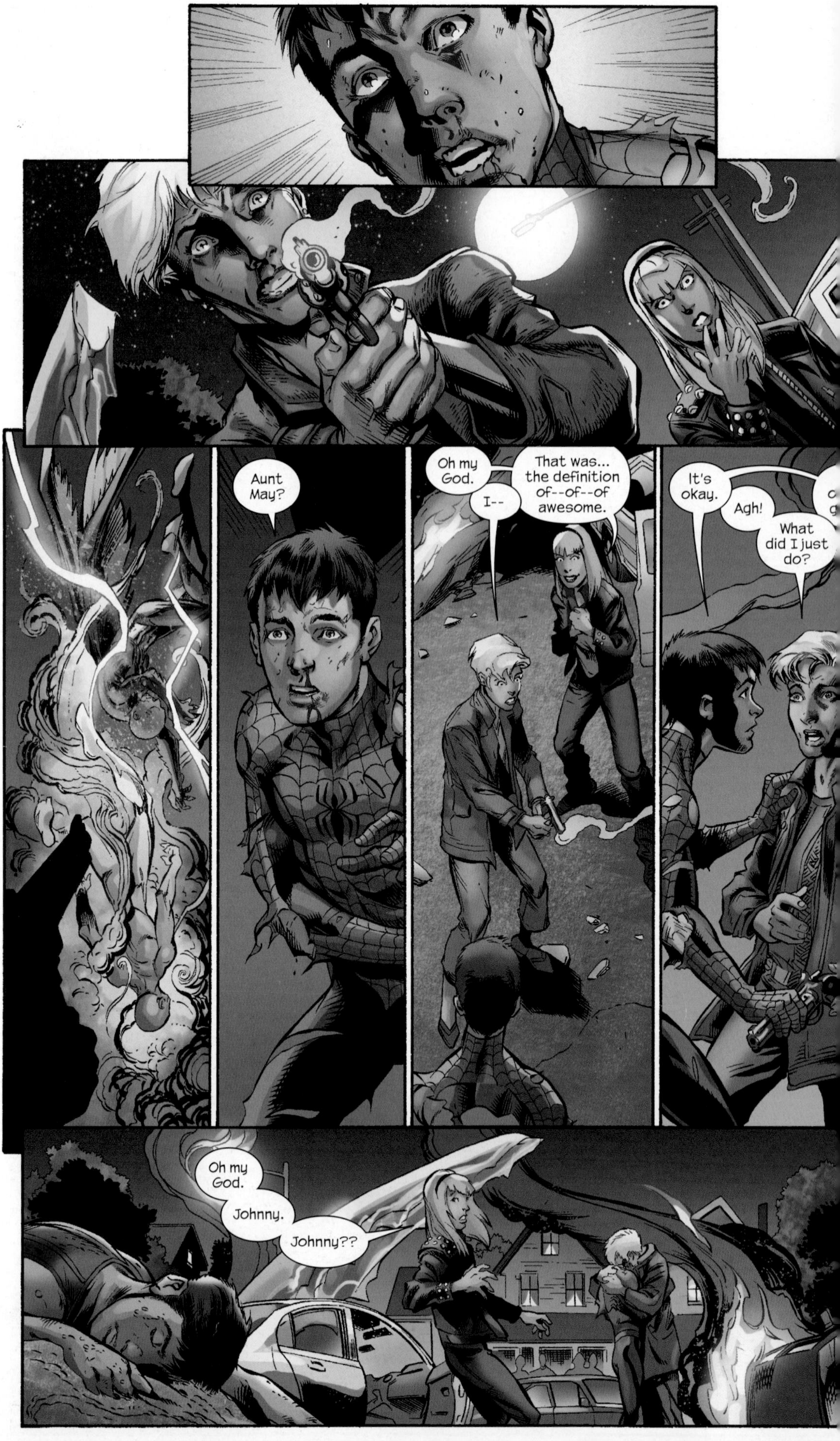
Aunt May?
Oh my God.
I--
That was... the definition of--of--of awesome.
It's okay.
Agh!
What did I just do?
Oh my God.
Johnny.
Johnny??

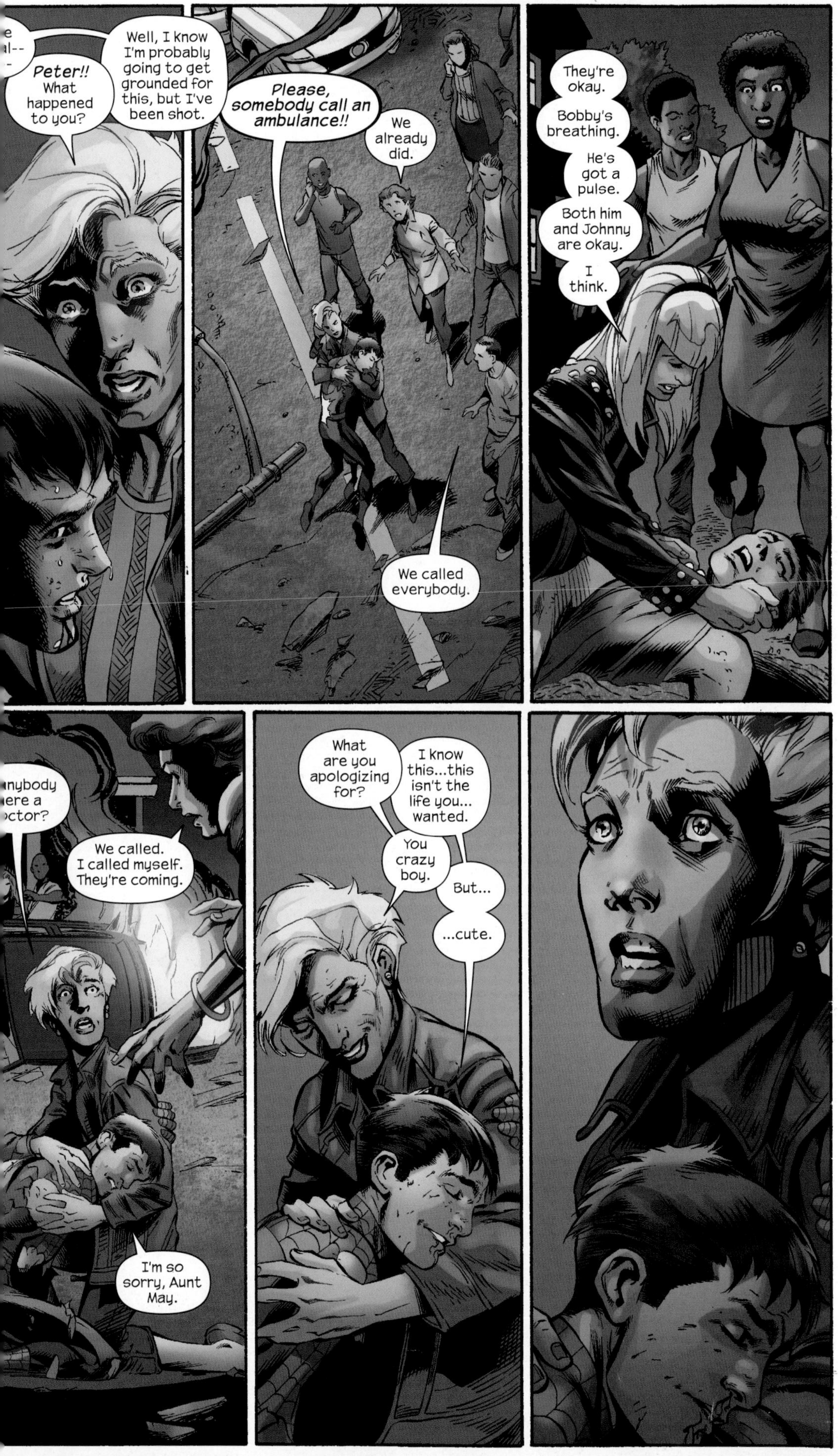
Peter!! What happened to you?
Well, I know I'm probably going to get grounded for this, but I've been shot.
Please, somebody call an ambulance!!
We already did.
We called everybody.
They're okay.
Bobby's breathing.
He's got a pulse.
Both him and Johnny are okay.
I think.
We called. I called myself. They're coming.
I'm so sorry, Aunt May.
What are you apologizing for?
I know this...this isn't the life you... wanted.
You crazy boy.
But...
...cute.

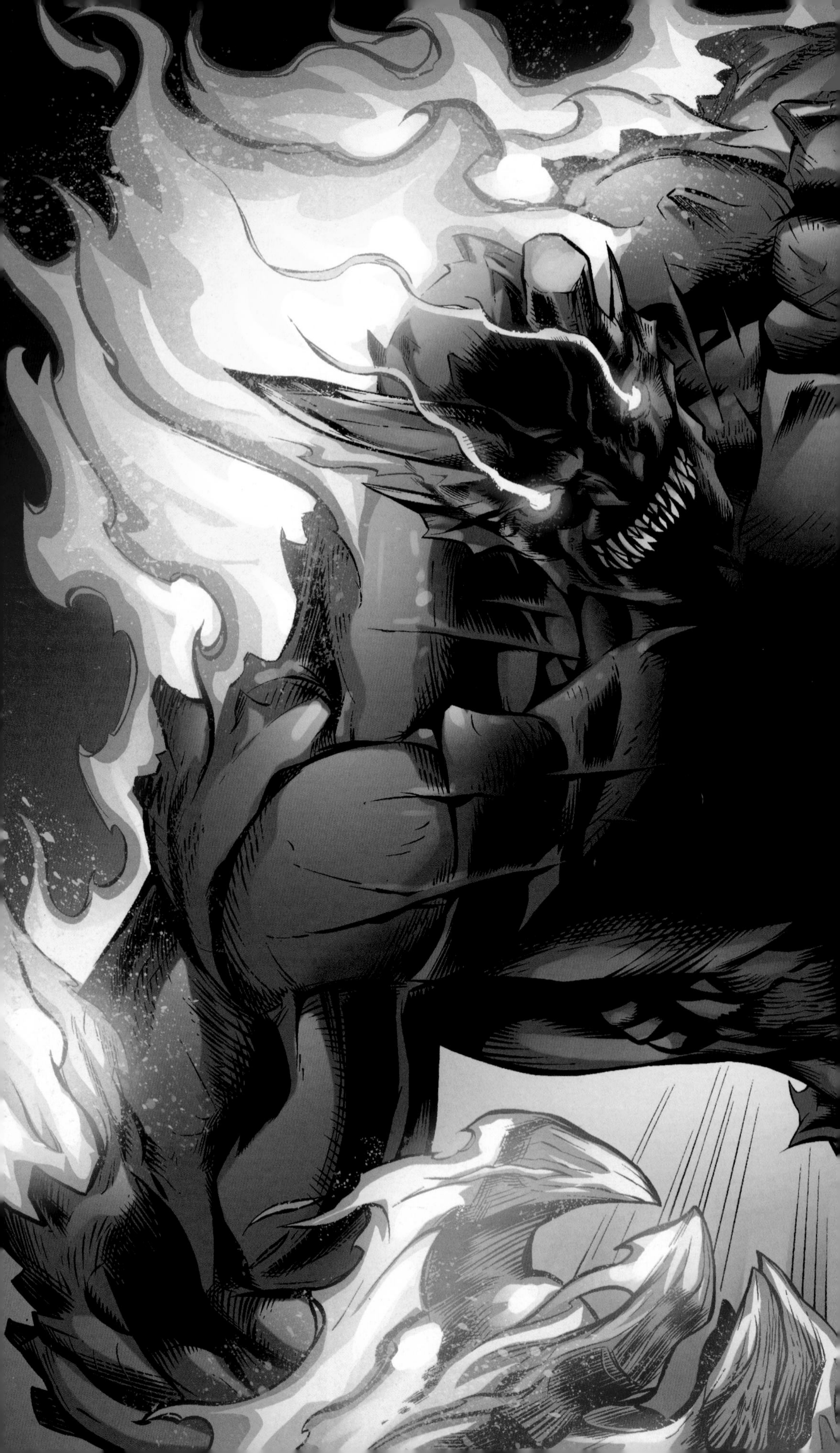

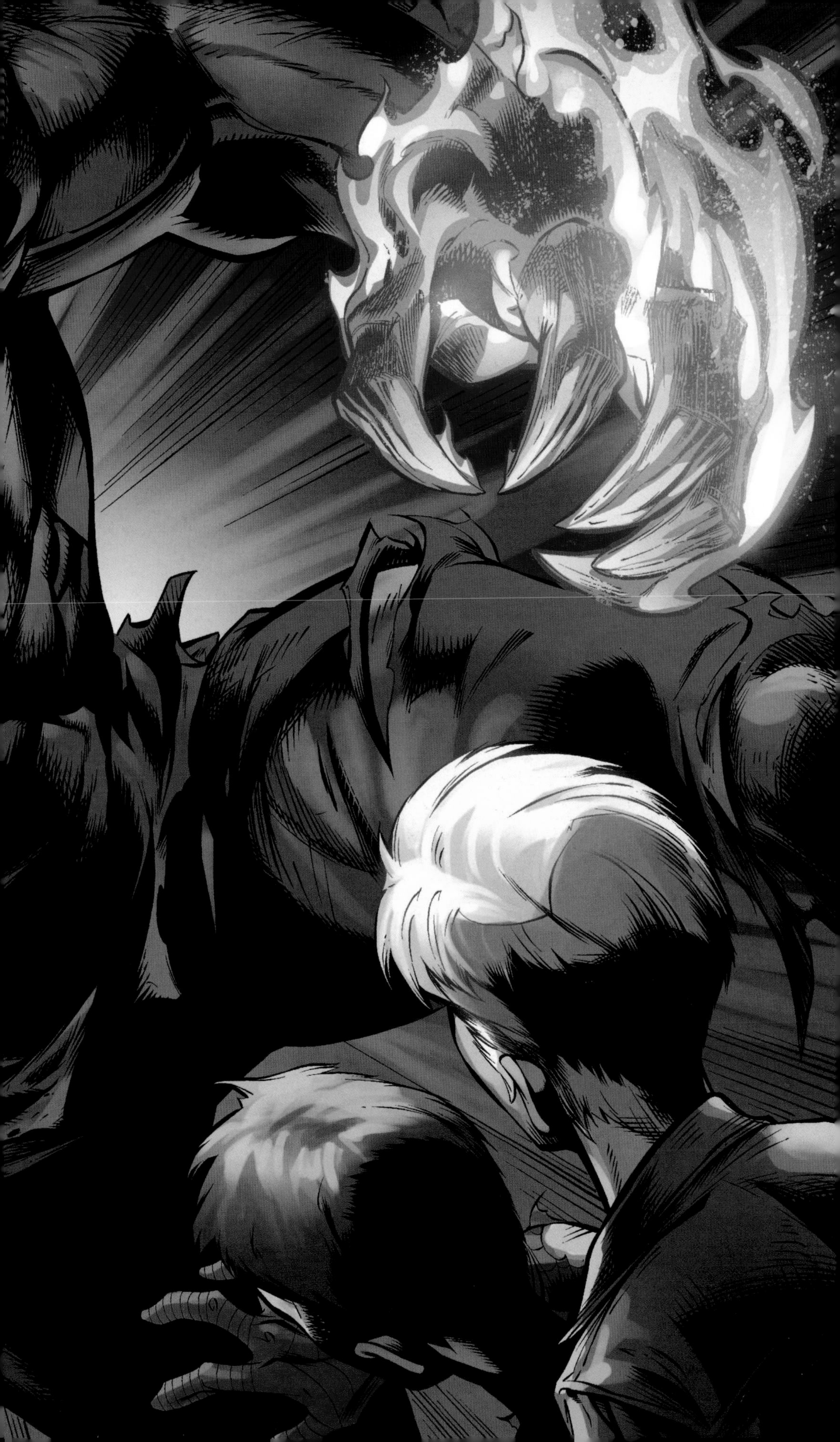

#158 VARIANT
BY STEVE MCNIVEN, DEXTER VINES & JUSTIN PONSOR

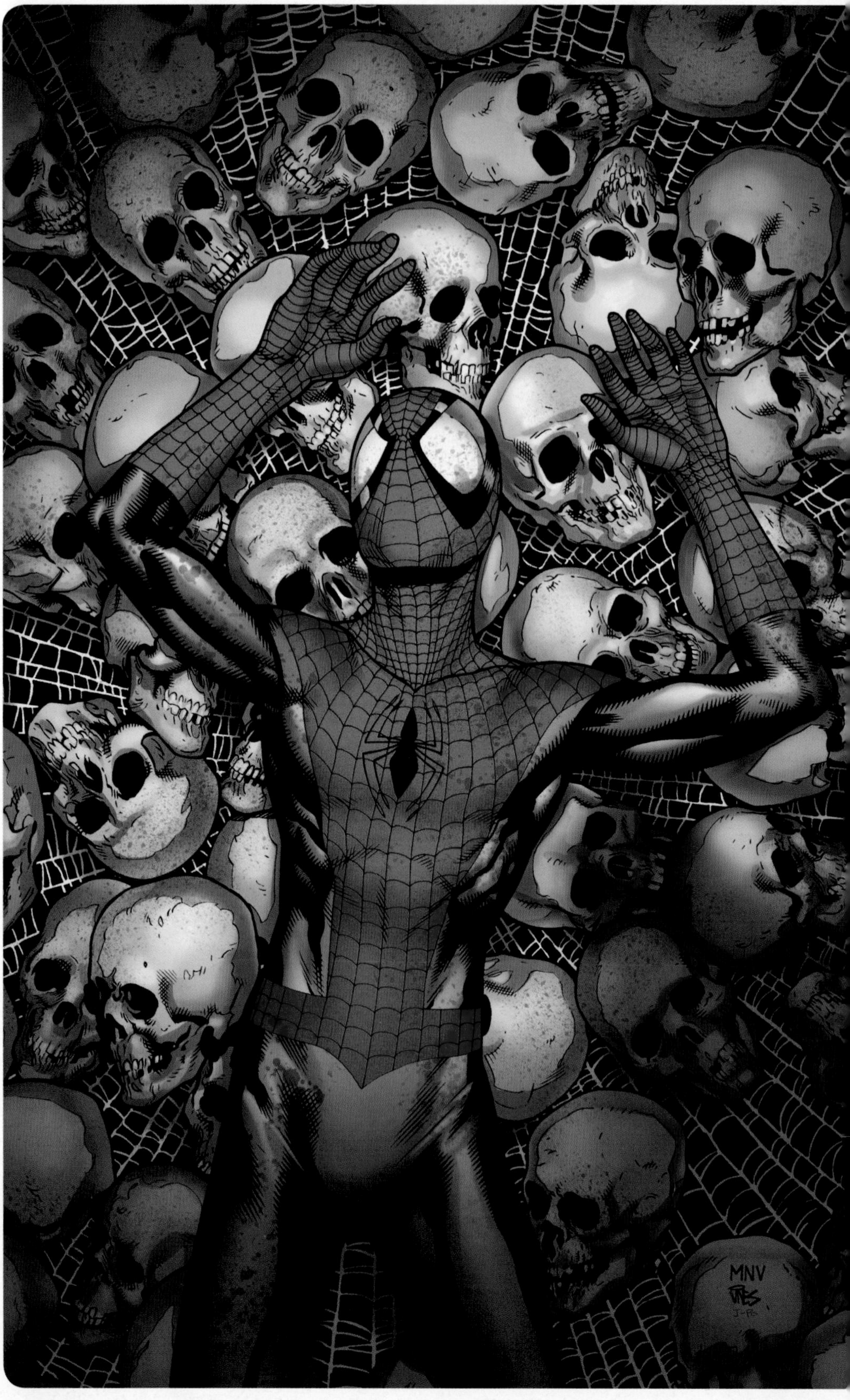

160

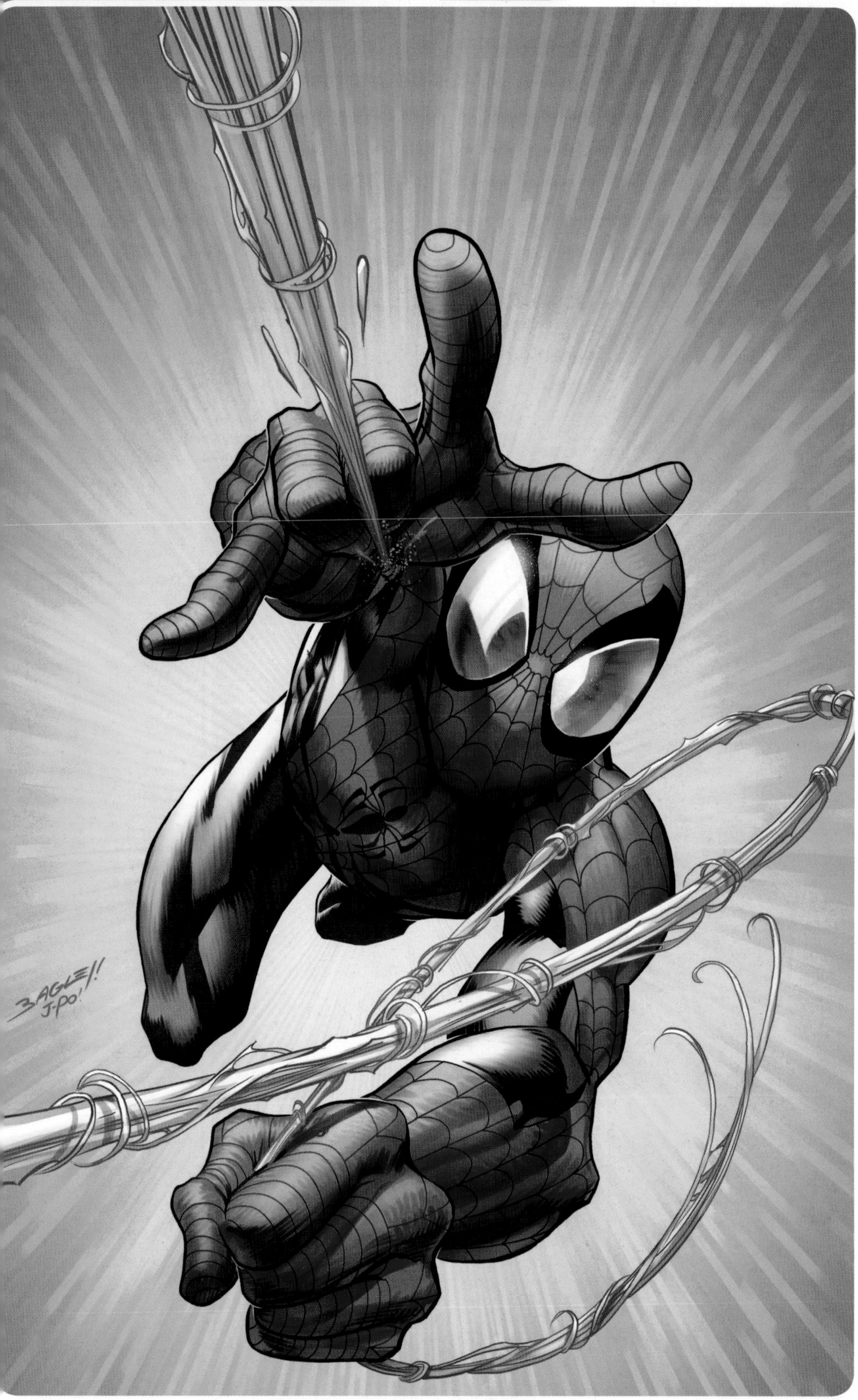
BAGLEY!!
J-PO!

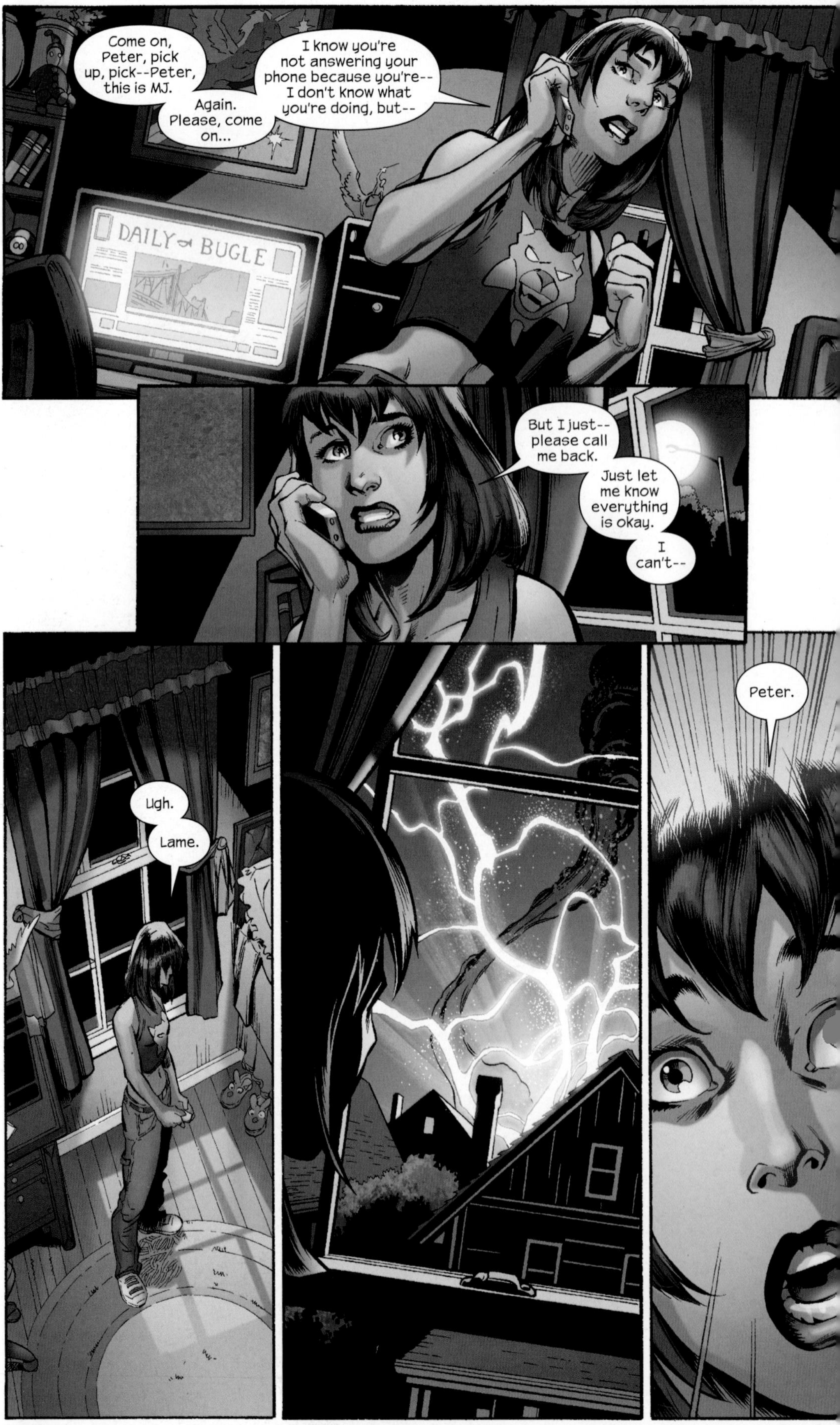

Come on, Peter, pick up, pick--Peter, this is MJ.
Again. Please, come on...
I know you're not answering your phone because you're-- I don't know what you're doing, but--
DAILY BUGLE
But I just-- please call me back.
Just let me know everything is okay.
I can't--
Ugh.
Lame.
Peter.

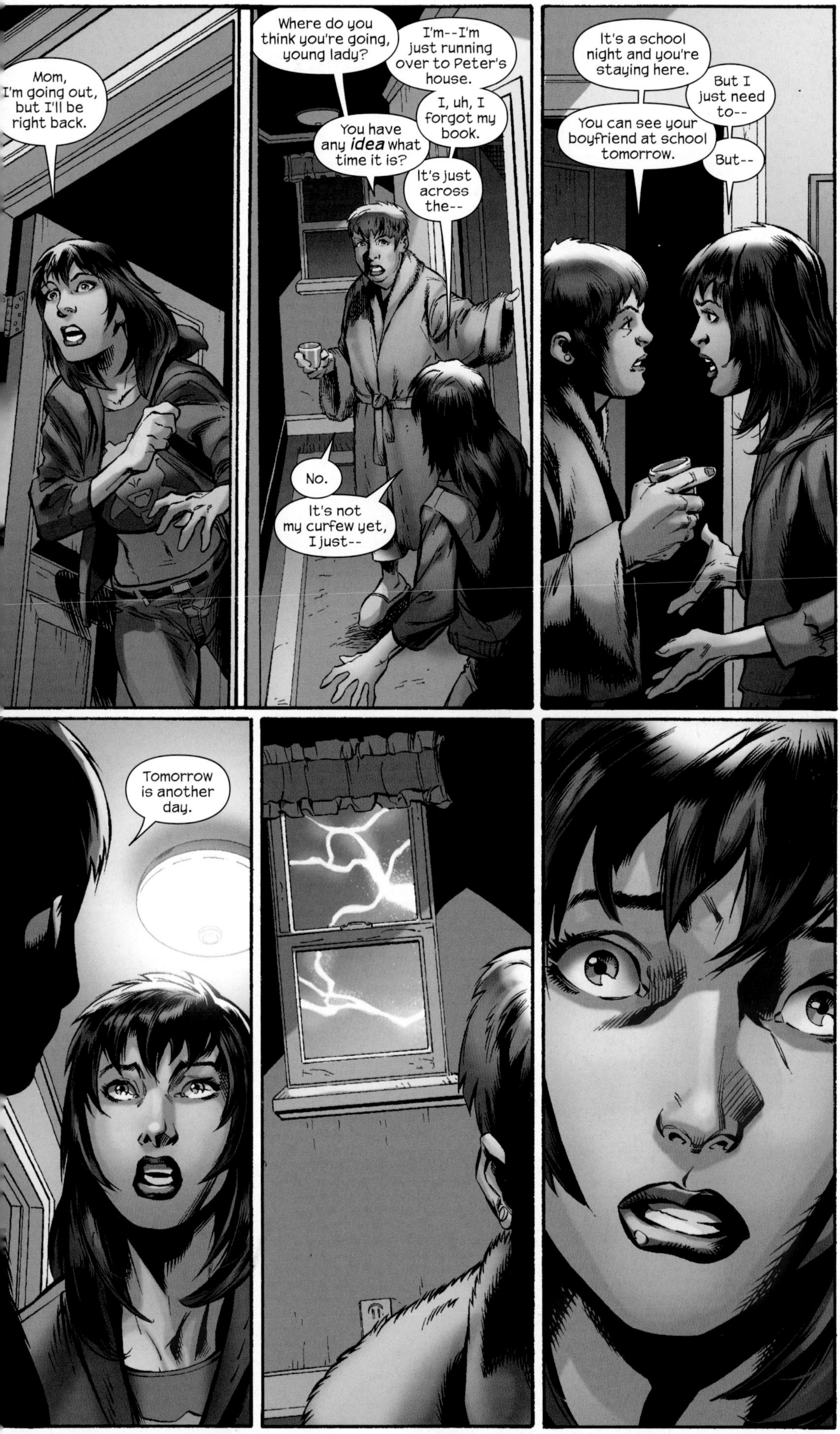
Mom, I'm going out, but I'll be right back.
Where do you think you're going, young lady?
I'm--I'm just running over to Peter's house.
You have any *idea* what time it is?
I, uh, I forgot my book.
It's just across the--
No.
It's not my curfew yet, I just--
It's a school night and you're staying here.
But I just need to--
You can see your boyfriend at school tomorrow.
But--
Tomorrow is another day.

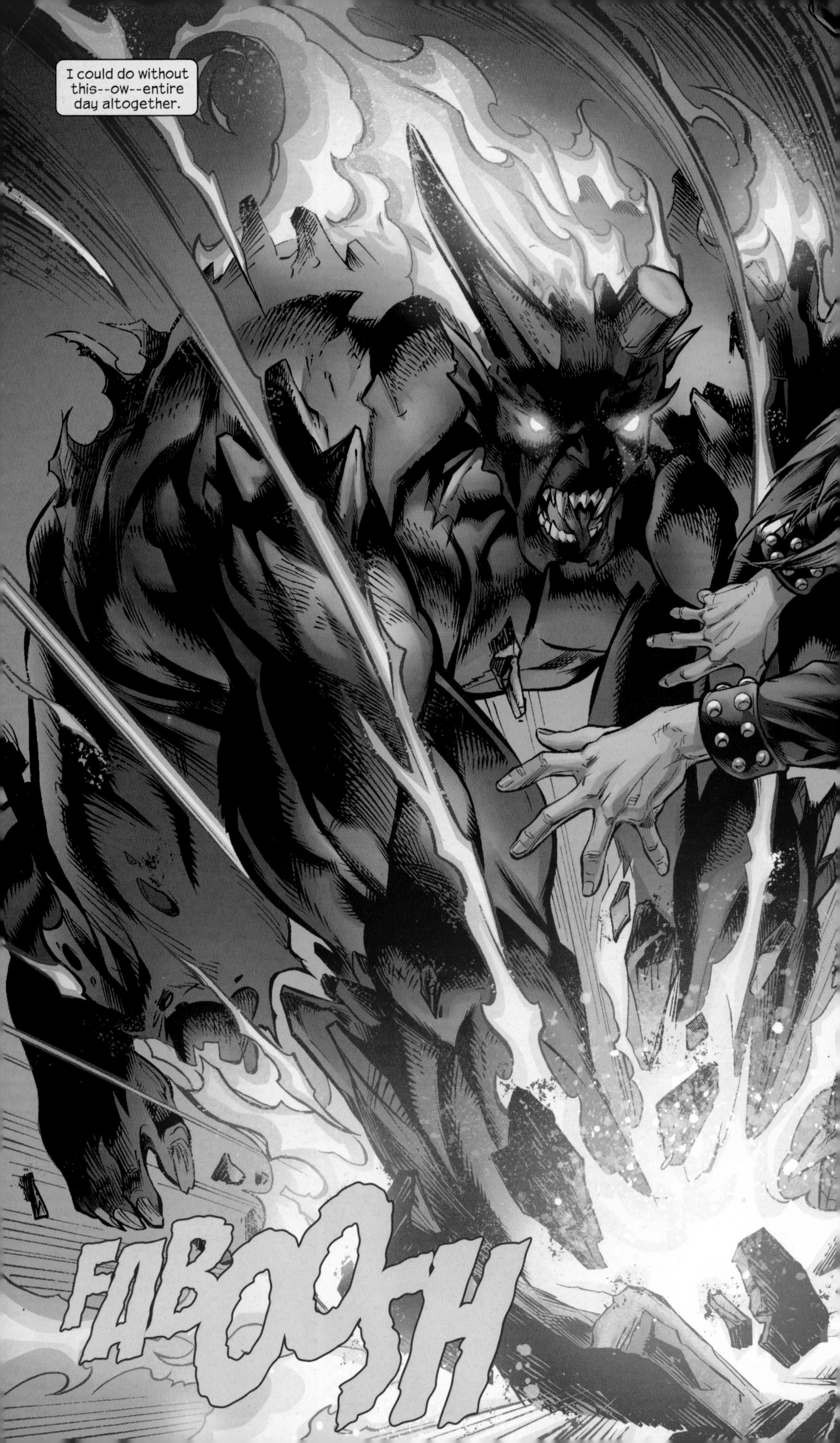
I could do without this--ow--entire day altogether.
FABOOOH

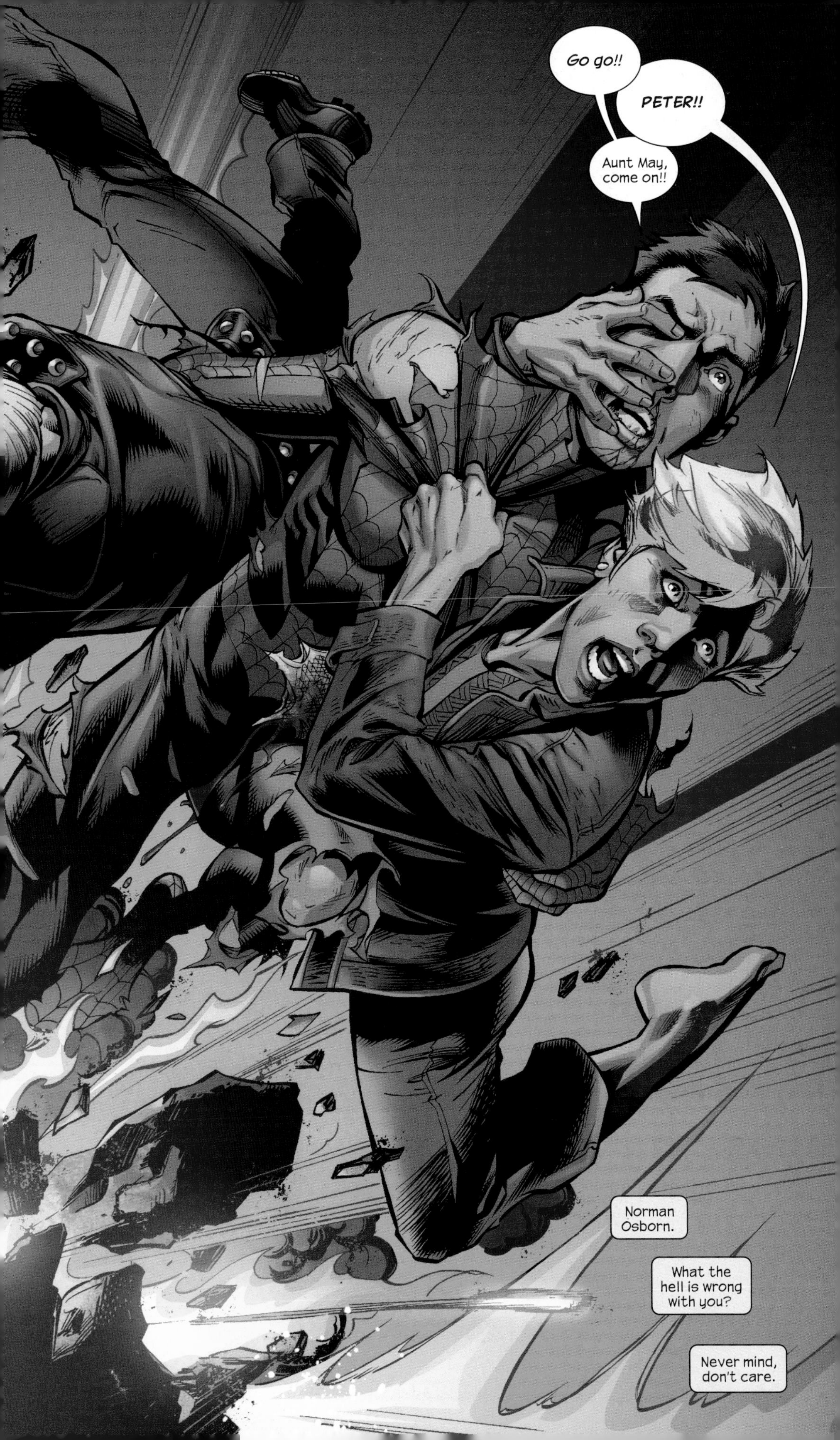
Go go!!
PETER!!
Aunt May, come on!!
Norman Osborn.
What the hell is wrong with you?
Never mind, don't care.

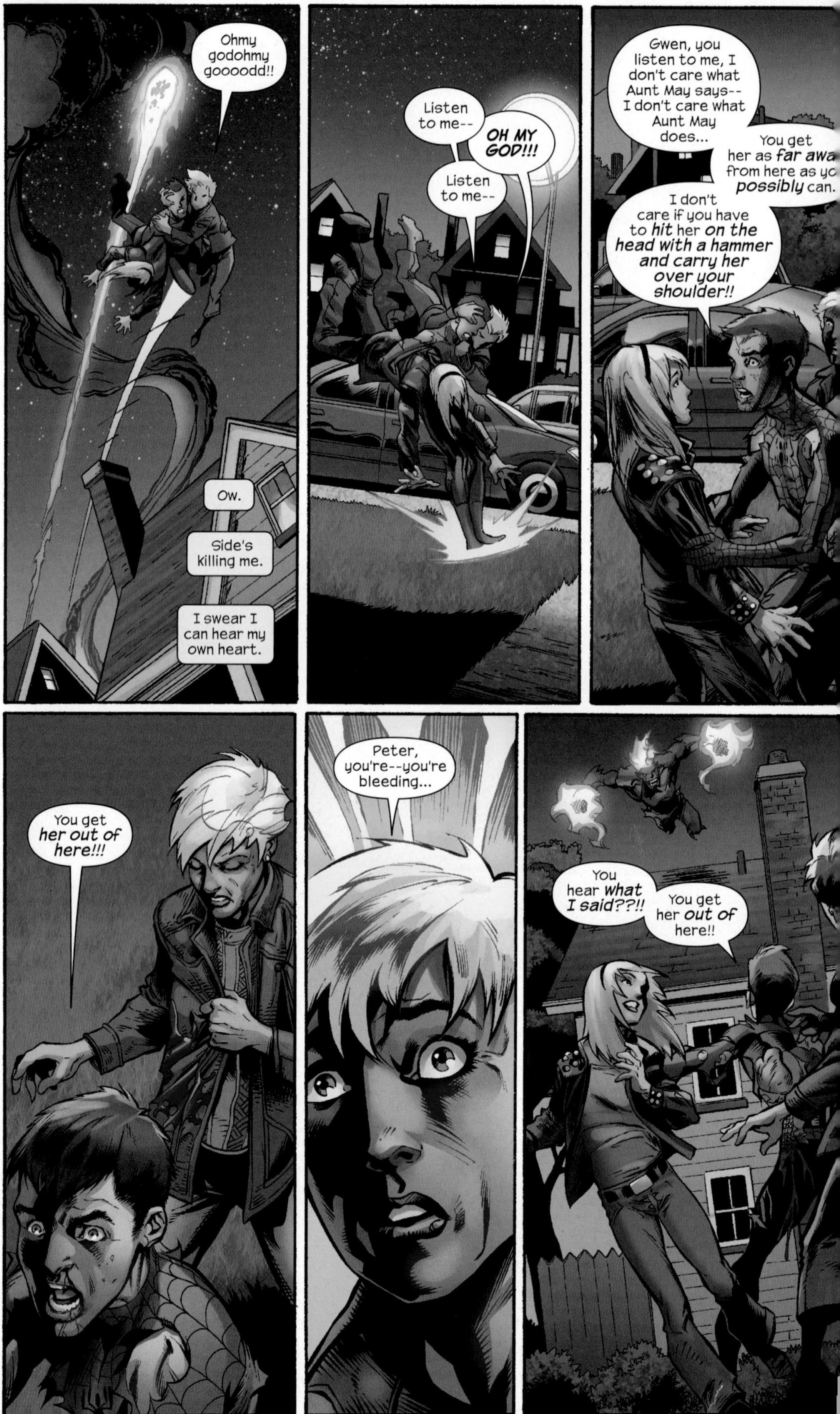
Ohmy godohmy goooodd!!
Ow.
Side's killing me.
I swear I can hear my own heart.
Listen to me--
OH MY GOD!!!
Listen to me--
Gwen, you listen to me, I don't care what Aunt May says-- I don't care what Aunt May does...
You get her as far awa from here as yo possibly can.
I don't care if you have to hit her on the head with a hammer and carry her over your shoulder!!
You get her out of here!!!
Peter, you're--you're bleeding...
You hear what I said??!!
You get her out of here!!

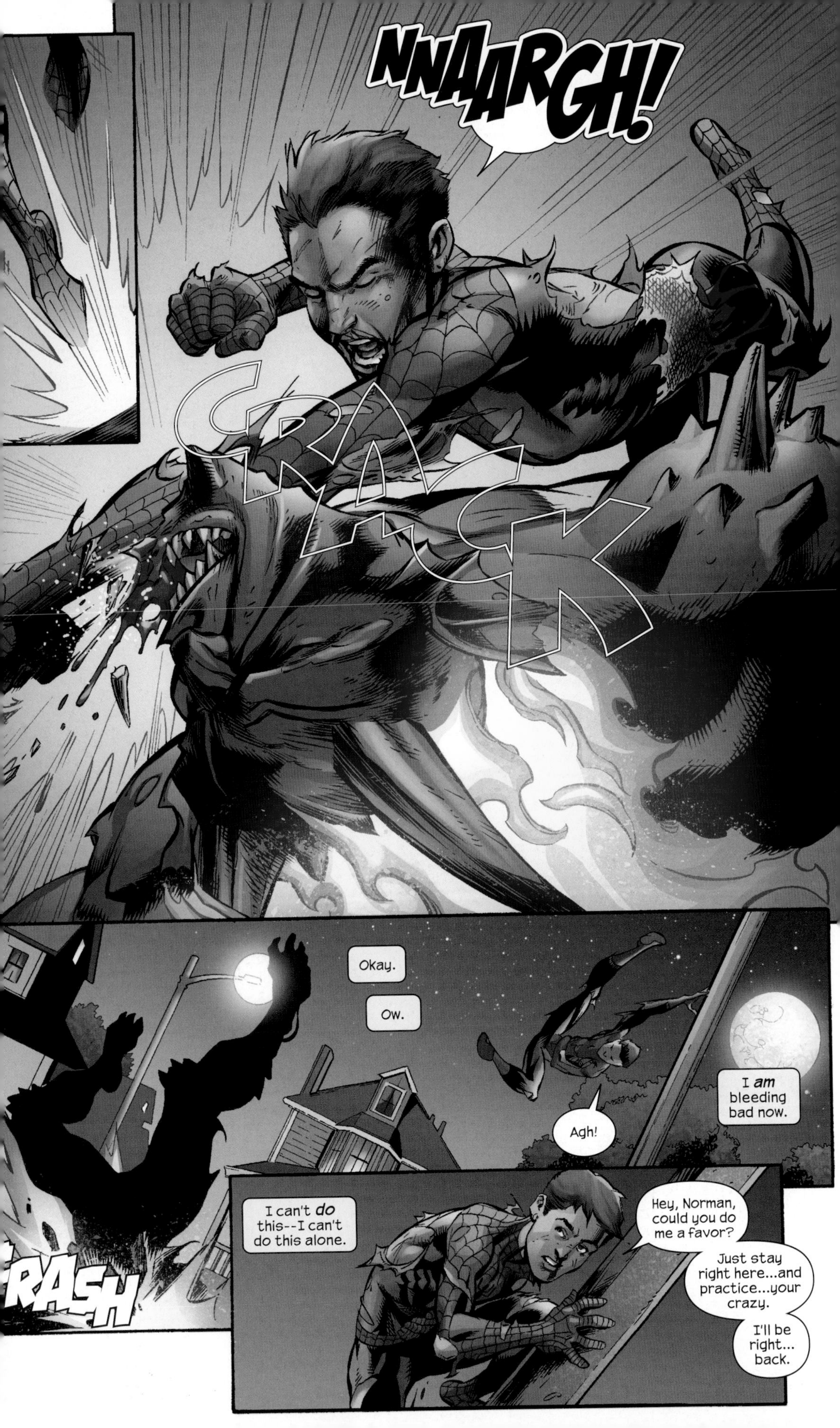
NNAARGH!
CRACK
Okay.
Ow.
Agh!
I am bleeding bad now.
RASH
I can't do this--I can't do this alone.
Hey, Norman, could you do me a favor?
Just stay right here...and practice...your crazy.
I'll be right... back.

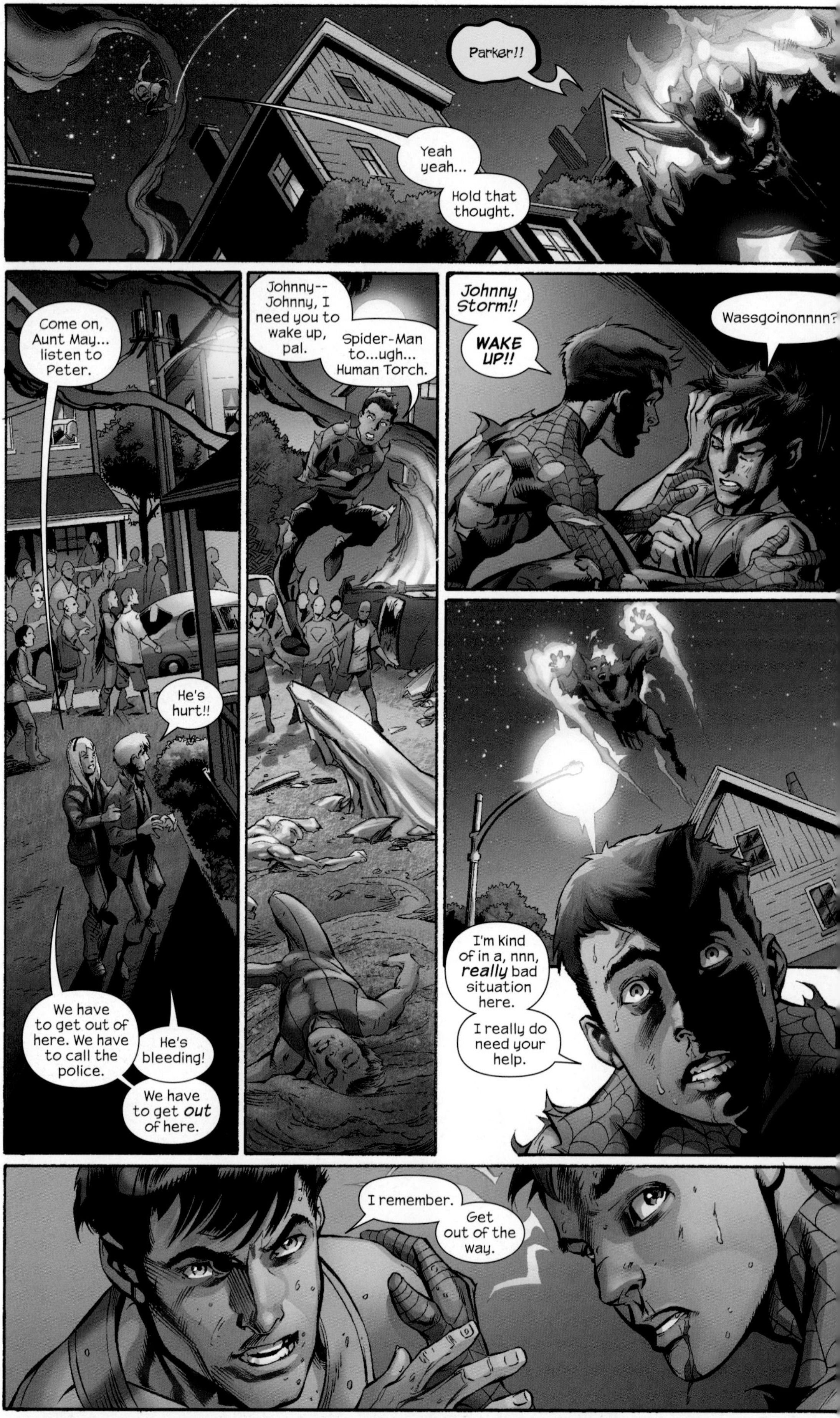
Parker!!
Yeah yeah...
Hold that thought.
Come on, Aunt May... listen to Peter.
He's hurt!!
We have to get out of here. We have to call the police.
He's bleeding!
We have to get out of here.
Johnny-- Johnny, I need you to wake up, pal.
Spider-Man to...ugh... Human Torch.
Johnny Storm!!
WAKE UP!!
Wassgoinonnnn?
I'm kind of in a, nnn, really bad situation here.
I really do need your help.
I remember.
Get out of the way.

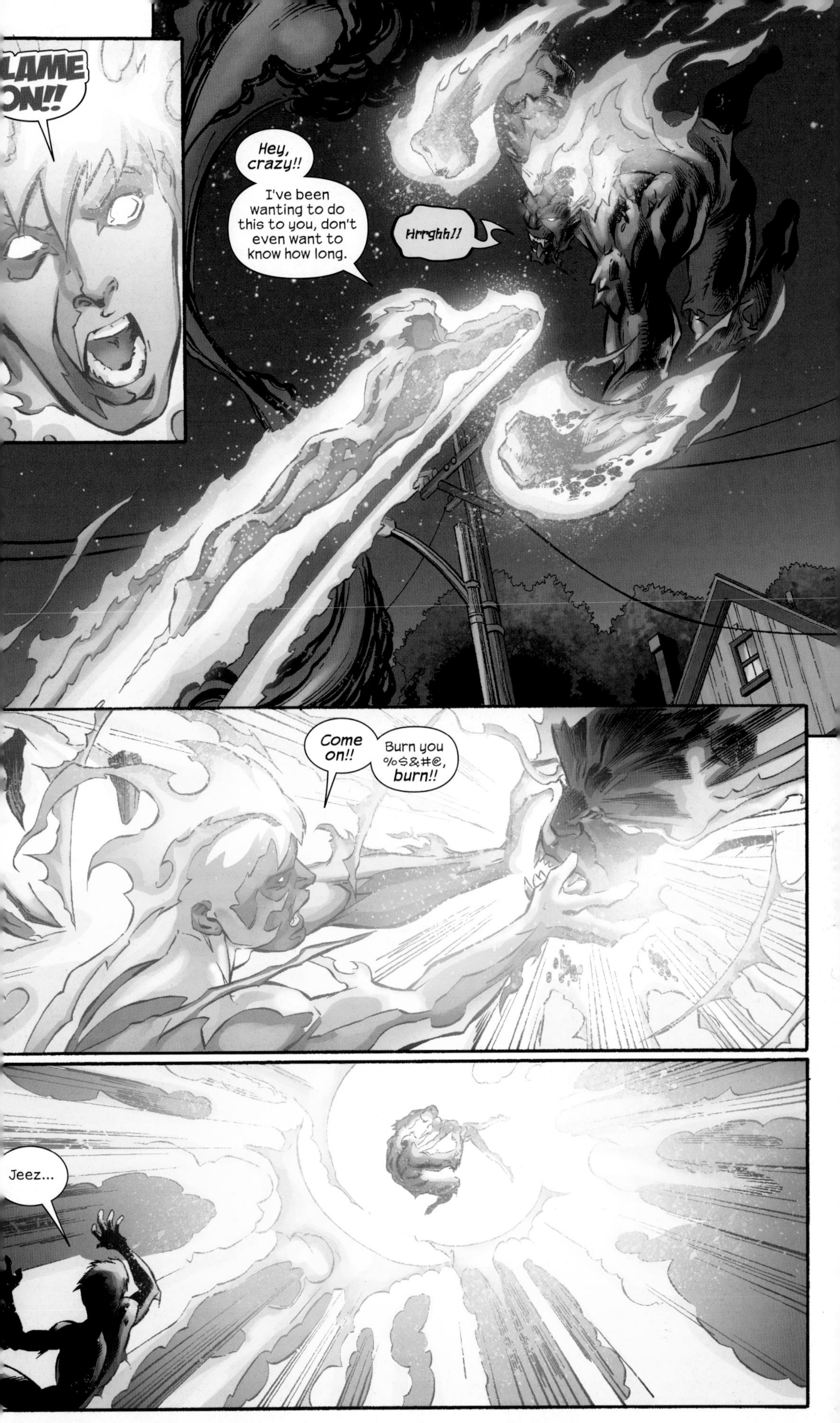
FLAME ON!!
Hey, crazy!!
I've been wanting to do this to you, don't even want to know how long.
Hrrghh!!
Come on!!
Burn you %$&#@, burn!!
Jeez...

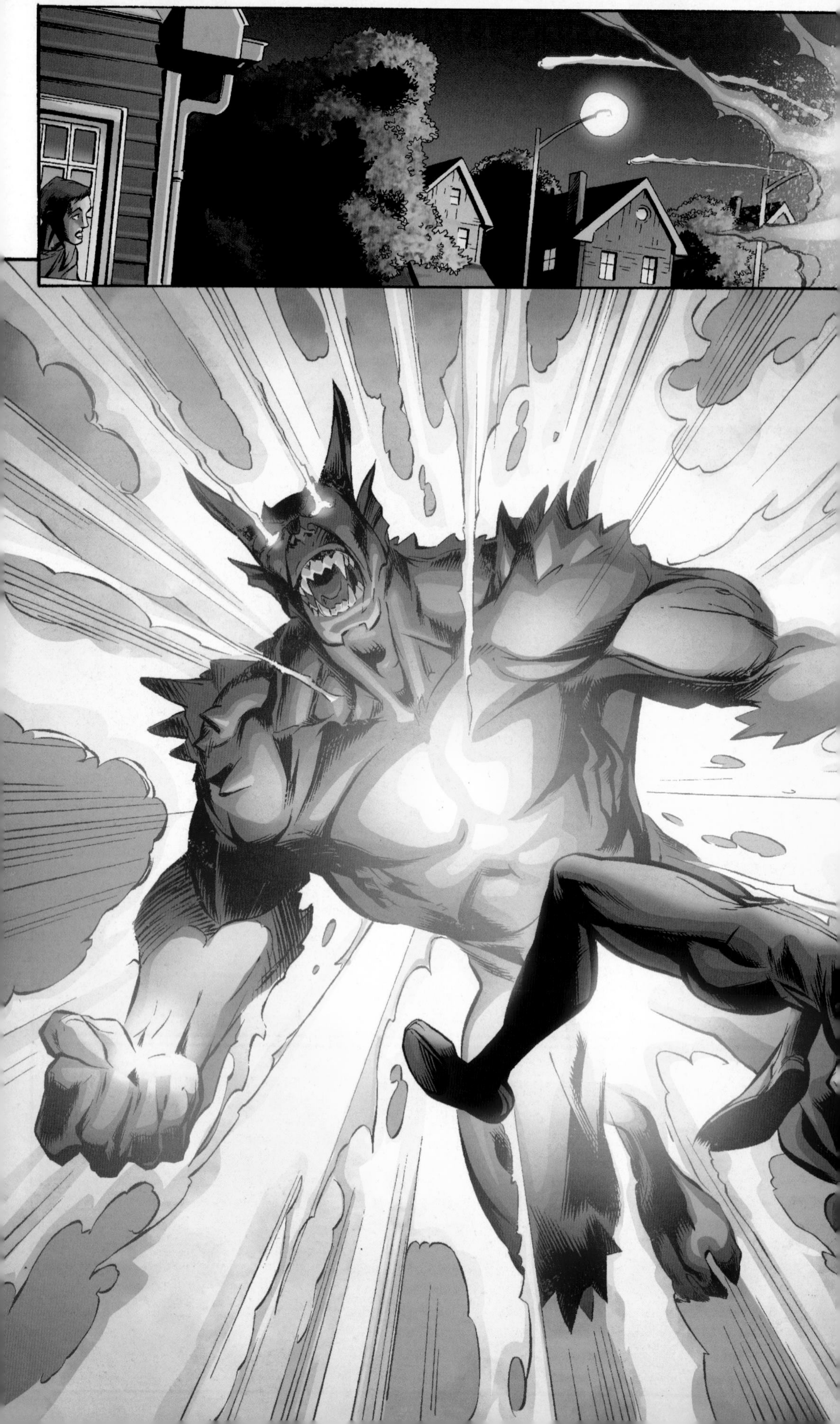

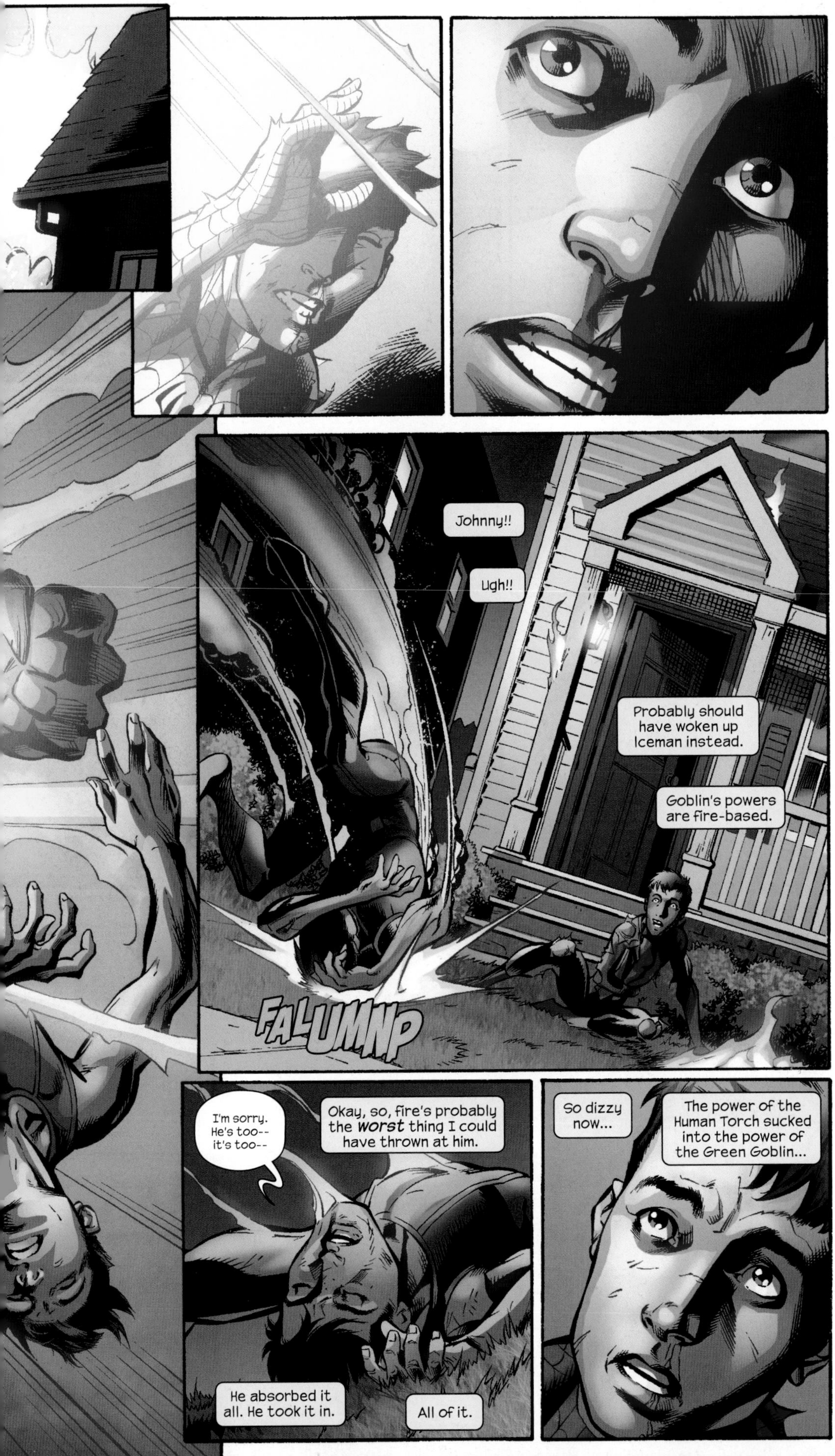
Johnny!!
Ugh!!
Probably should have woken up Iceman instead.
Goblin's powers are fire-based.
FALUMNP
I'm sorry. He's too-- it's too--
Okay, so, fire's probably the *worst* thing I could have thrown at him.
He absorbed it all. He took it in.
All of it.
So dizzy now...
The power of the Human Torch sucked into the power of the Green Goblin...

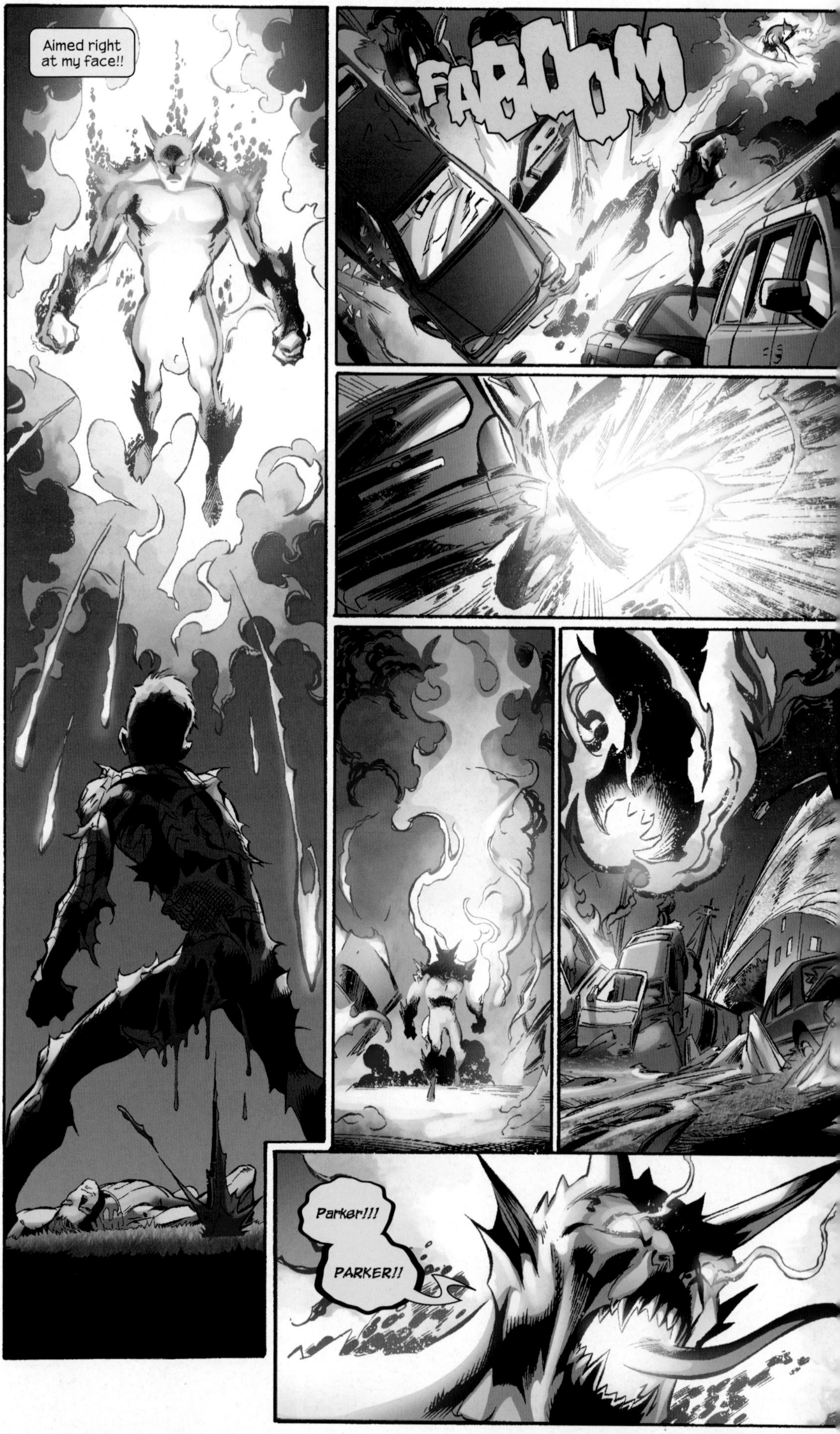
Aimed right at my face!!
FABOOM
Parker!!!
PARKER!!

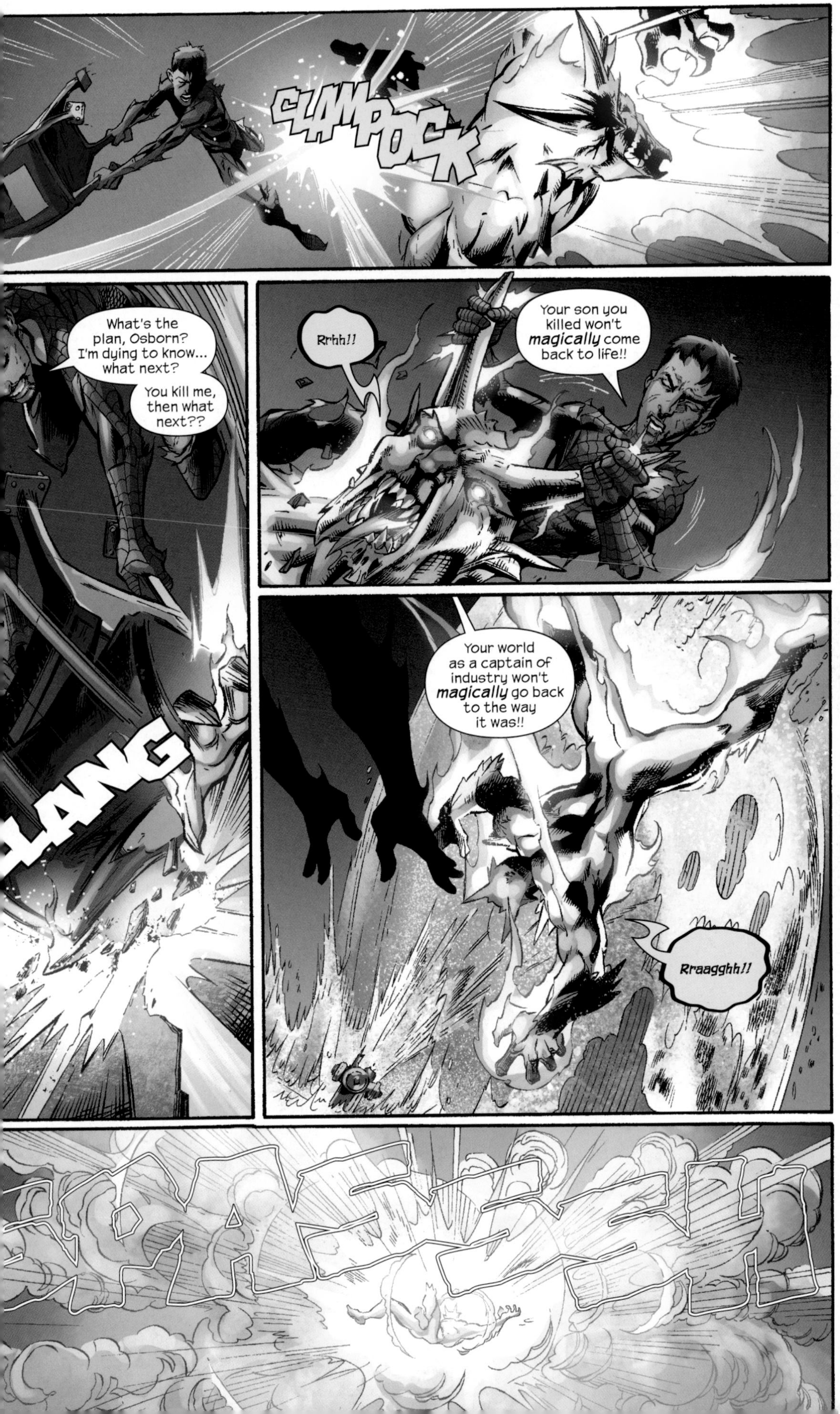
CLAMPOCK
What's the plan, Osborn? I'm dying to know... what next?
You kill me, then what next??
LANG
Rrhh!!
Your son you killed won't *magically* come back to life!!
Your world as a captain of industry won't *magically* go back to the way it was!!
Rraagghh!!

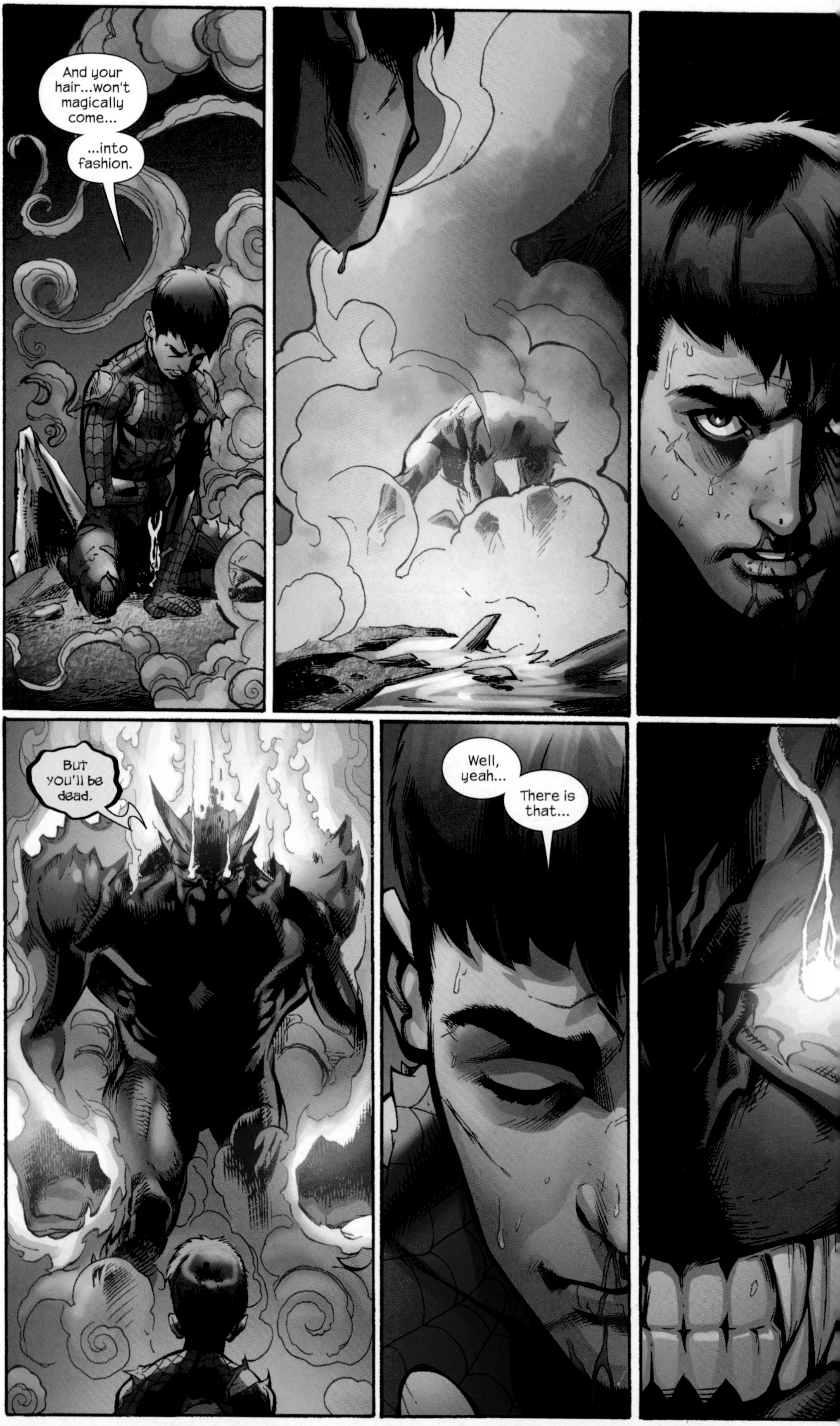
And your hair...won't magically come...
...into fashion.
But you'll be dead.
Well, yeah...
There is that...

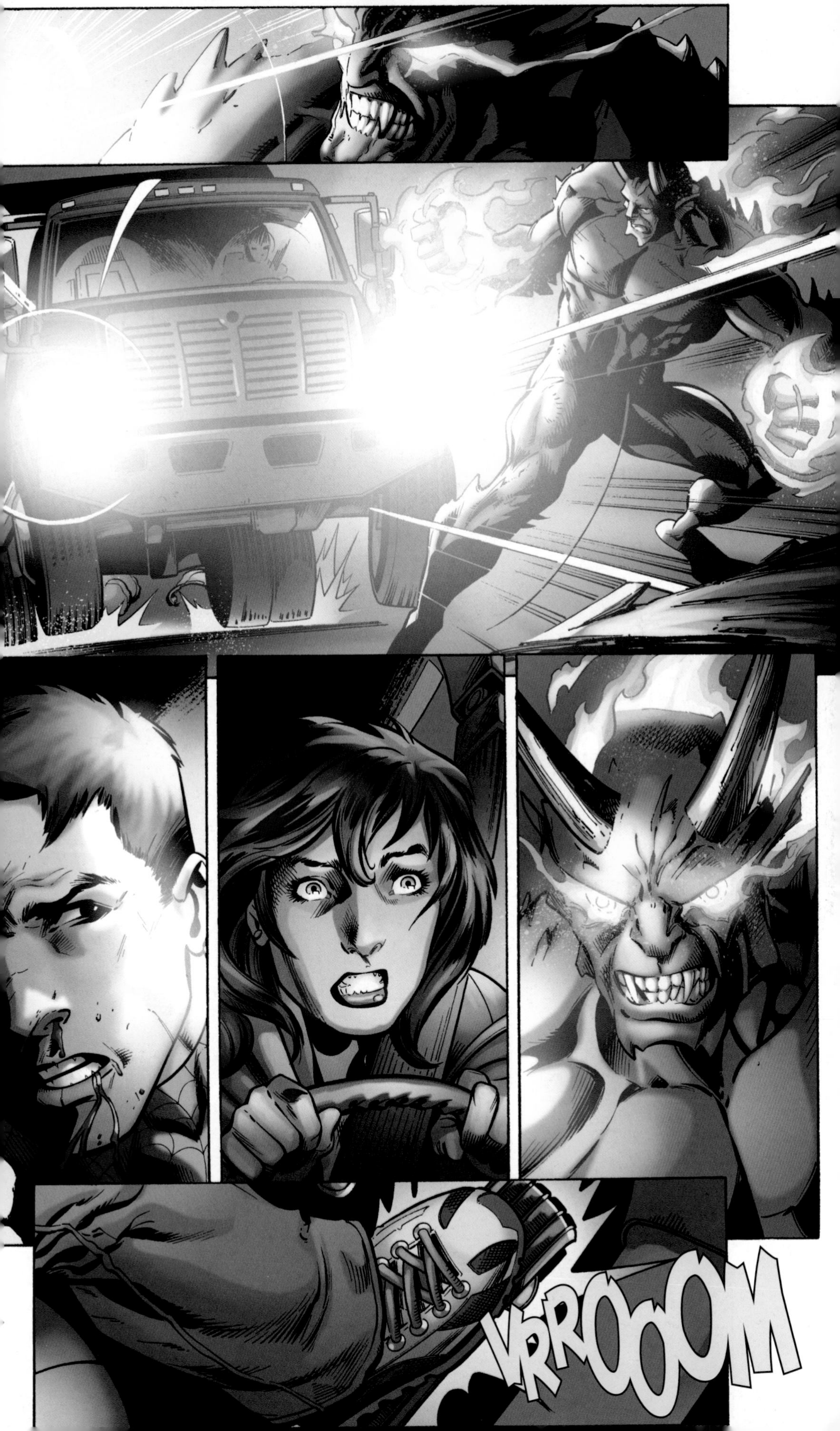
VRROOOM

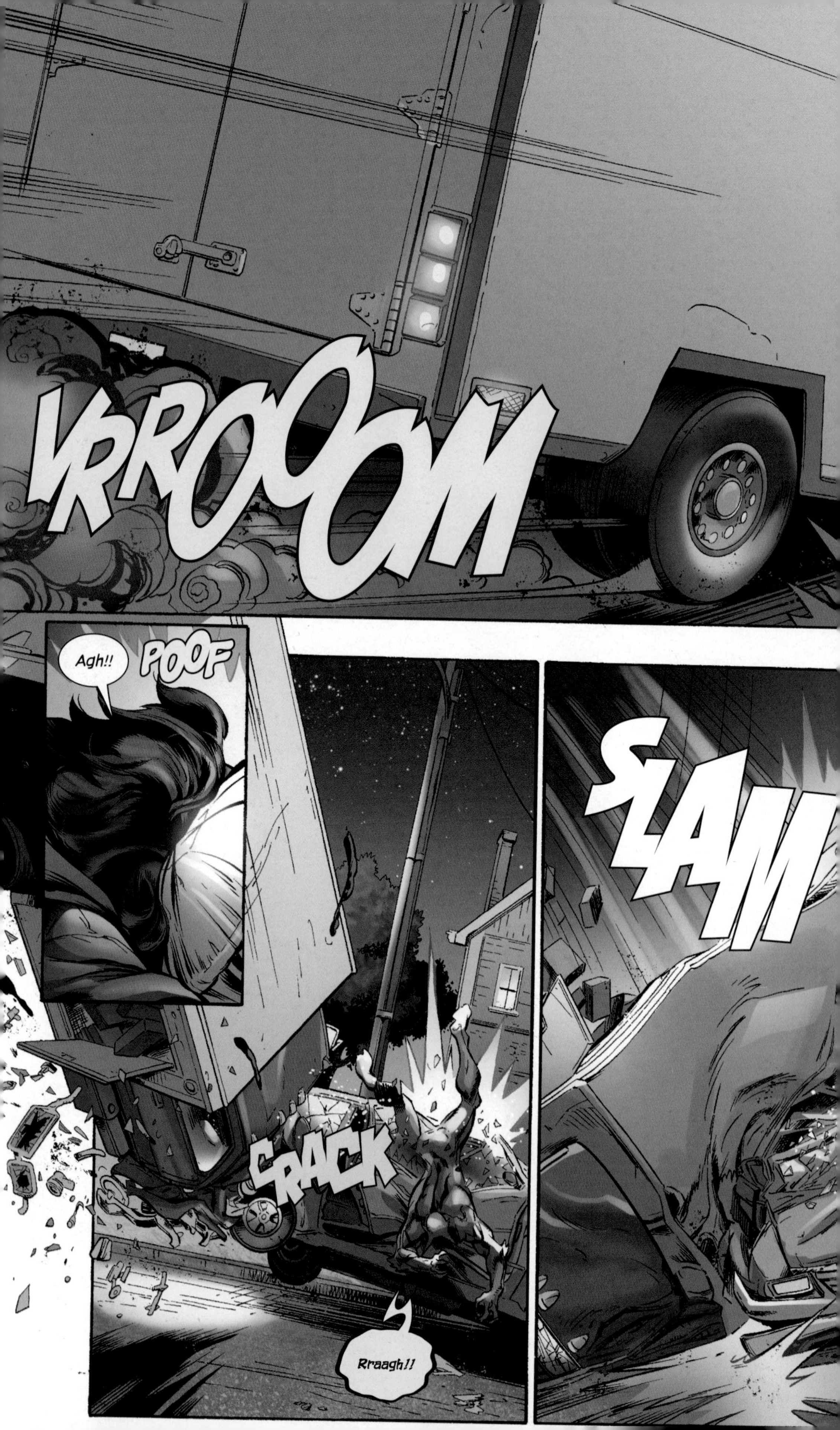
VRROOOM
Agh!!
POOF
CRACK
Rraagh!!
SLAM

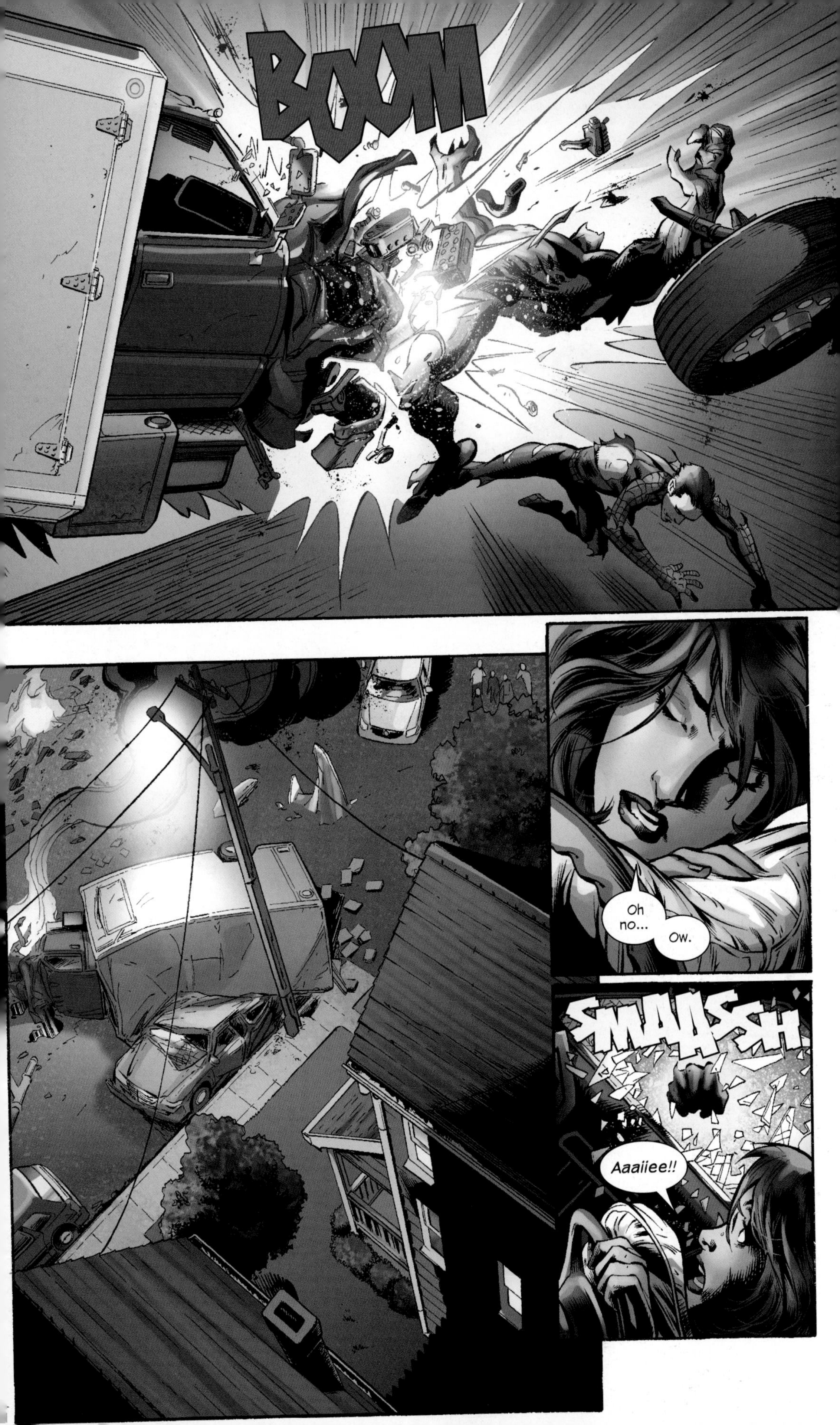
BOOM
Oh no...
Ow.
SMAASSH
Aaaiiee!!

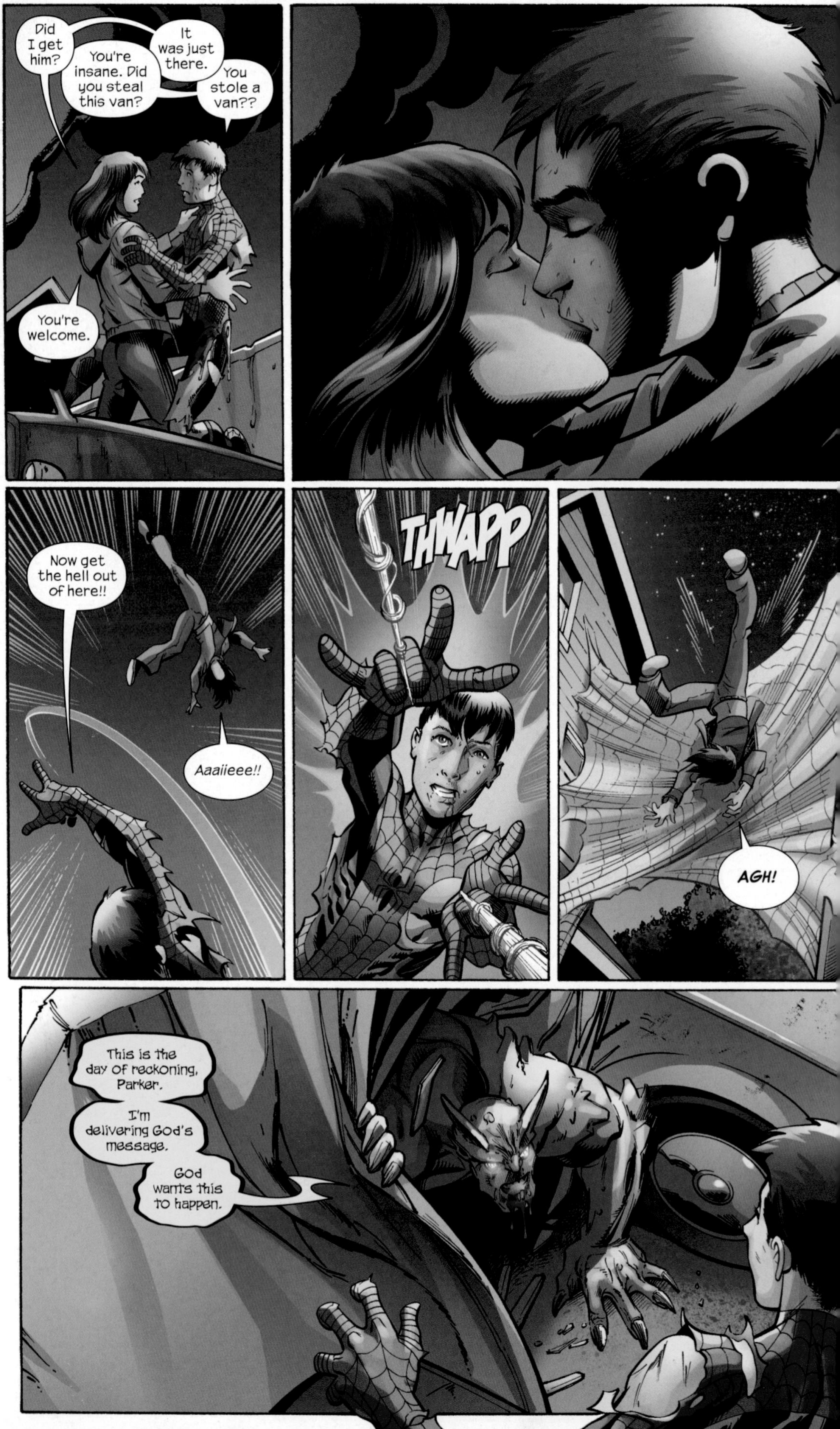
Did I get him?
You're insane. Did you steal this van?
It was just there.
You stole a van??
You're welcome.
Now get the hell out of here!!
Aaaiieee!!
THWAPP
AGH!
This is the day of reckoning, Parker.
I'm delivering God's message.
God wants this to happen.

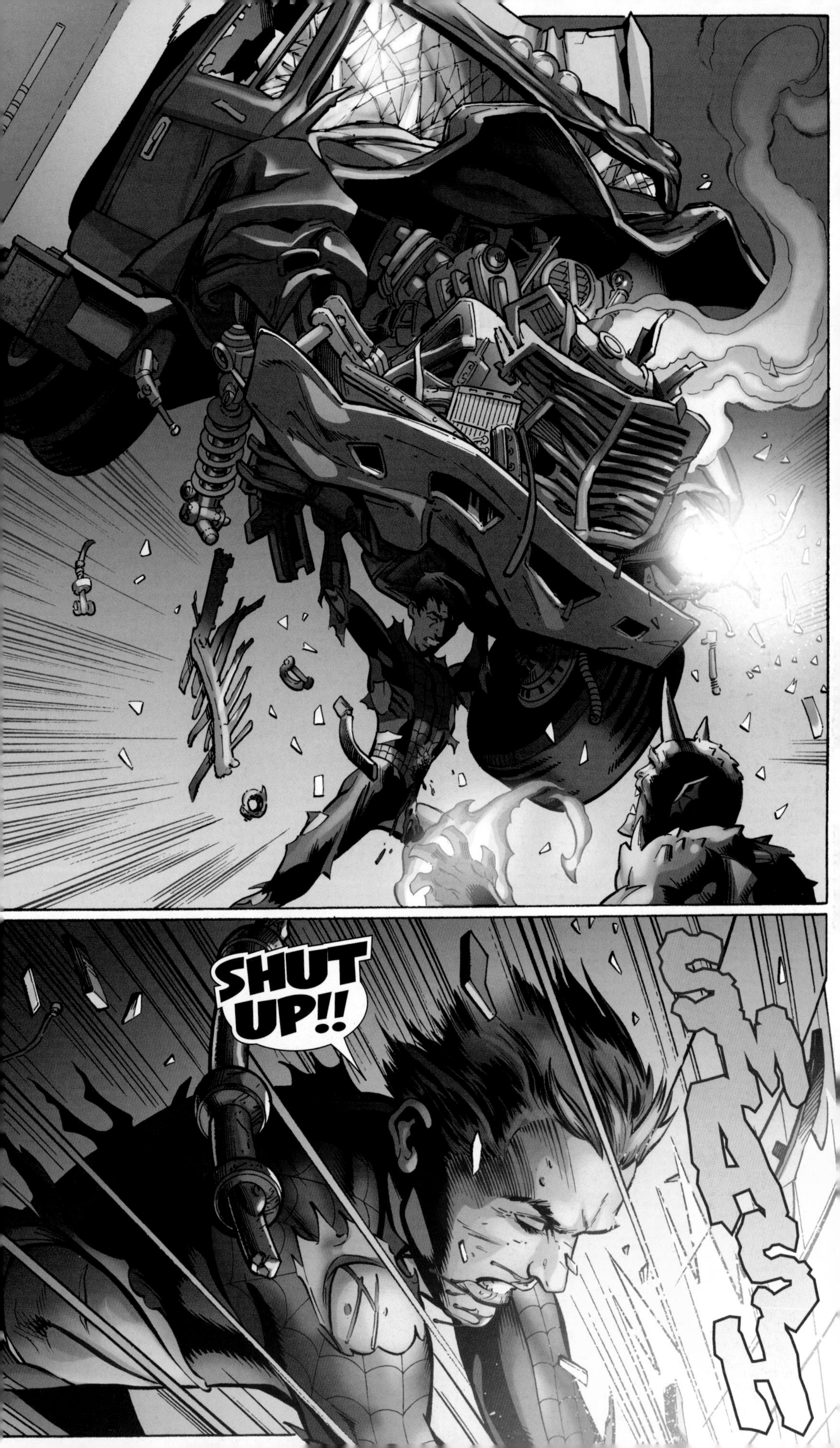
SHUT UP!!
SMASH

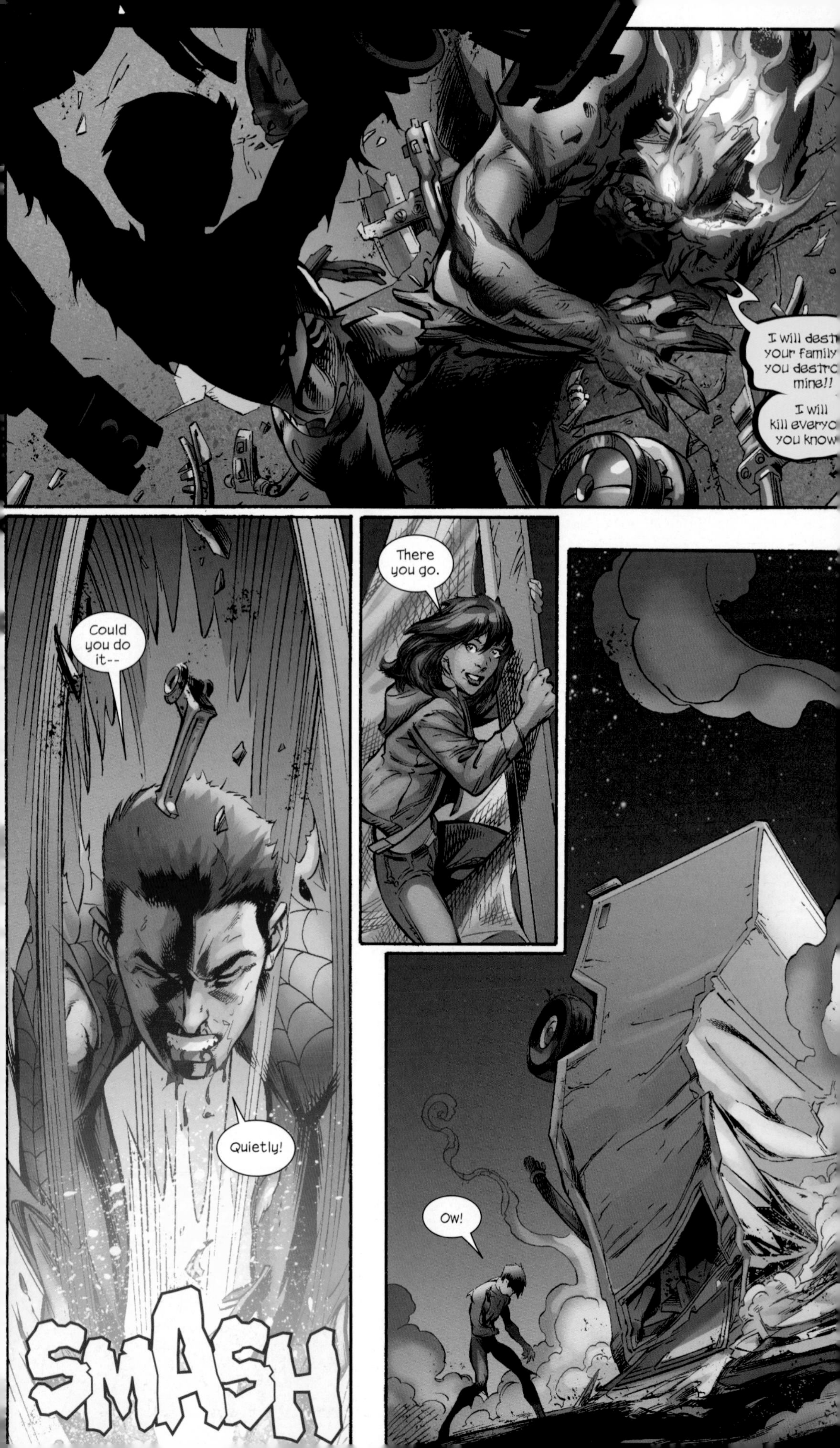
I will dest
your family
you destro
mine!!
I will
kill everyo
you know
Could you do it--
Quietly!
SMASH
There you go.
Ow!

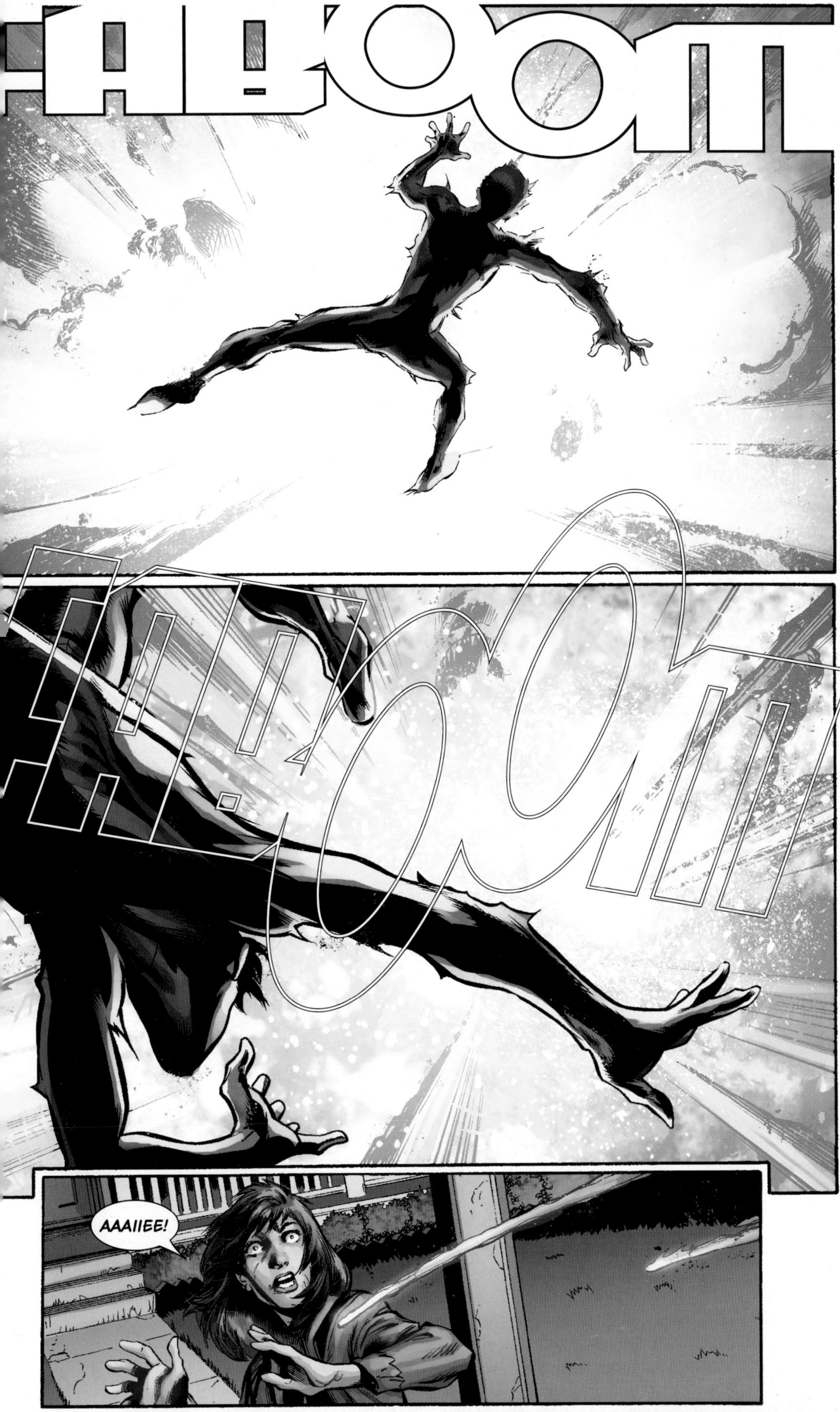
AAAIIEE!

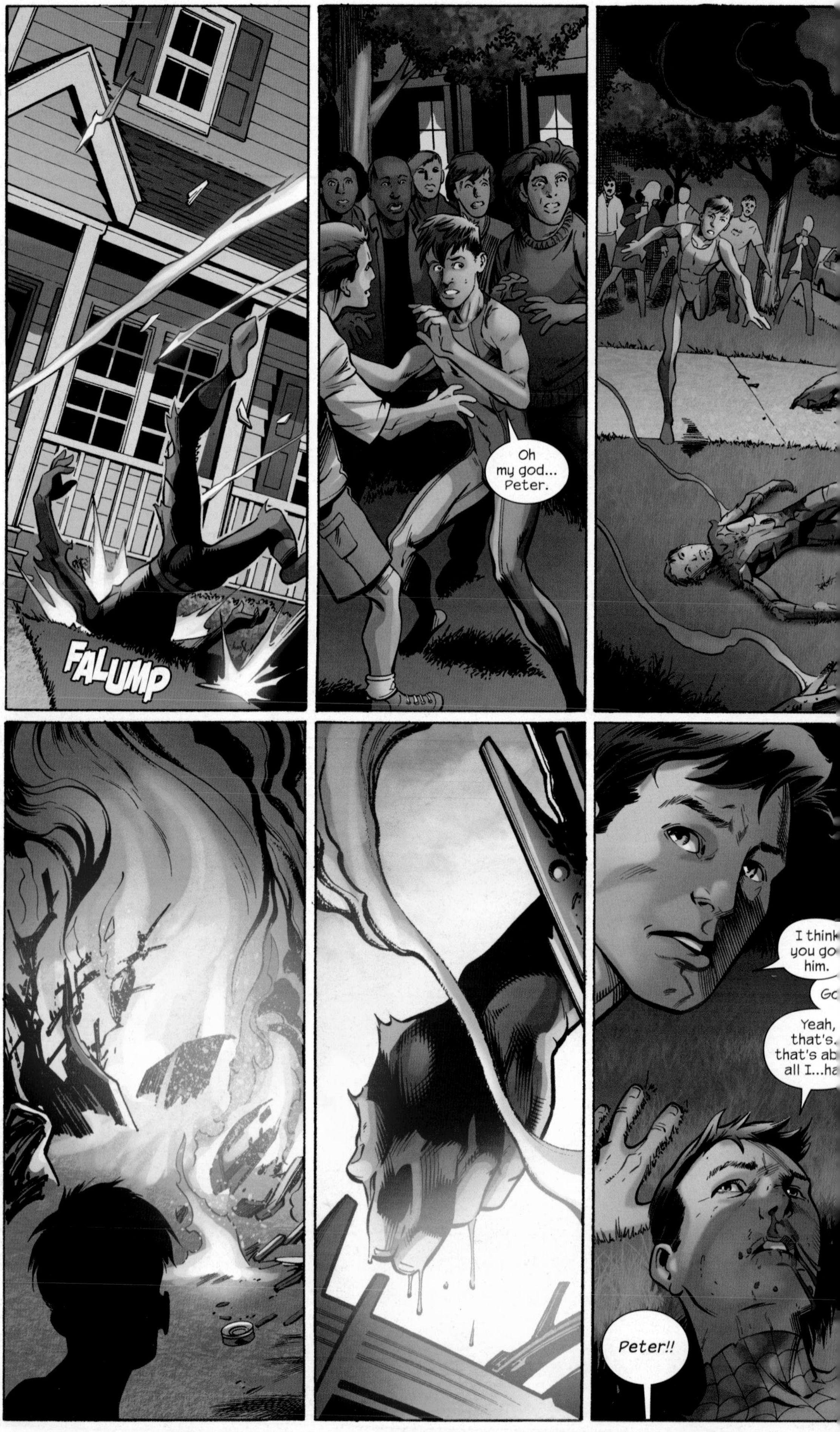
FALUMP
Oh my god... Peter.
I think you go
him.
Yeah, that's. that's ab all I...ha
Peter!!

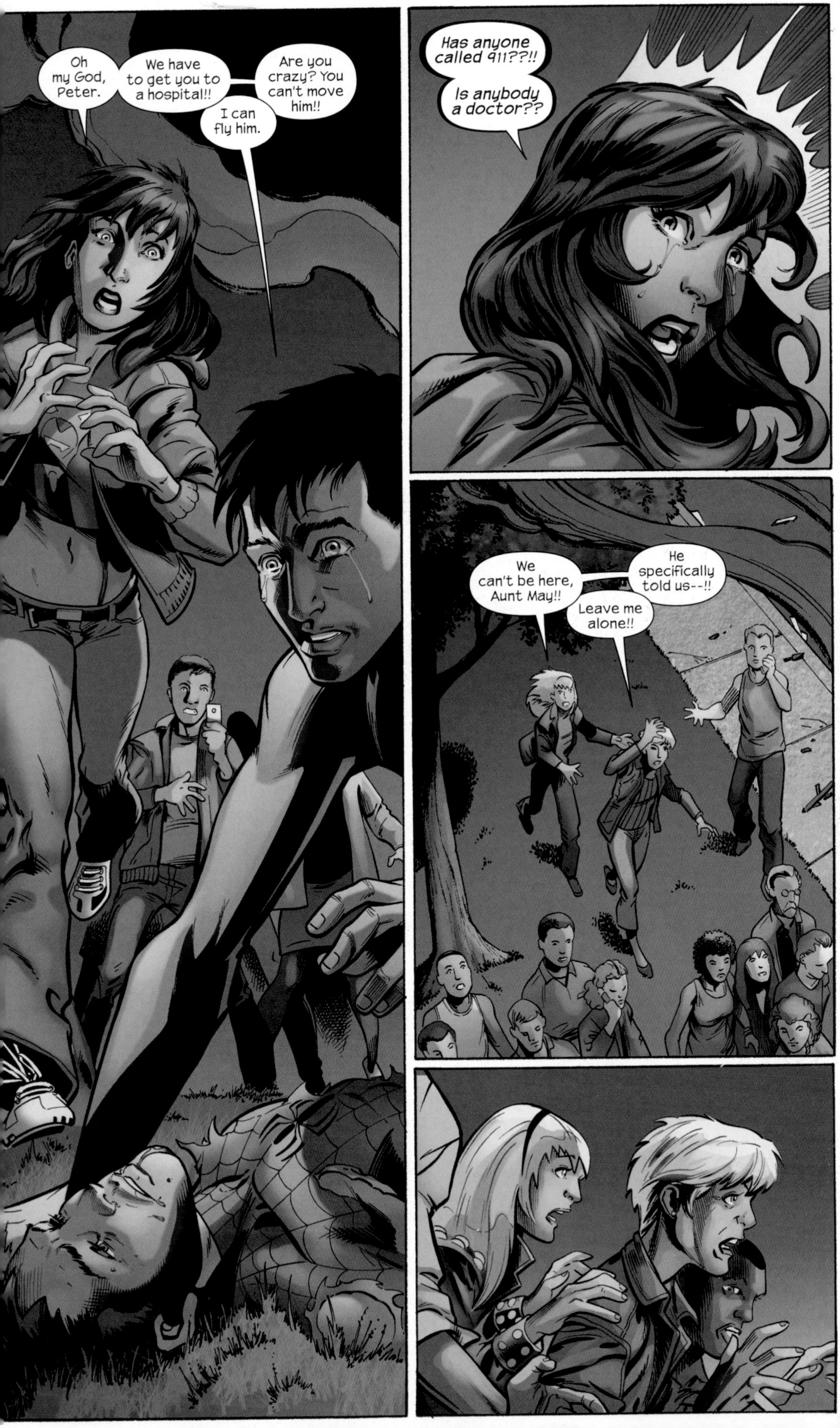
Oh my God, Peter.
We have to get you to a hospital!!
Are you crazy? You can't move him!!
I can fly him.
Has anyone called 911??!!
Is anybody a doctor??
We can't be here, Aunt May!!
He specifically told us--!!
Leave me alone!!

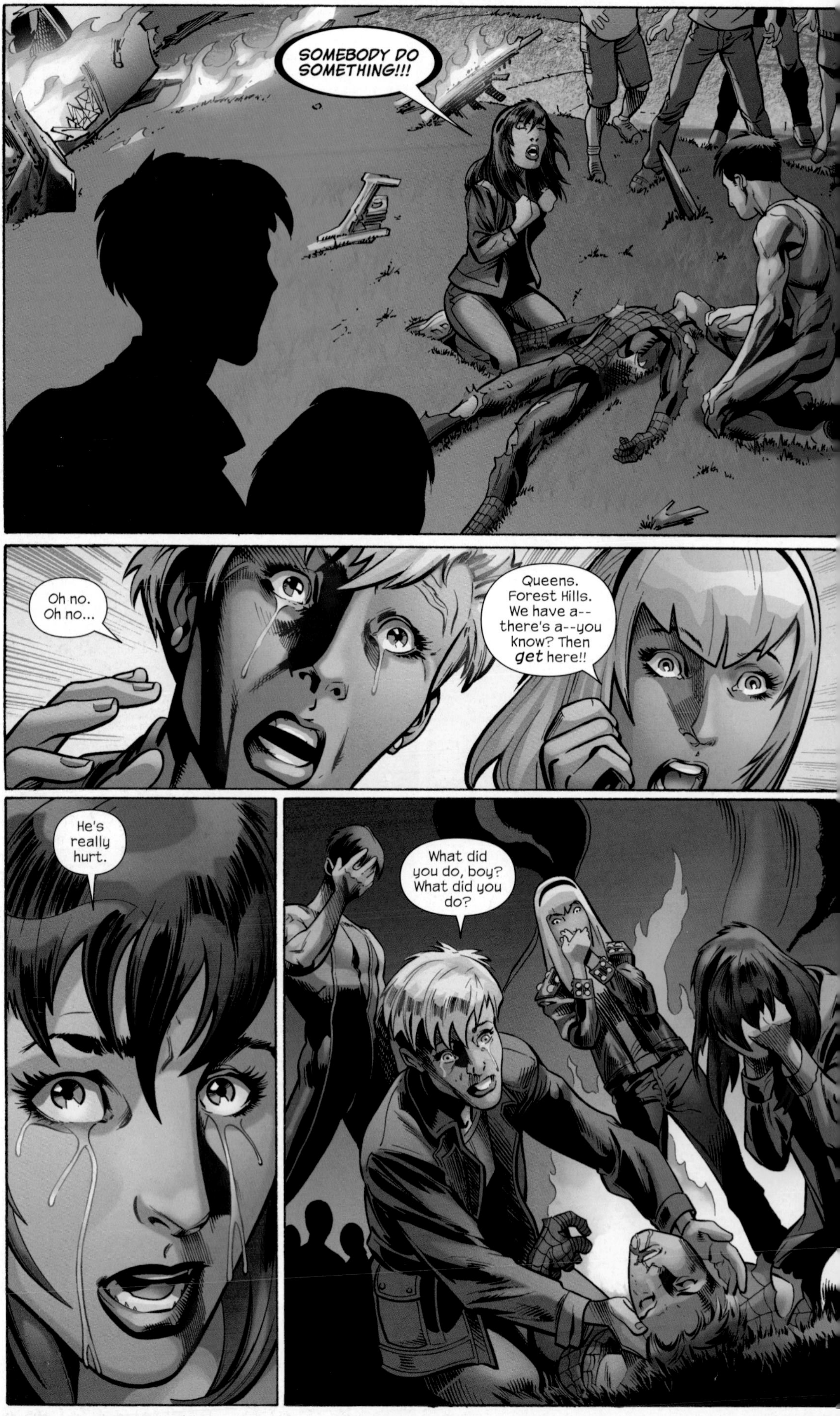
SOMEBODY DO SOMETHING!!!
Oh no. Oh no...
Queens. Forest Hills. We have a-- there's a--you know? Then get here!!
He's really hurt.
What did you do, boy? What did you do?

It's okay.

I--I did it.

Just--just hold on. The ambulance is--

Don't you see...it's okay.

I did it.

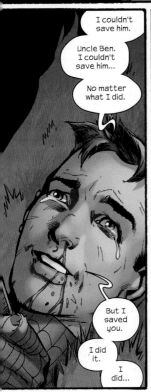

I couldn't save him.

Uncle Ben. I couldn't save him...

No matter what I did.

But I saved you.

I did it.

I did...

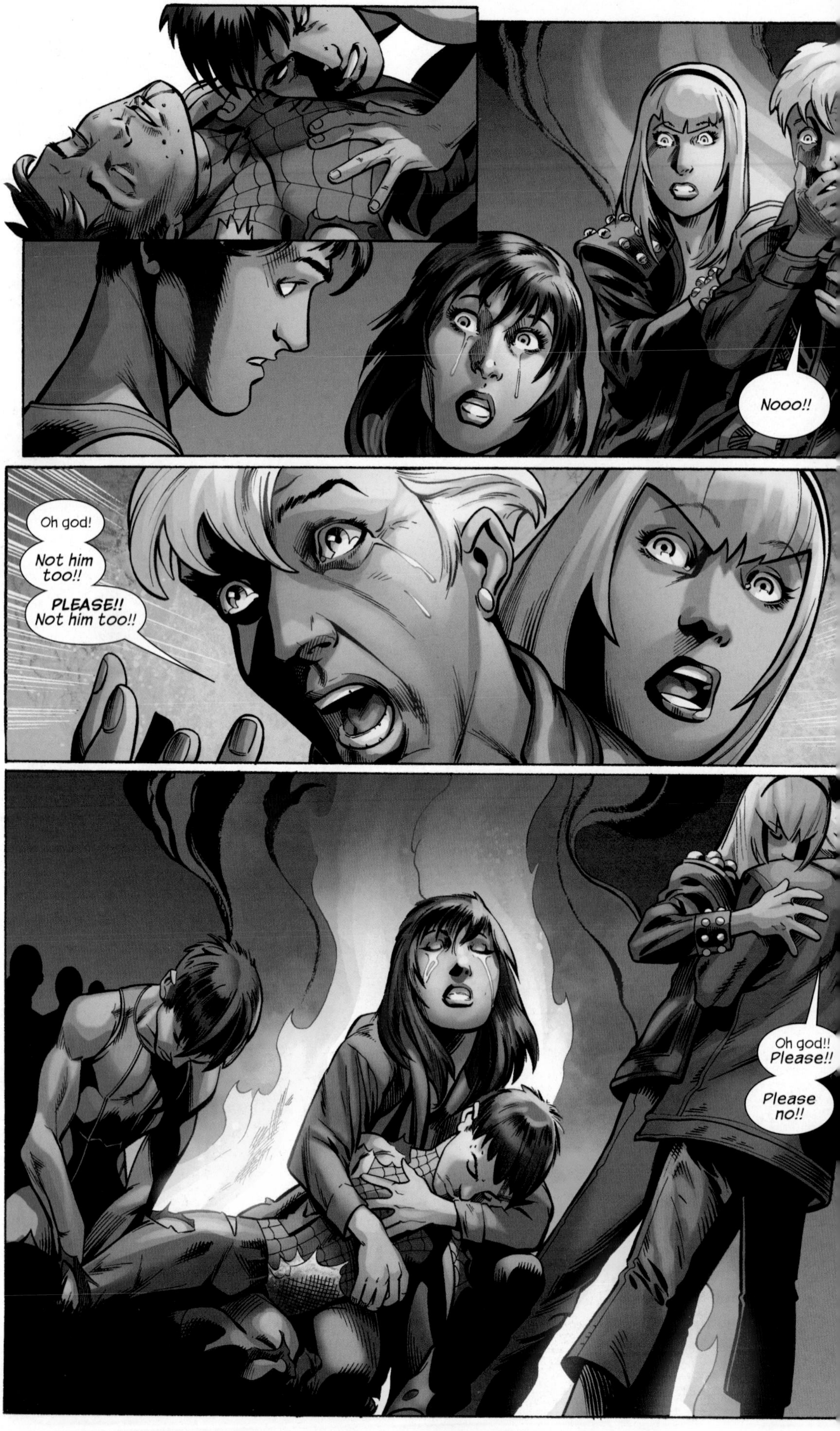
Nooo!!
Oh god!
Not him too!!
PLEASE!! Not him too!!
Oh god!! Please!!
Please no!!

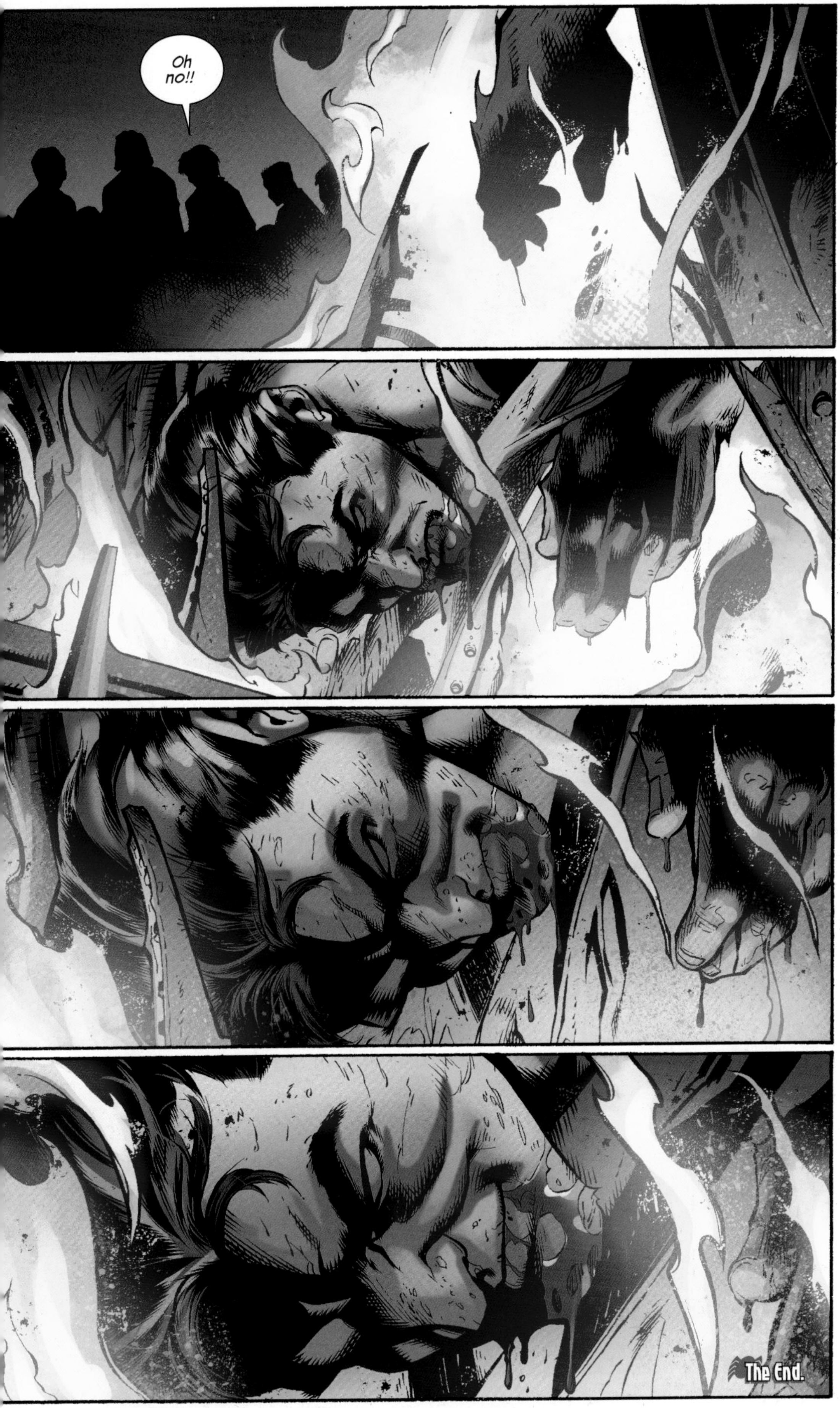
Oh no!!
The End.

#159 VARIANT
BY FRANK CHO & JASON KEITH

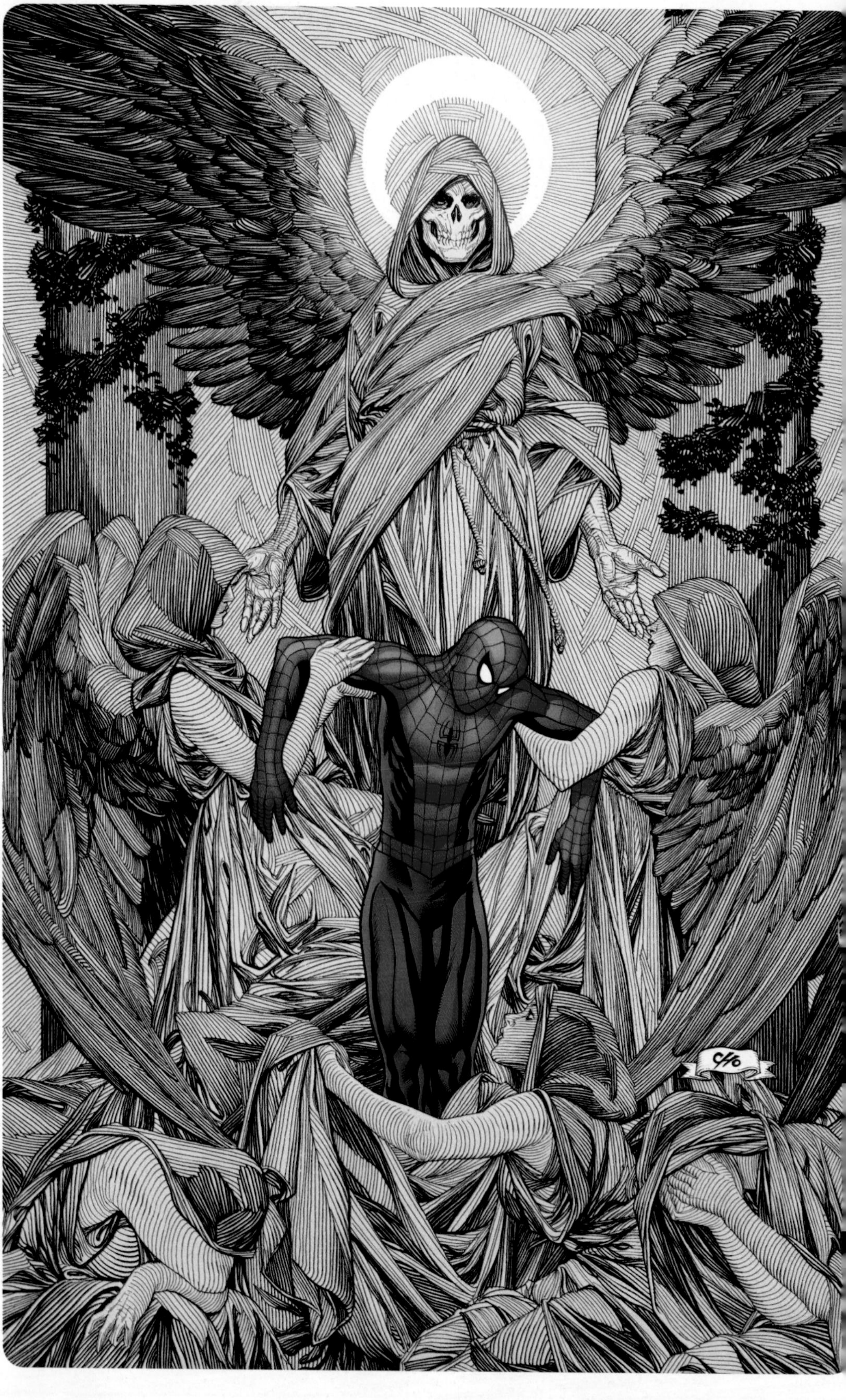
CHO

#160 SPOILER VARIANT

BY MARK BAGLEY, ANDY LANNING & JUSTIN PONSOR

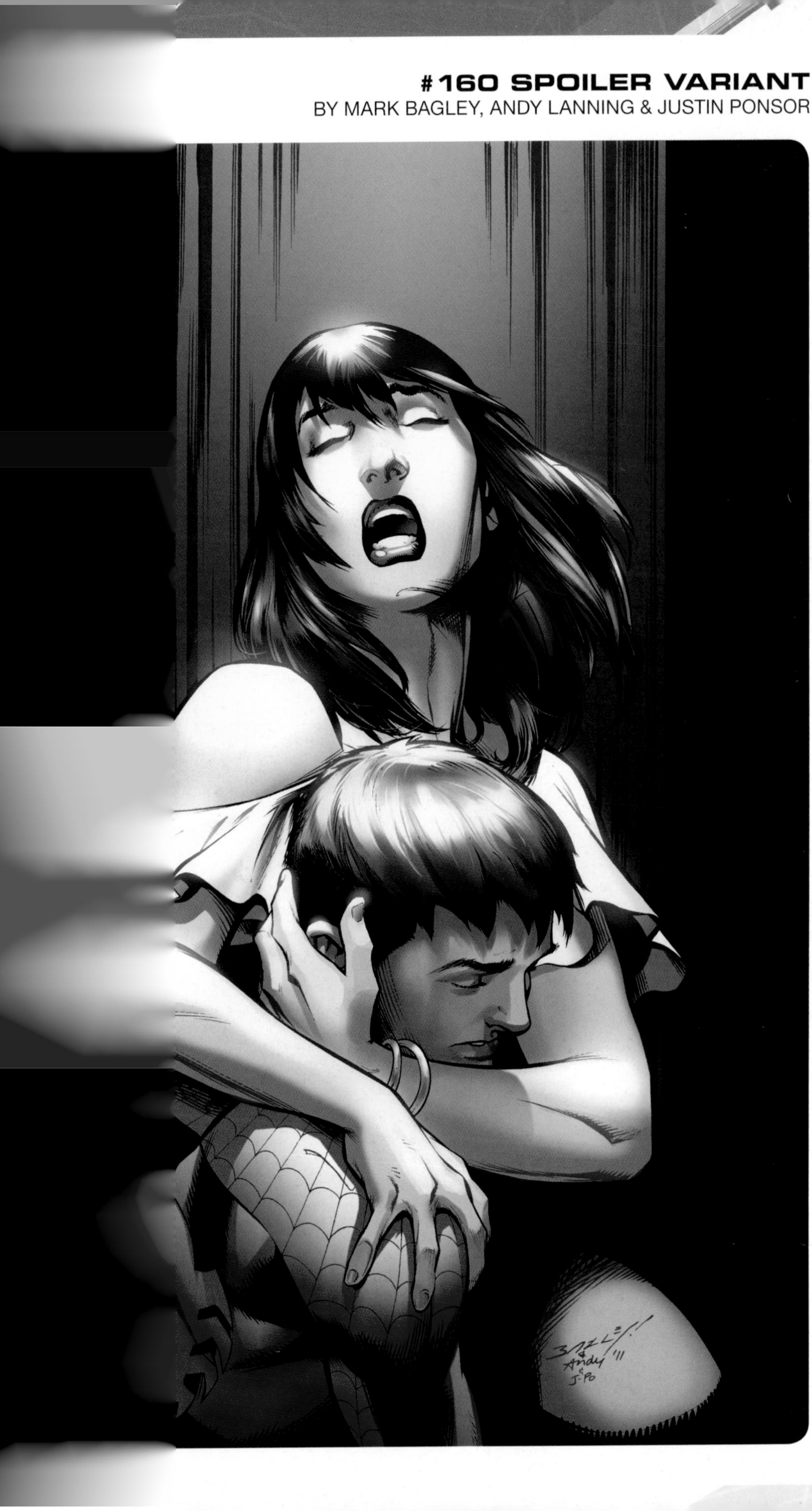

#160 VARIANT
BY JOE QUESADA, DANNY MIKI & RICHARD ISANOVE

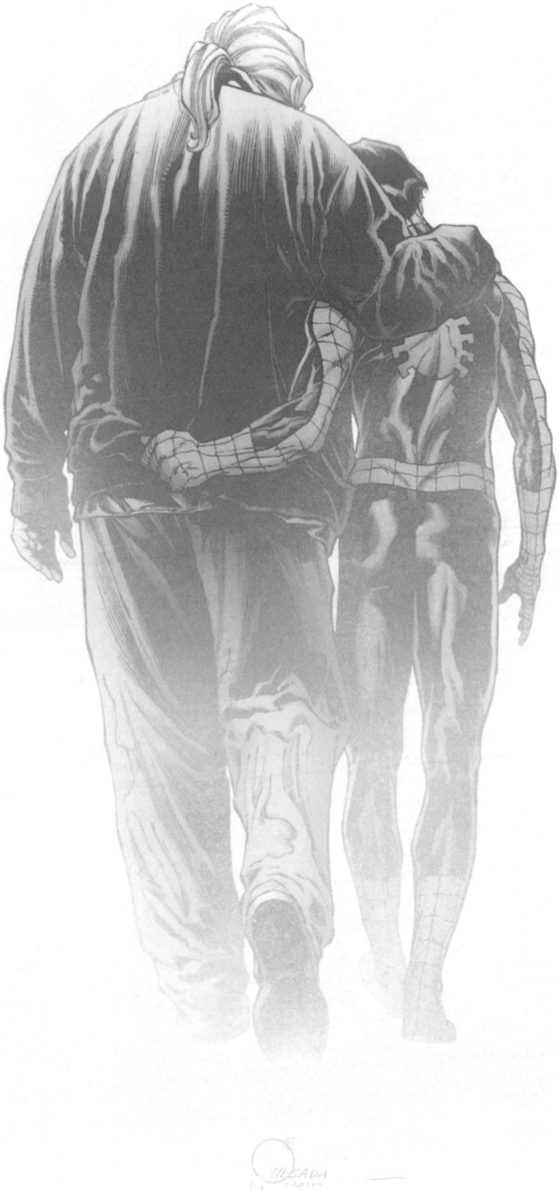

#160 SKETCH VARIANT
BY JOE QUESADA

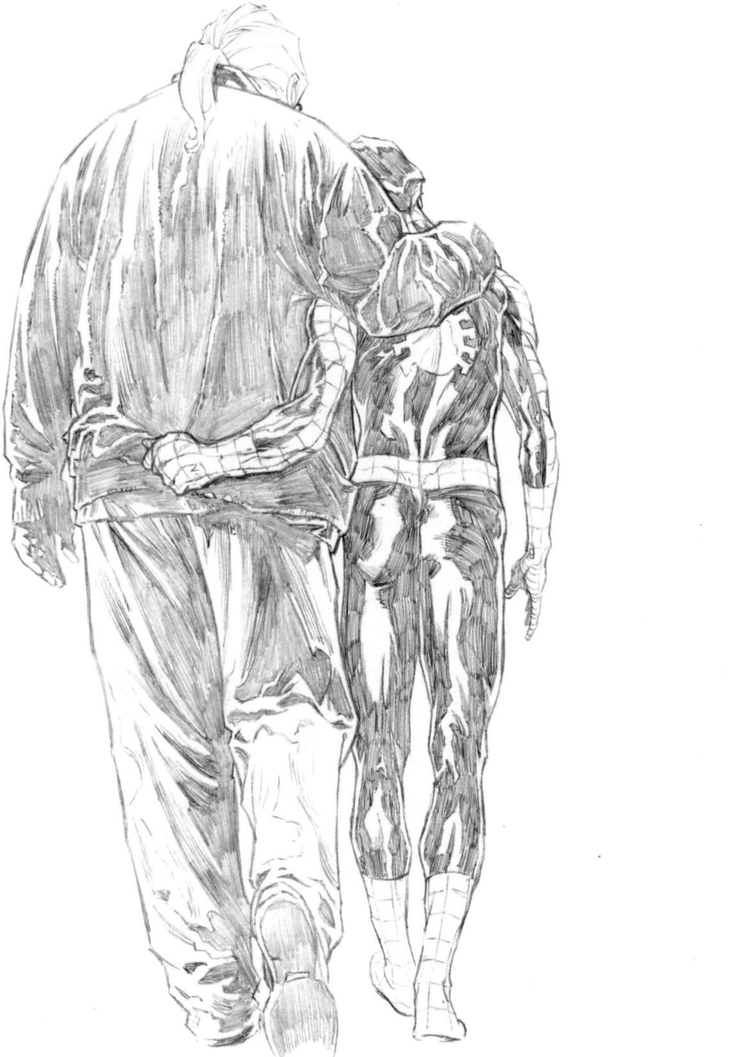

#160 VARIANT
BY MICHAEL KALUTA

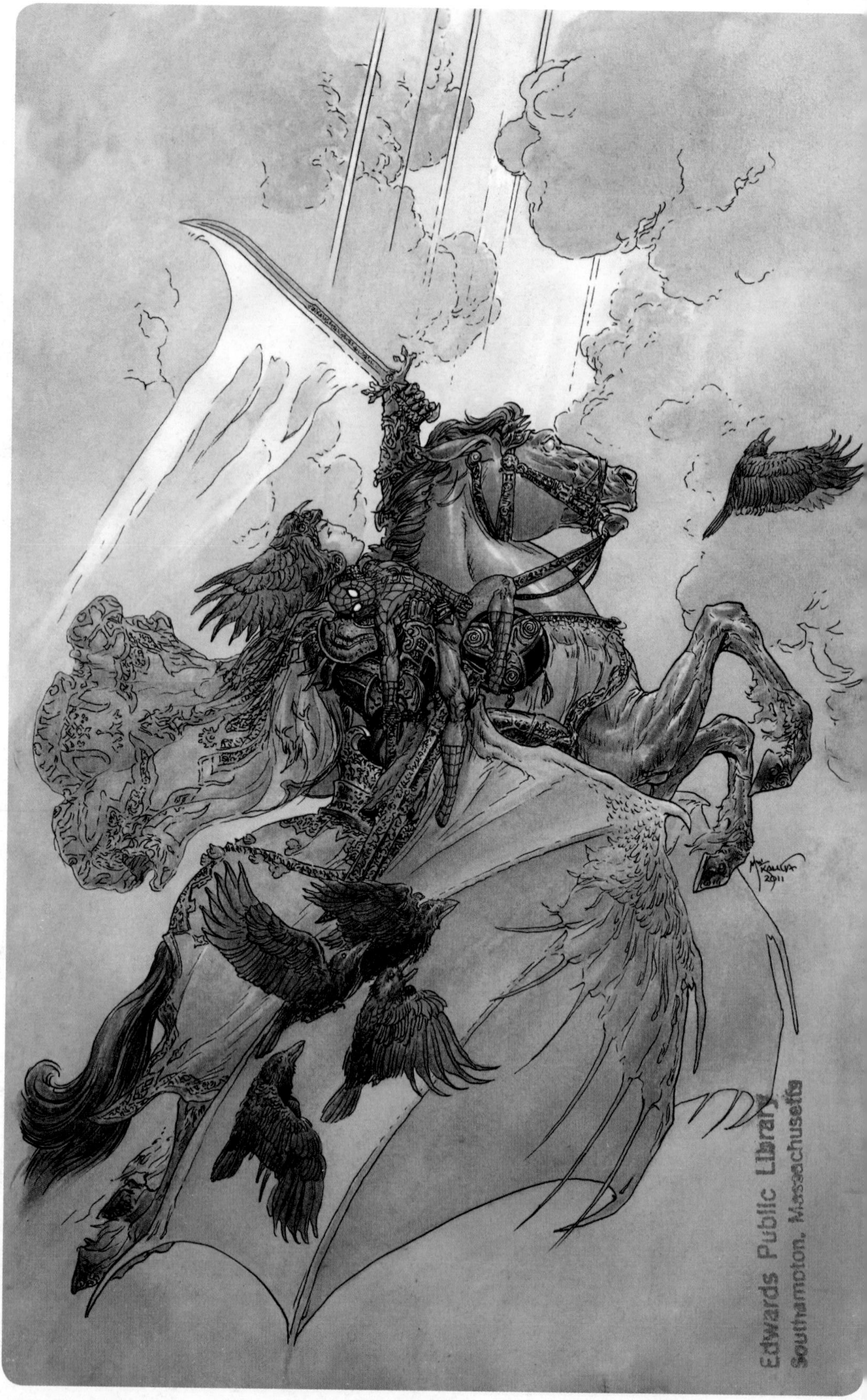